CentOS 7 Linux Server Cookbook
Second Edition

Over 80 recipes to get up and running with
CentOS 7 Linux server

Oliver Pelz

Jonathan Hobson

[PACKT] open source *
PUBLISHING   community experience distilled

BIRMINGHAM - MUMBAI

CentOS 7 Linux Server Cookbook
Second Edition

First published: April 2013

Second edition: January 2016

Production reference: 1250116

Published by Packt Publishing Ltd.
Livery Place
35 Livery Street
Birmingham B3 2PB, UK.

ISBN 978-1-78588-728-4

www.packtpub.com

Credits

Authors

Oliver Pelz

Jonathan Hobson

Reviewer

Mitja Resman

Commissioning Editor

Priya Singh

Acquisition Editor

Kevin Colaco

Content Development Editor

Pooja Mhapsekar

Technical Editor

Deepti Tuscano

Copy Editor

Angad Singh

Project Coordinator

Francina Pinto

Proofreader

Safis Editing

Indexer

Rekha Nair

Production Coordinator

Manu Joseph

Cover Work

Manu Joseph

About the Authors

Oliver Pelz has more than 10 years of experience as a software developer and system administrator. He graduated with a diploma degree in bioinformatics and is currently working at the German Cancer Research center in Heidelberg where he has authored and co-authored several scientific publications in the field of Bioinformatics. As well as developing web applications and biological databases for his department and scientists all over the world, he administers a division-wide Linux-based data center and has set up two high-performance CentOS clusters for the analysis of high-throughput microscope and genome sequencing data. He loves writing code, riding his mountain bike in the Black Forest of Germany and has been an absolute Linux and open source enthusiast for many years. He has contributed to several open-source projects in the past and also worked as a reviewer on the book *CentOS High Performance, Packt Publishing*. He maintains an IT tech blog at www.oliverpelz.de.

I would like to thank my family and especially my wonderful wife Beatrice and little son Jonah for their patience and understanding during all the long working hours while writing this book. Also I would like to thank the folks at Packt Publishing for all their support and the opportunity to to write this book, it was a great pleasure for me. Last but not least I would like to thank Jonathan Hobson for writing the first edition of this book: without him no second edition of this book would have been possible.

I would also like to thank all of the mentors that I've had over the years, especially Prof. Dr. Tobias Dykerhoff, who introduced me to the whole world of Linux a long time ago and infected me with his enthusiasm about open source and the free software movement.

Jonathan Hobson is a web developer, systems engineer, and applications programmer. For more than 20 years, he has been working behind the scenes to support companies, organizations, and individuals around the world to realize their digital ambitions. With an honors degree in both english and history and as a respected practitioner of many computer languages, Jonathan enjoys writing code, publishing articles, building computers, playing the video games, and getting 'out and about' in the big outdoors. He has been using CentOS since its inception, and over the years, it has not only earned his trust, but it has also become his first choice for a server solution. CentOS is a first class community-based enterprise class operating system. It is a pleasure to work with and because of this, Jonathan has written this book so that his knowledge and experience can be passed on to others.

About the Reviewer

Mitja Resman comes from a small, beautiful country called Slovenia, located in southern Central Europe. Mitja is a fan of Linux and an open source enthusiast, and also a Red Hat Certified Engineer and Linux Professional Institute professional. Working as a system administrator, Mitja got years of professional experience with open source software and Linux system administration on local and international projects worldwide. Swiss Army knife syndrome makes Mitja an expert in the fields of VMware virtualization, Microsoft system administration, and also Android system administration.

Mitja has a strong desire to learn, develop, and share knowledge with others. This is the reason he started a blog called GeekPeek.Net. This website provides CentOS Linux guides and "how to" articles covering all sorts of topics appropriate for beginners and advanced users. Mitja wrote a book called *CentOS High Availability, Packt Publishing*, covering how to install, configure, and manage cluster on CentOS Linux.

Mitja is also a devoted father and husband. His two daughters and wife take his mind off the geek stuff and make him appreciate life, looking forward to things to come.

www.PacktPub.com

Support files, eBooks, discount offers, and more

For support files and downloads related to your book, please visit www.PacktPub.com.

Did you know that Packt offers eBook versions of every book published, with PDF and ePub files available? You can upgrade to the eBook version at www.PacktPub.com and as a print book customer, you are entitled to a discount on the eBook copy. Get in touch with us at service@packtpub.com for more details.

At www.PacktPub.com, you can also read a collection of free technical articles, sign up for a range of free newsletters and receive exclusive discounts and offers on Packt books and eBooks.

https://www2.packtpub.com/books/subscription/packtlib

Do you need instant solutions to your IT questions? PacktLib is Packt's online digital book library. Here, you can search, access, and read Packt's entire library of books.

Why Subscribe?

- ▶ Fully searchable across every book published by Packt
- ▶ Copy and paste, print, and bookmark content
- ▶ On demand and accessible via a web browser

Free Access for Packt account holders

If you have an account with Packt at www.PacktPub.com, you can use this to access PacktLib today and view 9 entirely free books. Simply use your login credentials for immediate access.

This work is dedicated to my son Marlin Pelz who was tragically stillborn on 2.10.15, two weeks before his expected date of delivery while I was writing the last few chapters of this book. Marlin, words can not express how much I miss you!

Table of Contents

Preface

This is the second edition of the highly rated *CentOS Linux Server Cookbook*. With the advent of CentOS 7 in mid 2014, there has been a long list of significant changes and new features to this famous operating system. To name a few, there is a new installer, suite of system management services, firewall daemon, enhanced Linux container support, and a new standard filesystem. With all these new advances in the operating system, a major part of the recipes from the *CentOS 6 Linux Server Cookbook* became obsolete or even non-functional, making an update of the book's original content essential. But this book is not just a refresher of the topics covered in the first edition: two brand new chapters have been included as well to keep up to date with the latest open source technologies as well as providing better security: operating system-level virtualization and SELinux. Finally, to make the book a more comprehensive server-administration book, another chapter about server monitoring has been included as well.

Building a server can present a challenge. It is often difficult at the best of times and frustrating at the worst of times. They can represent the biggest of problems or give you a great sense of pride and achievement. Where the word "server" can describe many things, it is the intention of this book to lift the lid and expose the inner workings of this enterprise-class computing system with the intention of enabling you to build your professional server solution of choice. CentOS is a community-based enterprise class operating system. It is available free of charge, and as a fully compatible derivative of Red Hat Enterprise Linux (RHEL), it represents the first choice operating system for organizations, companies, professionals, and home users all over the world who intend to run a server. It's widely respected as a very powerful and flexible Linux distribution and regardless of whether you intend to run a web server, file server, FTP server, domain server, or a multi-role solution, it is the purpose of this book to deliver a series of turnkey solutions that will show you how quickly you can build a fully capable and comprehensive server system using the CentOS operating system. So with this in mind, you could say that this book represents more than just another introduction to yet another server-based operating system. This is a cookbook about an enterprise-class operating system that provides a step-by-step approach to making it work. So, regardless of whether you are a new or an experienced user, there is something inside these pages for everyone, as this book will become your practical guide to getting things done and a starting point to all things CentOS.

What this book covers

Chapter 1, Installing CentOS, is a series of recipes that introduces you to the task of installing your server, updating, and enhancing the minimal install with additional tools. It is designed to get you started and to provide a reference that shows you a number of ways to achieve the desired installation.

Chapter 2, Configuring the System, is designed to follow on from a successful installation to offer a helping hand and provide you with a number of recipes that will enable you to achieve the desired starting server configuration. Beginning with showing you how to work with text files, then changing language and time and date settings, you will not only learn how configure your network settings but also how to resolve a fully qualified domain name and work with kernel modules.

Chapter 3, Managing the System, provides the building blocks that will enable you to champion your server and take control of your environment. It is here where you will kick start your role as a server administrator by disseminating a wealth of information that will walk you through a variety of steps that are required to develop a fully considered and professional server solution.

Chapter 4, Managing Packages with YUM, serves to introduce you to working with software packages on CentOS 7. From upgrading the system to finding, installing, removing, and enhancing your system with additional repositories, it is the purpose of this chapter to explain the open source command-line package management utility known as the Yellowdog Updater Modified (YUM) as well as the RPM package manager.

Chapter 5, Administering the Filesystem, focuses on working with your server's file system. From creating mocking disk devices to test-drive concepts expert level formatting and partitioning commands, you will learn how to work with the Logical Volume Manager, maintain your file system and work with disk quotas.

Chapter 6, Providing Security, discusses the need to implement a series of solutions that will deliver the level of protection you need to run a successful server solution. From protecting your ssh and FTP services, to understanding the new firewalld manager and creating certificates, you will see how easy it is to build a server that not only considers the need to reduce risk from external attack but one that will provide additional protection for your users.

Chapter 7, Building a Network, explains the steps required to implement various forms of resource sharing within your network's computers. From IP addresses and printing devices to various forms of file sharing protocols, this chapter plays an essential role of any server whether you are intending to support a home network or a full corporate environment.

Chapter 8, Working with FTP, concentrates on the role of VSFTP with a series of recipes that will provide the guidance you need to install, configure and manage the File Transfer Protocol (FTP) you want to provide on a CentOS 7 server.

Chapter 9, Working with Domains, considers the steps required to implement domain names, domain resolution, and DNS queries on a CentOS 7 server. The domain name system is an essential role of any server and whether you are intending to support a home network or a full corporate environment, it is the purpose of this chapter to provide a series of solutions that will deliver the beginning of a future-proof solution.

Chapter 10, Working with Databases, provides a series of recipes that deliver instant access to MySQL and PostgreSQL with the intention of explaining the necessary steps required to deploy them on a CentOS 7 server.

Chapter 11, Providing Mail Services, introduces you to the process of enabling a domain-wide Mail Transport Agent to your CentOS 7 server. From building a local POP3/SMTP server to configuring Fetchmail, the purpose of this chapter is to provide the groundwork for all your future e-mail-based needs.

Chapter 12, Providing Web Services, investigates the role of the well-known Apache server technology to full effect, and whether you are intending to run a development server or a live production server, this chapter provides you with the necessary steps to deliver the features you need to become the master of your web based publishing solution.

Chapter 13, Operating System-Level Virtualization, introduces you to the word of Linux containers using the state-of-the-art open source platform Docker, and guides you through building, running, and sharing your first Docker image.

Chapter 14, Working with SELinux, helps to understand and demystify Security Enhanced Linux, which is one of the most little-known topics of CentOS 7.

Chapter 15, Monitoring IT Infrastructure, introduces and shows how to set up Nagios Core, the de-facto industry standard for monitoring your complete IT infrastructure.

What you need for this book

The requirements of this book are relatively simple and begin with the need to download the CentOS operating system. The software is free, but you will need a computer that is capable of fulfilling the role of a server, some free installation media (blank CD-R/DVD-R or USB device), an Internet connection, some spare time, and a desire to have fun.

In saying that, many readers will be aware that you do not need a spare computer to take advantage of this book as the option of installing CentOS on virtualization software is always available. This approach is quite common and where the recipes contained within these pages remain applicable, you should be aware that the use of virtualization software is not considered by this book. For this reason, any requests for support regarding the use of this software should be directed towards the appropriate supplier.

Who this book is for

This is a practical guide for building a server solution, and rather than being about CentOS itself, this is a book that will show you how to get CentOS up and running. It is a book that has been written with the novice-to-intermediate Linux user in mind who is intending to use CentOS as the basis of their next server. However, if you are new to operating systems as a whole, then don't worry; this book will also serve to provide you with the step-by-step approach you need to build a complete server solution with plenty of tricks of the trade thrown in for good measure.

Sections

In this book, you will find several headings that appear frequently (Getting ready, How to do it, How it works and There's more).

To give clear instructions on how to complete a recipe, we use these sections as follows:

Getting ready

This section tells you what to expect in the recipe, and describes how to set up any software or any preliminary settings required for the recipe.

How to do it...

This section contains the steps required to follow the recipe.

How it works...

This section usually consists of a detailed explanation of what happened in the previous section.

There's more...

This section consists of additional information about the recipe in order to make the reader more knowledgeable about the recipe.

Conventions

In this book, you will find a number of text styles that distinguish between different kinds of information. Here are some examples of these styles and an explanation of their meaning.

Code words in text, database table names, folder names, filenames, file extensions, pathnames, dummy URLs, user input, and Twitter handles are shown as follows: "For the purpose of this recipe, it is assumed that all the downloads will be stored on Windows in your personal `C:\Users\<username>\Downloads` folder, or if using an OS X system, in the `/Users/<username>/Downloads` folder."

A block of code is set as follows:

```
<?xml version="1.0" encoding="utf-8"?>
<service>
  <description>enable FTPS ports</description>
  <port protocol="tcp" port="40000-40100"/>
  <port protocol="tcp" port="21"/>
  <module name="nf_conntrack_ftp"/>
</service>
```

Any command-line input or output is written as follows:

```
sudo diskutil unmountDisk /dev/disk3
sudo dd if=./CentOS-7-x86_64-Minimal-XXXX.iso of=/dev/disk3
bs=1M
```

New terms and **important words** are shown in bold. Words that you see on the screen, for example, in menus or dialog boxes, appear in the text like this: "Clicking the **Next** button moves you to the next screen."

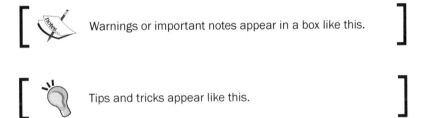

Warnings or important notes appear in a box like this.

Tips and tricks appear like this.

Reader feedback

Feedback from our readers is always welcome. Let us know what you think about this book—what you liked or disliked. Reader feedback is important for us as it helps us develop titles that you will really get the most out of.

To send us general feedback, simply e-mail feedback@packtpub.com, and mention the book's title in the subject of your message.

If there is a topic that you have expertise in and you are interested in either writing or contributing to a book, see our author guide at www.packtpub.com/authors.

Customer support

Now that you are the proud owner of a Packt book, we have a number of things to help you to get the most from your purchase.

Errata

Although we have taken every care to ensure the accuracy of our content, mistakes do happen. If you find a mistake in one of our books—maybe a mistake in the text or the code—we would be grateful if you could report this to us. By doing so, you can save other readers from frustration and help us improve subsequent versions of this book. If you find any errata, please report them by visiting http://www.packtpub.com/submit-errata, selecting your book, clicking on the **Errata Submission Form** link, and entering the details of your errata. Once your errata are verified, your submission will be accepted and the errata will be uploaded to our website or added to any list of existing errata under the Errata section of that title.

To view the previously submitted errata, go to https://www.packtpub.com/books/content/support and enter the name of the book in the search field. The required information will appear under the **Errata** section.

Piracy

Piracy of copyrighted material on the Internet is an ongoing problem across all media. At Packt, we take the protection of our copyright and licenses very seriously. If you come across any illegal copies of our works in any form on the Internet, please provide us with the location address or website name immediately so that we can pursue a remedy.

Please contact us at copyright@packtpub.com with a link to the suspected pirated material.

We appreciate your help in protecting our authors and our ability to bring you valuable content.

Questions

If you have a problem with any aspect of this book, you can contact us at questions@packtpub.com, and we will do our best to address the problem.

1
Installing CentOS

In this chapter, we will cover:

- ▸ Downloading CentOS and confirming the checksum on Windows or OS X
- ▸ Creating USB installation media on Windows or OS X
- ▸ Performing an installation of CentOS using the graphical installer
- ▸ Running a netinstall over HTTP
- ▸ Installing CentOS using a kickstart file
- ▸ Re-installing the boot loader
- ▸ Troubleshooting the system in rescue mode
- ▸ Getting started and customizing the boot loader
- ▸ Updating the installation and enhancing the minimal install with additional administration and development tools

Introduction

This chapter is a collection of recipes that covers the basic practice of installing the CentOS 7 operating system. The purpose of this chapter is to show you how quickly you can get CentOS up and running whilst enabling you to customize your installation with a few 'tricks of the trade' thrown in for good measure.

Downloading CentOS and confirming the checksum on Windows or OS X

In this recipe, we will learn how to download and confirm the checksum of one or more CentOS 7 disk images using a typical Windows or OS X desktop computer. CentOS is made available in various formats by HTTP, FTP, or the rsync protocol from a series of mirror sites located across the world or via the BitTorrent network. For downloading very important files from the Internet, such as operating system images, it is considered best practices to validate those files' checksum, in order to ensure that any resulting media would function and perform as expected when installing. This also makes certain that the files are genuine and come from the original source.

Getting ready

To complete this recipe, it is assumed that you are using a typical Windows-based (Windows 7, Windows Vista, or similar) or OS X computer with full administration rights. You will need an Internet connection to download the required installation files and also need access to a standard DVD/CD disk burner with the appropriate software, in order to create the relevant installation disks from the image files. For the purpose of this recipe, it is assumed that all the downloads will be stored on Windows in your personal `C:\Users\<username>\Downloads` folder, or if using an OS X system, in the `/Users/<username>/Downloads` folder.

How to do it...

Regardless of the type of installation files you download, the following techniques can be applied to all the image files supplied by the CentOS project:

1. Let's begin by visiting `http://www.centos.org` in a web browser and navigate to the button link **Get CentOS Now**. Then click the link **list of the current mirrors** in the text.

2. The mirror sites are categorized, so from the resulting list of links, choose a mirror that is geographically near your current location. For example, if you are in London (UK), you can choose a mirror from **EU** and **United Kingdom**. Now choose a mirror site by selecting either the HTTP or the FTP link.

3. Having made your selection, you will now see a list of directories of all the available CentOS versions. To proceed, simply click the appropriate folder that reads 7. Next, you will see an additional list of directories, such as `atomic`, `centosplus`, `cloud`, and so on. We proceed by choosing the `isos` directory.

4. CentOS 7 currently only supports the 64-bit architecture, so browse to the only directory available labeled `x86_64`, which is a container for the 64-bit version.

5. You will now be presented with a series of files available for download. Begin by downloading a copy of the valid checksum result identified as `md5sum.txt`.

6. If you are new to CentOS or are intending to follow the recipes found throughout this book, then the minimal installation is ideal. This contains the least amount of packages to have a functional system, so choose the following (XXXX is the month stamp of this release):

```
CentOS-7-x86_64-Minimal-XXXX.iso
```

7. On a Windows-based system only (on Mac, this tool is already available in the system), visit http://mirror.centos.org/centos/dostools/ in your browser and download the program md5sum.exe.

8. Now on Windows, open the command prompt (typically found at **Start** | **All Programs** | **Accessories** | **Command Prompt**) and type the following commands into the window that will open (press the *Enter* key at the end of all the lines):

```
cd downloads
dir
```

9. On OS X, open the program **Finder** | **Applications** | **Utilities** | **Terminal**, then type the following commands (press the *Enter* key at the end of all the lines):

```
cd ~/Downloads
ls
```

10. You should now see all the files in your download folder (including all the downloaded CentOS installation image files, the md5sum.txt file and on Windows, the md5sum.exe program).

11. Based on the file names shown, modify the following command in order to check the checksum of your downloaded ISO image file. On Windows, type the following command (change the XXXX month stamp accordingly):

```
md5sum.exe CentOS-7-x86_64-Minimal-XXXX.iso
```

12. On OS X, use instead:

```
md5 CentOS-7-x86_64-Minimal-XXXX.iso
```

13. Press the *Return* key to proceed and then wait for the command prompt to respond. The response is known as the MD5 sum and the result could look like the following:

```
d07ab3e615c66a8b2e9a50f4852e6a77  CentOS-7-x86_64-Minimal-
1503-01.iso
```

14. Now look at the the sum and compare against the relevant listing for your particular image file in md5sum.txt (open in a text editor). If both the numbers match, then you can be confident that you have indeed downloaded a valid CentOS image file. If not, your downloaded file is probably corrupted, so please restart this procedure by downloading the image file again.

15. When you have finished, simply burn your image file(s) to a blank CD-ROM or DVD-ROM using your preferred desktop software, or create a USB installation media from it, as we will show you in the next recipe in this chapter.

How it works...

So what have we learned from this experience?

The act of downloading a CentOS installation image is just the first step towards building the perfect server. Although this process is very simple, many do forget the need to confirm the checksum. In this book, we will work with the minimal installation image, but you should be aware that there are other installation options available to you, such as NetInstall, DVD, Everything, and various LiveCDs.

Creating USB installation media on Windows or OS X

In this recipe, we will learn how to create a USB installation media on Windows or OS X. Nowadays, more and more server systems, desktop PCs, and laptops get shipped without any optical drive. Installing a new operating system, such as CentOS Linux using USB devices gets essential for them as no other installation option is available, as there is no other way to boot the installation media. Also, installing CentOS using USB media can be considerably faster than using the CD/DVD approach.

Getting ready

Before we begin, it is assumed that you have followed the previous recipe in which you were shown how to download a minimal CentOS image and confirm the checksum of the relevant image files. It is also assumed that all the downloads (including the downloaded ISO file) are stored on Windows in your `C:\Users\<username>\Downloads` folder or if using a OS X system, in the `/Users/<username>/Downloads` folder. Next, you will need a free USB device which can be discovered by your operating system, with enough total space, and which is empty or with data on it that can be discarded. The total space of the USB device needed for preparing as an installation media for CentOS 7 for the minimal version must be roughly 700 megabyte. If you are working on a Windows computer, you will need a working Internet connection to download additional software. On OS X, you need an administrator user account.

How to do it...

To begin this recipe, start up your Windows or OS X operating system, then connect a free USB device with enough capacity, and wait until it gets discovered by **File Manager** under Windows or **Finder** under OS X.

1. On a Windows based system, we need to download an additional software called `dd`. Visit `http://www.chrysocome.net/dd` in your favorite browser. Now download the latest `dd-XX.zip` file you can find there, with `XX` being the latest stable version number. For example, `dd-0.5.zip`.

2. On Windows, navigate to your `Downloads` folder using **File Manager**. Here you will find the `dd-05.zip` file. Right-click on it and click on **Extract All**, and extract the `dd.exe` file without creating any subdirectory.

3. On Windows, open the command prompt (typically found at **Start | All Programs | Accessories | Command Prompt**) and type the following commands:

   ```
   cd downloads
   dd.exe --list
   ```

4. On OS X, open the program **Finder | Applications | Utilities | Terminal**, and then type the following commands:

   ```
   cd ~/Downloads
   diskutil list
   ```

5. On Windows, to spot the name of the right USB device you want to use as installation media, look into the output of the command under the `removable media` section. Below that, you should find a line starting with `Mounting on` and then a drive letter, for example, `\.\e:`. This cryptic written drive letter is the most important part we need in the next step, so please write it down.

6. On OS X, the device path can be found in the output of the former command and has the format of `/dev/disk<number>`, where `number` is a unique identifier of the disk. The disks are numbered, starting with zero (`0`). Disk `0` is likely to be the OS X recovery disk, and disk `1` is likely to be your main OS X installation. To identify your USB device, try to compare the `NAME`, `TYPE`, and `SIZE` columns to the specifications of your USB stick. If you have identified the device name, write it down, for example, `/dev/disk3`.

7. On Windows, type the following command, assuming your USB device selected as a installation media has the Windows device name `\\.\e:` (change this as required and be careful what you type – this can create tremendous data loss). Also, substitute `XXXX` with the correct `iso` file version number in the next command:

   ```
   dd.exe if=CentOS-7-x86_64-Minimal-XXXX.iso of=\\.\e: bs=1M
   ```

8. On OS X, you need two commands which will ask for the administrator password (replace `XXXX` and `disk3` with the correct version number and the correct USB device path):

   ```
   sudo diskutil unmountDisk /dev/disk3
   sudo dd if=./CentOS-7-x86_64-Minimal-XXXX.iso of=/dev/disk3 bs=1m
   ```

9. After the `dd` program finishes, there will be some output statistics on how long it took and how much data has been transferred during the copy process. On OS X, ignore any warning messages about the disk not being readable.

10. Congratulations! You now have created your first CentOS 7 USB installation media. You now can safely remove the USB drive in Windows or OS X, and physically unplug the device and use it as a boot device for installing CentOS 7 on your target machine.

How it works...

So what have we learned from this experience?

The purpose of this recipe was to introduce you to the concept of creating an exact copy of a CentOS installation ISO file on a USB device, using the `dd` command-line program. The `dd` program is a Unix based tool which can be used to copy bits from a source to a destination file. This means that the source gets read bit by bit and written to a destination without considering the content or file allocation; it just involves reading and writing pure raw data. It expects two file name based arguments: input file (`if`) and output file (`of`). We will use the CentOS image file as our input filename to clone it exactly `1:1` to the USB device, which is accessible through its device file as our output file parameter. The `bs` parameter defines the block size, which is the amount of data to be copied at once. Be careful, it is an absolute expert tool and overwrites any existing data on your target while copying data on it without further confirmation or any safety checks. So at least double-check the device drive letters of your target USB device and never confuse them! For example, if you have a second hard disk installed at `D:` and your USB device at `E:` (on OS X, at `/dev/disk2` and `/dev/disk3` respectively) and you confuse the drive letter `E:` with `D:` (or `/dev/disk3` with `/dev/disk2`), your second hard disk would be erased with little to no chances of recovering any lost data. So handle with care! If you're in doubt of the correct output file device, never start the `dd` program!

In conclusion, it is fair to say that there are other far more convenient solutions available for creating a USB installation media for CentOS 7 than the `dd` command, such as the Fedora Live USB Creator. But the purpose of this recipe was not only to create a ready-to-use CentOS USB installer but also to get you used to the `dd` command. It's a common Linux command that every CentOS system administrator should know how to use. It can be used for a broad variety of daily tasks. For example, for securely erasing hard disks, benchmarking network speed, or creating random binary files.

Performing an installation of CentOS using the graphical installer

In this recipe, we will learn how to perform a typical installation of CentOS using a new graphical installer interface introduced in CentOS 7. In many respects, this is considered to be the recommended approach to installing your system, as it not only provides you with the ability to create the desired hard disk partitions but also to customize your installation in lots of ways (for example, keyboard layout, package selection, installation type, and so on). Your installation will then form the basis of a server on which you can build, develop, and run any type of service you may want to provide in the future.

Getting ready

Before we begin, it is assumed that you have followed the previous recipe in which you were shown how to download a CentOS image, confirm the checksum of the relevant image files, and create the relevant installation optical disks or USB media. Your system must be a 64 bit (x64_86) architecture, must have at least 406 MB RAM to load the graphical installer 1 GB or more is recommended if installing a graphical window manager such as Gnome), and have at least 10 GB free hard disk space.

How to do it...

To begin this recipe, insert your installation media (CD/DVD or USB device), restart the computer, and press the correct key for selecting the boot device during startup. Then choose the inserted device from the list (for many computers, this can be reached using *F11* or *F12* but can be different on your system. Please refer to your motherboard's manual).

1. On the welcome splash screen, the option **Test this media & install CentOS 7** is preselected and we will use this option. When you are ready, press the *Return* key to proceed.

2. After loading some initial files, the installer then starts to test the installation media. A single test should take between 30 seconds to five minutes and will report if there are any errors on your installation media. When this process is complete, the system will finally load the graphical installer.

3. The CentOS installer will now present the graphical installation welcome screen. From this point onwards, you can use your keyboard and mouse (the latter is highly recommended), but remember to enable the number lock on your keyboard if you intend to use the keypad.

4. On the left side you see the main language category and on the right side, the sub-languages for the installer. You can also search for a language using the textbox on the left bottom. All changes to your language settings will take effect immediately, so when you are ready, choose the **Continue** button to proceed.

5. Now we reach the main installation menu, which is called **Installation summary**.

6. Most options shown here already have some predefined values and can be used without changing, others which do not have any default value and which need your attention are labeled with a red exclamation mark like the **Installation Destination** under **System** category. So let's click on it using the mouse.

7. After clicking the **Installation Destination** button, you will see a graphical list of all the hard disk devices currently connected to your computer, which you can use for installing the operating system on. You can select your target hard disk by clicking on the correct hard disk symbol. It will then put a check mark on it. If you are unsure about the right hard disk, try to identify it by comparing its brand and total size shown in the menu. Before the installation can proceed, you must select a hard disk. Be careful and choose your target hard disk wisely as it will erase any existing data on it during the installation. When you are ready, click the **Done** button.

8. If your selected hard disk already contained data, then when clicking on **Done,** you may see what could be described as a warning/error message. The message may read: **You don't have enough space available to install CentOS**. Don't worry! This is to be expected and the message is simply asking you to re-initialize your hard disk because CentOS can only be installed on an empty disk. In most cases, especially if you have more than one partition on the hard disk, simply click on **Reclaim space** which will show a new window with a detailed list of all the partitions on this drive. Here just click on **Delete All** and then again on **Reclaim space** to discard any data on this disk, which will complete the task of disk initialization and enable you to proceed to the next step. When finished, click the **Done** button.

9. Back at the **Installation Summary** screen, the exclamation mark on the **Installation Destination** item should be gone now.

10. Optionally, we can click on **Network & Hostname** under **System category**. On the following page, on the left side, you can choose the primary network adapter you would like to connect to the Internet and select it by clicking on it. For the selected device, click on the switch on the right side to enable and connect it automatically using the **On** position of the switch. Finally, before closing this submenu, change the hostname in its text field to something appropriate. Click **Done**.

11. Now back at the **Installation Summary** screen, all the important settings have been made or have got predefined values, and all the exclamation marks are gone. If you are happy with these settings, click on the **Start installation** button or change the settings appropriately.

12. On the next screen, you will be required to create and confirm a root password for the root user while the new system gets installed in the background. Choose a secure password with not less than six characters.

13. Here on this screen you can also create a standard user account which is highly recommended. If you create a new user do not check **Make this user administrator**. When you are ready, click **Done** (if you entered a weak password, you have to confirm this by clicking twice)

14. CentOS will now partitionate and format your hard disk in the background and resolve any dependencies, and the installer will begin writing to the hard disk. This may take some time, but a progress bar will indicate the status of your installation. When finished, the installer will inform you that the entire process is complete and that the installation was successful. So when you are ready, click on the **Reboot** button. Now release your installation media from the drive.

15. Congratulations! You have now installed CentOS 7 on your computer.

How it works...

In this recipe, you have discovered how to install the CentOS 7 operating system. Having covered the typical approach to the graphical installation process, you are now in a position to develop the server with additional configuration changes and packages that will suit the role you intend the server to fulfill. This graphical installer has been built with the aim to be very intuitive and flexible, and makes installation very easy as it will guide the user through some mandatory tasks that he has to fulfill before the installation of the main system can be started.

Running a netinstall over HTTP

In this recipe, we will learn how to initiate the process of running a netinstall over HTTP (using the URL method) in order to install CentOS 7. It is a process in which a small image file is used to boot the computer and let the user select and install only the software packages and services he wants and nothing more over a network connection thus providing great flexibility.

Getting ready

Before we begin, it is assumed that you already know how to download and checksum a CentOS 7 installation image and how to create the relevant installation media from it. For this recipe here, we will need to download and create installation media for the netinstall image (download the latest CentOS-7-x86_64-NetInstall-XXXX.iso file) instead of the minimal ISO shown in another recipe in this chapter. Also, it is assumed that you have at least gone through the graphical installation procedure once to exactly know how to boot from your installation media and work with the installer program.

How to do it...

To begin this recipe, insert your prepared netinstall media, boot your computer from it, and wait for the welcome screen to appear:

1. On the welcome splash screen, the option **Test this media & install CentOS 7** is preselected and we will use this option. When you are ready, press the *Return* key to proceed.

2. After the tests finish, the graphical installer will load and present the typical graphical installation summary screen.

> Here the installer should be configured exactly as in the normal graphical installation recipe, besides the following mandatory changes to the **Network & Host name** and **Installation source** menu items (which is shown by the red exclamation marks).

3. Before we can install CentOS over the network, we have to make sure that we have a working network connection. Therefore, you should first click on the **Network & Host name** menu entry and activate one of your network adapters to the connected state. Refer to the normal installation recipe for more details.

4. Next, click on **Installation source** to enter the settings. As we will be installing over HTTP (also referred to as the URL method), you should leave the default **On the network** selected in the **Which installation source would you like to use?** section.

5. Now type in the following URL in the standard `http://` textfield, which we will use to download all the required installation packages at `http://mirror.centos.org/centos/7/os/x86_64/`.

6. Alternatively, you can also use a personal repository which you would have to create in advance (see *Chapter 4, Managing Packages with YUM*)

7. When you are ready, click on **Done** to start the initialization process.

8. On success, the installer will begin to retrieve the appropriate `install.img` file. This may take several minutes to complete, but once resolved, a progress bar will indicate all the download activity. When this process finishes successfully, the exclamation mark at the **installation source** will go away but another one will pop up which will tell the user that it is missing the **software selection**. Click on it and choose whatever fits your need. As for the purpose of this recipe, just select **Minimal install** under **Base environment** and then click on **Done**.

9. If the **Which installation source** would you like to use stays greyed out and cannot be changed, then there are connection problems with your network adapter. If this is the case, go back to configure **Network & Hostname** and change the network settings until the connected state can be reached.

10. CentOS 7 will now install the operating system the usual way and will congratulate you when this process finishes. It may be slower than installing from a physical installation media since all the packages have to be retrieved from the Internet.

How it works...

The purpose of this recipe was to introduce you to the concept of the CentOS network installation process, in order to show you just how simple this approach can be. By completing this recipe you have not only saved time by limiting your initial download to those files that are required by the installation process, but you have also been able to take advantage of the full graphical installation method without the need for a complete DVD suite.

Installing CentOS 7 using a kickstart file

While installing CentOS 7 manually using the graphical installer utility is fine on a single server, doing so on a multiple number of systems can be tedious. Kickstart files can automate the installation process of a server system and here we will show how this can be done. They are simple text based configuration files which provide detailed and exact instructions on how the target system should be set up and installed (for example, which keyboard layout or additional software packages to install).

Getting ready

To successfully complete this recipe, you will need access to an already installed CentOS 7 system to retrieve the kickstart configuration file we want to work with and use for automated installation. On this pre-installed CentOS server, you also need a working Internet connection to download additional software.

Next, we will need to download and create installation media for the DVD or the Everything image (download the latest `CentOS-7-x86_64-DVD-XXXX.iso` or `CentOS-7-x86_64-Everything-XXXX.iso` file), instead of the minimal iso file shown in another recipe in this chapter. Then you need another USB device which must be read and writable on Linux systems (formatted as FAT16, FAT32, EXT2, EXT3, EXT4, or XFS filesystem).

How to do it...

For this recipe to work, we first need physical access to an existing kickstart file from another finished CentOS 7 installation, which we will use as a template for a new CentOS 7 installation.

1. Log in as root on the existing CentOS 7 system and make sure the kickstart configuration file exists by typing the following command and pressing the *Return* key to execute (this will show you the details of the file):

   ```
   ls -l /root/anaconda-ks.cfg
   ```

2. Next, physically plug in a USB device and then type the following command, which will give you a list of all the hard disk devices currently connected to the computer:

   ```
   fdisk -l
   ```

3. Try to identify the device name by comparing its size, partitions, and identified filesystems with the specifications of your USB device. The device name will be of kind /dev/sdX, where X is an alphabetical character, such as b, c, d, e, ... and so on. If you cannot find the right device name for your USB media using the fdisk command, try the following trick: run fdisk -l twice - first with plugged-out and then with plugged-in USB device and compare how the second output changed - it has one device name more than the first output: your device name of interest !

4. If you have found the right device name in the list, create a directory to mount it to the current filesystem:

   ```
   mkdir /mnt/kickstart-usb
   ```

5. Next, actually mount the stick to this folder, assuming that your USB partition of choice is at /dev/sdc1 (change this as required):

   ```
   mount /dev/sdc1 /mnt/kickstart-usb
   ```

6. Now we will create our working copy of the kickstart file on the USB device for customizing:

   ```
   cp /root/anaconda-ks.cfg /mnt/kickstart-usb
   ```

7. Next, open the copied kickstart file on the USB device with your favorite text editor (here we will use the editor nano, if you have not installed it yet type yum install nano):

   ```
   nano /mnt/kickstart-usb/anaconda-ks.cfg
   ```

8. We will now modify the file for installing CentOS on a new target system. In nano, use the up and down arrow keys to go to the line which starts with (<your_hostname> will be the name of the hostname you gave during installation e.g. minimal.home):

   ```
   network   --hostname=<your_hostname>
   ```

9. Now edit the `<your_hostname>` string to give it a new unique hostname. For example, add a `-2` to the end of any existing name, as shown next:

    ```
    network    --hostname=minimal-2.home
    ```

10. Next, move the cursor down using the up and down arrow keys until it stops at the line which says `%packages`. Append the following lines right below it (you can further customize this and provide additional packages that you want to install automatically):

    ```
    mariadb-server

    httpd

    rsync

    net-tools
    ```

11. Now save and close the file, to do this in the nano editor use the key combination *Ctrl+o* (which means, hold down the *Ctrl* key on the keyboard and then the *o* key without releasing the *Ctrl* key) to write the changes. Then press *Return* to confirm the filename and *Ctrl+x* to exit the editor.

12. Next, install the following CentOS package:

    ```
    yum install system-config-kickstart
    ```

13. Now we validate the syntax of our kickstart file using the `ksvalidator` program, which is included in the package we just installed:

    ```
    ksvalidator /mnt/kickstart-usb/anaconda-ks.cfg
    ```

14. If the `config` file is error-free, unmount the USB stick now by using the following commands:

    ```
    cd

    umount /mnt/kickstart-usb
    ```

15. When you get a new command prompt again, unplug the USB device with the kickstart file for using on the target machine physically from the system.

16. Now you need physical access to the target machine you want to install CentOS on, using the kickstart file just created. Disconnect any other external file storage(s) that you do not need during the installation.

17. Power on the computer and put in your prepared CentOS installation media (must be a CentOS DVD or Everything installation disk image prepared on a CD/DVD disc or a USB device installer). Also connect to the computer the USB stick containing the kickstart file you just created in the earlier steps (if you using a USB drive for installing CentOS then you will need two free USB ports in total to complete this recipe).

18. Next, start the server and press the correct key during the initial bootup screen, associated with booting the CentOS installation media you just connected.

19. After the CentOS installer starts loading, the common standard CentOS 7 installation welcome screen will show up and the option **Test this media & install CentOS 7** will be pre-selected by the cursor.

20. Next, press the *Esc* key on your keyboard once to switch to the `boot:` prompt.

21. Now we are ready to start the kickstart installation. To do this, you need to know the exact partition name on the USB device where the kickstart file is located. Type the following command, assuming that your partition is at `/dev/sdc1` (change this as required), and press the *Return* key to start the kickstart installation process:

```
linux ks=hd:sdc1:/anaconda-ks.cfg
```

 If you cannot find out the right device and partition name of the USB stick, you have to start the target system in rescue mode (refer to the *Troubleshooting the system in rescue mode* recipe) to identify the right device name and partition number by comparing its size, partitions, and identified filesystems with the specifications of your stick.

22. The new system now gets installed automatically using the instructions from the provided kickstart file. You can watch the installation output messages as it is showing the user detailed installation progress.

23. If the system has finished installing, reboot the system and log in to your new machine to verify that the new system has been setup the way we described using the kickstart file.

How it works...

In this recipe, you have seen that every server running a CentOS 7 installation keeps the kickstart file in its root directory, which contains detailed information on how the system had been set up during the installation. The kickstart files can be used to automate the installations of multiple systems with the same configuration. This can save a lot of time doing repetitive work as no user interaction during installation is needed. Also, we can use this method if the target machines don't meet the minimum requirement in RAM for graphical based installations but when needed other features the text mode installer does not provide such as custom partitioning of the system. Kickstart configuration files are simple plain text files which can be created manually from scratch. Because there are quite a number of different commands available to construct your system using the kickstart syntax, we used an existing file as a template and customized it to fit our needs, instead of starting out completely new. We did not use the minimal installation image to drive our kickstart installation because we installed some extra packages not included on the minimal ISO file, such as the Apache webserver.

Getting started and customising the boot loader

When you turn on your computer, the boot loader is the first program that starts up and is responsible for loading and transferring control to an underlying operating system. Nowadays, almost any modern Linux distribution uses the **GRand Unified Bootloader version 2** (**GRUB2**) for starting the system. It has a lot of flexibility in configuration and supports a lot of different operating systems. In this recipe, we will show how to customize the GRUB2 boot loader by disabling the waiting time of the menu display and therefore improving the time it takes for booting the system.

Getting ready

To complete this recipe, you will require access to an already installed CentOS 7 operating system (minimal or any other CentOS 7 installation type will work) with root privileges. Also, you need to have some basic experiences with a text based editor, such as nano, for changing the configuration files.

How to do it...

We begin this recipe by opening the main GRUB2 configuration file with our text editor of choice and modifying it.

1. First log in as root into your system and create a copy of the GRUB2 configuration file for backup and rollback, if needed. Press the *Return* key to finish:

    ```
    cp /etc/default/grub /etc/default/grub.BAK
    ```

2. Open the main GRUB2 configuration file that we want to edit with the following command and press the *Return* key (here we will use the editor nano, if you have not installed it yet type `yum install nano`):

    ```
    nano /etc/default/grub
    ```

3. Press the *Return* key in the first line where the cursor is at to insert a new line at the top, and then insert the following line:

    ```
    GRUB_HIDDEN_TIMEOUT=0
    ```

4. Add a # sign to the beginning of the following line, as shown:

    ```
    GRUB_TIMEOUT=0
    ```

5. Now save the file in the nano using *Ctrl+o* (and *Return* to confirm the filename to save). Use *Ctrl+x* to exit the editor and then run the following command:

    ```
    dmesg | grep -Fq "EFI v"
    ```

6. If the preceding command does not produce any output, run the following command:

```
grub2-mkconfig -o /boot/grub2/grub.cfg
```

7. Otherwise, if there is an output, run:

```
grub2-mkconfig -o /boot/efi/EFI/centos/grub.cfg
```

8. If `grub2-mkconfig` is successful, it will print `Done`. Now reboot your system using the following command:

```
reboot
```

9. During the rebooting process, you will notice that the GRUB2 boot menu will not appear any more and the system will boot up faster.

How it works...

Having completed this recipe, we now know how to customize the GRUB2 boot loader. In this very easy recipe, we only showed you very basic modifications to the boot loader but it can do much more! It supports a broad variety of filesystems and can boot almost any compatible operating system. This is also particularly useful if you plan to run multiple operating systems on the same machine. To learn more about GRUB2's configuration file syntax type the `info grub2 | less` command and go to the section `6.1 Simple configuration handling` (read the recipe *Navigating text files with less* in *Chapter 2, Configuring the System* to learn how to browse this document).

Troubleshooting the system in rescue mode

We all make mistakes and this is especially true for novice Linux system administrators. Linux can have a steep learning curve and sooner or later there will be a point in your career where your CentOS installation does not start up due to broad number of reasons, including hardware problems or human mistakes such as configuration errors. If this has happened to you then you can use the CentOS rescue mode in order to boot an otherwise unbootable system and try to undo your mistakes or find out the root of the problems. In this recipe, we will show you three common use cases when to use this option:

▸ Accessing the filesystem for recovering important data or undoing changes to configuration files if CentOS is not booting up

▸ Changing the root password if you forgot it

▸ Re-installing the boot loader which can be damaged when installing another operating system on the same harddisk where CentOS is installed

Getting ready

To complete this recipe, you will require a standard installation media (CD/DVD or USB device) of the CentOS 7 operating system. For recovering the data from the system, you will need to connect some sort of external storage device to the system, such as an external hard disk or a working network connection to another computer to copy all your precious data to a different location.

How to do it...

To begin this recipe, you should boot your server from the CentOS installation CD/DVD or the USB device and wait until the first welcome splash screen appears with the cursor waiting at the **Test this media & install CentOS 7** menu option.

Reaching rescue mode

1. From the main menu, use the down arrow key to select **Troubleshooting** and then press the *Return* key to proceed.

2. On the **Troubleshooting** screen, use the down arrow key to highlight **Rescue a CentOS system**. When you are ready, press the *Return* key to proceed.

3. After some loading time, we enter the rescue screen, which includes various confirmation sub-screens. To begin this section, use the left and right arrow keys to choose **Continue** and press the *Return* key to proceed.

4. On the first sub-screen, choose **OK** and press the *Return* key to proceed.

5. Again, in the following sub-screen, choose **OK** and press the *Return* key to proceed.

6. On the next screen, choose the **Start** shell and by using the *Tab* key, highlight **OK** and press the *Return* key to proceed.

7. By completing the preceding steps, you will launch a shell session. You will notice this at the bottom of your display. The current status of the shell session will read as follows:

    ```
    bash-4.2#_
    ```

8. At the prompt, type the following instruction to change the root filesystem, before pressing the *Return* key to complete your request:

    ```
    chroot /mnt/sysimage
    ```

9. Congratulations! You just reached the rescue mode. To exit it at any time, simply type the following command and then press the *Return* key to complete your request (don't do this right now as this will restart the system):

    ```
    reboot
    ```

10. After the basic rescue mode is reached, we have the following options, depending on the type of problem.

Accessing the filesystem

If you are now in the rescue mode and need to backup important files from the filesystem, you need a destination location for the data transfer. For transferring the data we want to recover from the server to another computer please physically connect an external USB device to it. You can also use network storages for the recovery. For example, you could import an NFS server share and copy data to it. Refer to the *Working with NFS* recipe in *Chapter 7, Building a Network*.

1. On the rescue mode command line, type in the following command, which will show you all the current partitions connected to the system, and then press the *Return* key to complete your request:

   ```
   fdisk -l
   ```

2. You now need to find out the right device name with the partition number of your connected device; comparing the total size or the filesystem output of the various devices with the specifications from your stick can help you in this process. You can also try the following trick: run the `fdisk -l` command twice, first with the plugged-in USB device and then again with the USB device unplugged, and compare the output of both the commands. It should be different by one device name which you are searching for!

3. If you have found the right device name in the list, create a directory to mount the stick to the filesystem:

   ```
   mkdir /mnt/hdd-recovery
   ```

4. Next, mount the disk partition to this folder. Here we assume that the USB device of interest has the device name `sdd1` (please change if different on your system):

   ```
   mount /dev/sdd1 /mnt/hdd-recovery
   ```

5. The original system's hard disk's root partition has been mounted under a specific folder by the rescue system automatically (under `/mnt/sysimage`), if you need to access it for example to change configuration files which caused startup problems or make a full or partial backup. For example, if you need to backup your Apache webserver configuration files, use:

   ```
   cp -r /mnt/sysimage/etc/http /mnt/hdd-recovery
   ```

6. If you need to access the data that lives on partitions other than the currently mounted root partition, use `fdisk -l` to identify the partition of interest. Then create a directory and mount the partition to it and change to that directory to access your data similar you did when mounting the USB device.

7. To finish backing up the files, type:

   ```
   reboot
   ```

Accessing the filesystem

1. If you are in the rescue mode for changing the root password, just use the following command and provide a new password:

   ```
   passwd
   ```

2. To complete changing the password, type:

   ```
   reboot
   ```

Re-install the CentOS boot loader

1. We will now use the `fdisk` command to find the name of all the current partitions. To do this, type the following instruction and then press the *Return* key to complete your request:

   ```
   fdisk -l
   ```

2. Now run the following command:

   ```
   dmesg | grep -Fq "EFI v"
   ```

3. If the preceding command does not produce any output look for the * symbol in the `fdisk` listing in the boot column to find the correct start partition, and assuming that your boot disk is on `/dev/sda1` (change this as required), type the following:

   ```
   grub2-install /dev/sda
   ```

4. Otherwise, if there is an output, run instead:

   ```
   yum reinstall grub2-efi shim
   ```

5. If no error is reported, the console should respond as follows:

   ```
   # this device map was generated by anaconda
   (hd0) /dev/sda
   ```

6. The console output from the last step has confirmed that GRUB has now been successfully restored.

7. To reboot the computer, type:

   ```
   reboot
   ```

How it works...

There are a broad variety of problems which can be resolved by the tools provided through the rescue mode environment. Often these problems refer to booting problems but can also be from different types, such as forgetting the root password. Rescue mode can be a life-saver and an understanding of it is a very important skill to learn. It was felt that such a recipe should thus remain close at hand.

Remember to always be careful when working with bootloader commands as improper use can make your operating system unbootable.

Updating the installation and enhancing the minimal install with additional administration and development tools

In this recipe, we will learn how to enhance the minimal install with additional tools that will give you a variety of administrative and development options, which in turn will prove vital during the lifetime of your server and which are essential for some recipes in this book. The minimal install is probably the most efficient way you can install a server, but having said that, a minimal install does require some additional features in order to make it a more compelling model.

Getting ready

To complete this recipe, you will require a minimal installation of the CentOS 7 operating system with root privileges and a connection to the Internet in order to facilitate the download of additional packages.

How to do it...

We will begin this recipe by updating the system.

1. To update the system, log in as root and type:

    ```
    yum -y update
    ```

2. CentOS will now search for the relevant updates and, if available, they will be installed. On completion and depending on what was updated (that is, kernel and new security features to name but a few), you can decide to reboot your computer. To do this, type:

    ```
    reboot
    ```

3. Your server will now reboot and return to the login screen. We will now complete this recipe and enhance our current installation with a series of package groups that will prove to be very useful in the future. To do this, log in as root and type:

    ```
    yum -y groupinstall "Base" "Development Libraries" "Development Tools"
    yum -y install policycoreutils-python
    ```

How it works...

The purpose of this recipe is to enhance the minimal installation of the CentOS 7 operating system and by doing this you have not only introduced yourself to the **Yellowdog Updater Modified** (**YUM**) package manager (something to which we will return to later on in this book), but you now have a system that is capable of running a vast amount of applications right out-of-the-box.

So what have we learned from this experience?

We started the recipe by updating the system in order to ensure that it is up to date. At this stage, it is often a good idea to reboot the system. It is not expected that we will do this very often but it is expected when updating for the first time after the installation of the operating system, as it is most likely that there are major changes available. The reason behind this is typically based on the desire to take advantage of a new kernel or revised security updates. In the next phase, the recipe showed you how to add a series of package groups that may prove to be more than useful in the future. To save time, we wrapped the instruction to install the three main package groups: `Base`, `Development Libraries`, and `Development Tools`. The preceding action alone installs over 200 individual packages, thereby giving your server the ability to compile the code and run a vast array of applications out-of -the-box, that you may need over the life time of your server. To see a list of all the packages within a group, for example, from `Base`, run the `yum groupinfo Base` command. Another package we installed was `policycoreutils-python` which provides tools and programs to manage the security enhanced access control to Linux, which we will use quite often throughout the chapters of this book.

2
Configuring the System

In this chapter, we will cover the following topics:

- ▶ Navigating text files with less
- ▶ Introduction to Vim
- ▶ Speaking the right language
- ▶ Synchronizing the system clock with NTP and the chrony suite
- ▶ Setting your hostname and resolving the network
- ▶ Becoming a superuser
- ▶ Building a static network connection
- ▶ Customizing your system banners and messages
- ▶ Priming the kernel

Introduction

This chapter is a collection of recipes that covers the basic practice of establishing the basic needs of a server. For many, building a server can often seem to be a daunting task, and so the purpose of this chapter is to provide you with an instant method to achieve the desired goals.

Navigating text files with less

Throughout this book, you will often use programs and tools that use the program less or a less-like navigation to view and read file content or display output. At first, the control can seem a bit unintuitive .Here, in this recipe, we will show you the basics of how to navigate through a file using less controls.

Getting ready

To complete this recipe, you will require a working installation of the CentOS 7 operating system with root privileges.

How to do it...

1. To begin, log in as root and type the following command to open a program that uses less for navigation:

   ```
   man man
   ```

2. To navigate, press the *up* and *down* key to scroll up and down one line at a time, the *spacebar* to scroll down a page, and the *b* key to scroll up a page. You can search within the text using the forward slash key, /,followed by the search term, then press *Return* to search. Press *n* to jump to the next search result. Press the *q* key to exit.

How it works...

Here, in this short recipe, we have shown you the very basics of less navigation, which is essential for reading man pages and is used by a lot of other programs throughout this book to display text. We only showed you the basic commands and there is much more to learn. Please read the less manual to find out more on `man less` command.

Introduction to Vim

In this recipe, we will give you a very brief introduction to the text editor, Vim, which is used as the standard text editor throughout this book. You can also use any other text editor you prefer, such as nano or emacs, instead.

Getting ready

To complete this recipe, you will require a working installation of the CentOS 7 operating system with root privileges.

How to do it...

We will start this recipe by installing the `vim-enhanced` package, as it contains a tutorial you can use to learn working with Vim:

1. To begin, log in as root and install the following package:

   ```
   yum install vim-enhanced
   ```

2. Afterwards, type the following command to start the Vim tutorial:

   ```
   vimtutor
   ```

3. This will open the Vim tutorial in the Vim editor. To navigate, press the *up* and *down* key to scroll up and down single-line wise. To exit the tutorial, press the *Esc* key, then type `:q!`, followed by the *Return* key to exit.

4. You should now read through the file and go through the lessons to get a basic understanding of Vim, to learn how to edit your text documents.

How it works...

The tutorial shown in this recipe should be seen as a starting point from which to learn the basics for working with one of the most powerful and effective text editors available for Linux. Vim has a very steep learning curve, but after dedicating about half an hour to the vimtutor guide you should be able to do all the common text editing tasks without any problem, such as opening, editing, and saving text files.

Speaking the right language

In this recipe, we will show you how to change the language settings of your CentOS 7 installation for the whole system and for single users. The need to change this is rare but can be important, for example if we accidentally chose the wrong language during installation.

Getting ready

To complete this recipe, you will require a working installation of the CentOS 7 operating system with root privileges, and a console-based text editor of your choice. You should have read the *Navigating text files with less* recipe, because some commands in this recipe will use less for printing output.

How to do it...

There are two categories of settings that you have to adjust if you want to change the system-wide language settings of your CentOS 7 system. We begin by changing the system locale information and then the keyboard settings:

1. To begin, log in as root and type the following command to show the current locale settings for the console, graphical window managers (X11 layout), and also the current keyboard layout:

```
localectl status
```

2. Next, to change these settings, we first need to know all the available locale and keyboard settings on this system (both commands use `less` navigation):

```
localectl list-locales
localectl list-keymaps
```

3. If you have picked the right locale from the output above in our example, `de_DE.utf8` and `keymap de-mac` (change to your own appropriate needs), you can change your locale and keyboard settings using:

```
localectl set-locale LANG=de_DE.utf8
localectl set-keymap de-mac
```

4. Now, verify the persistence of your changes using the same command again:

```
localectl status
```

How it works...

As we have seen, the `localectl` command is a very convenient tool that can take care of managing all important language settings in a CentOS 7 system.

So what have we learned from this experience?

We started by logging in to our command line with the root user. Then, we ran the `localectl` command with the parameter `status`, which gave us an overview of the current language settings in the system. The output of this command showed us that language properties in a CentOS 7 system can be separated into locale (system locale) and keymap (VC keymap and all X11 layout properties) settings.

Locales on Linux are used to set the system's language as well as other language-specific properties. This can include texts from error messages, log output, user interfaces, and, if you are using a window manager such as Gnome, even **Graphical User Interfaces** (**GUI**). Locale settings can also define region-specific formatting such as paper sizes, numbers and their natural sorting, currency information, and so on. They also define character encoding, which can be important if you chose a language that has characters that cannot be found in the standard ASCII encoding.

Keymap settings on the other hand define the exact layout of each key on your keyboard.

Next, to change these settings, we first issued the `localctl` command with the `list-locales` parameter to retrieve a full list of all locales on the system, and `list-keymaps` to show a list of all keyboard settings available in the system. Locales as outputted from the `list-locales` parameter use a very compact annotation for defining a language:

Language[_Region][.Encoding][@Modificator]

Only the `Language` part is mandatory, all the rest is optional. Examples for language and region are: `en_US` for English and region United States or American English, `es_CU` would be language Spanish and Region Cuba or Cuban Spanish.

Encodings are important for special characters such as German umlaut or accents in the French language. The memory representation of these special characters can be interpreted differently depending on the used encoding type. In general UTF-8 should be used as it is capable of encoding almost any character in every language.

Modificators are used to change settings defined by the locale. For example, `sr_RS.utf8@latin` is used if you want to have Latin settings for serbian Serbia, which normally uses Cyrillic definitions. This will change to western settings such as sorting, currency information, and so on.

To change the actual locale, we used the `set-locale LANG=de_DE.utf8` parameter. Here, the encoding was selected to display proper German umlauts. Please note that we used the `LANG` option to set the same locale value (for example, `de_DE.utf8`) for all available locale options. If you don't want to have the same locale value for all available options, you can use a more fine-grained control over single locale options. Please refer to the locale description using the man page, `man 7 locale` (on minimal installation; you need to install all Linux documentation man pages before using the `yum install man-pages` command). You can set these additional options using a similar syntax, for example, to set the time locale use:

localctl set-locale LC_TIME="de_DE.utf8"

Next, we showed all available keymap codes using the `list-keymaps` parameter. As we have seen from running `localctl status`, the keymaps can be separated in non-graphical (VC keymap) and graphical (X11 layout) settings, which allows the flexible configuration of different keyboard layouts when using a window manager such as Gnome and for the console. Running `localctl` with the parameter, `set-keymap de-mac`, sets the current keymap to a German Apple Macintosh keyboard model. This command applies the given keyboard type to both the normal VC and the X11 keyboard mappings. If you want different mappings for X11 than for the console, use `localctl --no-convert set-x11-keymap cz-querty`, where we use `cz-querty` for the keymap code to a Czech querty keyboard model (change this accordingly).

There's more...

Sometimes, single system users need different language settings than the system's locale (which can only be set by the root user), according to their regional keyboard differences and for interacting with the system in their preferred human language. System-wide locales get inherited by every user as long as they are not overwritten by local environment variables.

 Changing system-wide locales does not necessarily have an effect on your user's locales if they have already defined something else for themselves.

To print all the current locale environment variables for any system user, we can use the command, `locale`. To set single environment variables with the appropriate variable name; for example, to set the time locale to US time we would use the following line:

```
export LC_TIME="en_US.UTF-8"
```

But, most likely we would want to change all the locales to the same value; this can be done by setting `LANG`. For example, to set all the locales to American English, use the following line:

```
export LANG="en_US.UTF-8"
```

To test the effect of locale changes, we can now produce an error message that will be shown in the language set by the `locale` command. Here is the different language output for changing locale from English to German:

```
export LANG="en_US.UTF-8"
ls !
```

The following output will be printed:

```
ls: cannot access !: No such file or directory
```

Now, change to German locale settings:

```
export LANG="de_DE.UTF-8"
ls !
```

The following output will be printed:

```
ls: Zugriff auf ! nicht möglich: Datei oder Verzeichnis nicht gefunden
```

Setting a locale in an active console using the `export` command will not survive closing the window or opening a new terminal session. If you want to make those changes permanent, you can set any locale environment variables, such as the `LANG` variable, in a file called `.bashrc` in your home directory, which will be read everytime a shell is opened. To change the locale settings permanently to `de_DE.UTF-8` in our example (change this to your own needs) use the following line:

```
echo "export LANG='de_DE.UTF-8'" >> ~/.bashrc
```

Synchronizing the system clock with NTP and the chrony suite

In this recipe, we will learn how to synchronize the system clock with an external time server using the **Network Time Protocol** (**NTP**) and the chrony suite. From the need to time-stamp documents, e-mails, and log files, to securing, running, and debugging a network, or to simply interact with shared devices and services, everything on your server is dependent on maintaining an accurate system clock, and it is the purpose of this recipe to show you how this can be achieved.

Getting ready

To complete this recipe, you will require a working installation of the CentOS 7 operating system with root privileges, a console-based text editor of your choice, and a connection to the Internet to facilitate downloading additional packages.

How to do it...

In this recipe, we will use the `chrony` service to manage our time synchronization. As chrony is not installed by default on CentOS minimal, we will start this recipe by installing it:

1. To begin, log in as root and install the `chrony` service, then start it and verify that it is running:

```
yum install -y chrony
systemctl start chronyd
systemctl status chronyd
```

2. Also, if we want to use chrony permanently, we will have to enable it on server startup:

```
systemctl enable chronyd
```

3. Next, we need to check whether the system already uses NTP to synchronize our system clock over the network:

```
timedatectl | grep "NTP synchronized"
```

4. If the output from the last step showed No for NTP synchronized, we need to enable it using:

```
timedatectl set-ntp yes
```

5. If you run the command (from step 3) again, you should see that it is now synchronizing NTP.

6. The default installation of chrony will use a public server that has access to the atomic clock, but in order to optimize the service we will need to make a few simple changes to streamline and optimize at what time servers are used. To do this, open the main chrony configuration file with your favorite text editor, as shown here:

```
vi /etc/chrony.conf
```

7. In the file, scroll down and look for the lines containing the following:

```
server 0.centos.pool.ntp.org iburst
server 1.centos.pool.ntp.org iburst
server 2.centos.pool.ntp.org iburst
server 3.centos.pool.ntp.org iburst
```

8. Replace the values shown with a list of preferred local time servers:

```
server 0.uk.pool.ntp.org iburst
server 1.uk.pool.ntp.org iburst
server 2.uk.pool.ntp.org iburst
server 3.uk.pool.ntp.org iburst
```

 Visit http://www.pool.ntp.org/ to obtain a list of local servers geographically near your current location. Remember, the use of three or more servers will have a tendency to increase the accuracy of the NTP service.

9. When complete, save and close the file before synchronizing your server using the sytstemctl command:

```
systemctl restart chronyd
```

10. To check whether the modifications in the `config` file were successful, you can use the following command:

   systemctl status chronyd

11. To check whether chrony is taking care of your system time synchronization, use the following:

   chronyc tracking

12. To check the network sources chrony uses for synchronization, use the following:

   chronyc sources

How it works...

Our CentOS 7 operating system's time is set on every boot based on the hardware clock, which is a small-battery driven clock located on the motherboard of your computer. Often, this clock is too inaccurate or has not been set right, therefore it's better to get your system time from a reliable source over the Internet (that uses real atomic time). The chrony daemon, `chronyd`, sets and maintains system time through a process of synchronization with a remote server using the NTP protocol for communication.

So, what have we learned from this experience?

As a first step, we installed the `chrony` service, since it is not available by default on a CentOS 7 minimal installation. Afterwards, we enabled the synchronization of our system time with NTP using the `timedatectl set-ntp yes` command.

After that, we opened the main chrony configuration file, `/etc/chrony.conf`, and showed how to change the external time servers used. This is particularly useful if your server is behind a corporate firewall and have your own NTP server infrastructure.

Having restarted the service, we then learned how to check and monitor our new configuration using the `chronyc` command. This is a useful command line tool (c stands for client) for interacting and controlling a chrony daemon (locally or remotely). We used the `tracking` parameter with `chronyc`, which showed us detailed information of the current NTP synchronization process with a specific server. Please refer to the `man` pages of the `chronyc` command if you need further help about the properties shown in the output (`man chronyc`).

We also used the `sources` parameter with the `chronyc` program, which showed us an overview of the used NTP time servers.

You can also use the older `date` command to validate correct time synchronization. It is important to realize that the process of synchronizing your server may not be instantaneous, and it can take a while for the process to complete. However, you can now relax in the full knowledge that you now know how to install, manage and synchronize your time using the NTP protocol.

There's more...

In this recipe, we set our system's time using the `chrony` service and the NTP protocol. Usually, system time is set as **Coordinated Universal Time** (**UTC**) or world time, which means it is one standard time used across the whole world. From it, we need to calculate our local time using time zones. To find the right time zone, use the following command (read the *Navigating textfiles with less* recipe to work with the output):

```
timedatectl list-timezones
```

If you have found the right time zone, write it down and use it in the next command; for example, if you are located in Germany and are near the city of Berlin, use the following command:

```
timedatectl set-timezone Europe/Berlin
```

Use `timedatectl` again to check if your local time is correct now:

```
timedatectl | grep "Local time"
```

Finally, if it is correct, you can synchronize your hardware clock with your system time to make it more precise:

```
hwclock --systohc
```

Setting your hostname and resolving the network

The process of setting the hostname is typically associated with the installation process. If you ever need to change it or your server's **Domain Name System** (**DNS**) resolver, this recipe will show you how.

Getting ready

To complete this recipe, you will require a working installation of the CentOS 7 operating system with root privileges, and a console-based text editor of your choice.

How to do it...

To begin this recipe, we shall start by accessing the system as root and opening the following file in order to name or rename your current server's hostname:

1. Log in as root and type in the following command to see the current hostname:
   ```
   hostnamectl status
   ```

2. Now, change the hostname value to your preferred name. For example, if you want to call your server `jimi`, you would type (change appropriately):

```
hostnamectl set-hostname jimi
```

 Static hostnames are case-sensitive and restricted to using an Internet-friendly alphanumeric string of text. The overall length should be no longer than 63 characters, but try to keep it much shorter.

3. Next, we need the IP address of the server. Type in the following command to find it (you need to identify the correct network interface in the output):

```
ip addr list
```

4. Afterwards, we will set the **Fully Qualified Domain Name** (**FQDN**), in order to do this, we will need to open and edit the hosts file:

```
vi /etc/hosts
```

5. Here, you should add a new line appropriate to your needs. For example, if your server's hostname was called jimi, (with an IP address of `192.168.1.100`, and a domain name of `henry.com`) your final line to append will look like this:

```
192.168.1.100          jimi.henry.com jimi
```

 For a server found on a local network only, it is advisable to use a non-Internet based top-level address. For example, you could use `.local` or `.lan`, or even `.home`, and by using these references you will avoid any confusion with the typical `.com`, `.co.uk`, or `.net` domain names.

6. Next, we will open the `resolv.conf` file, which is responsible for configuring static DNS server addresses that the system will use:

```
vi /etc/resolv.conf
```

7. Replace the content of the file with the following:

```
# use google for dns
nameserver 8.8.8.8
nameserver 8.8.4.4
```

8. When complete, save and close your file before rebooting your server to allow the changes to take immediate effect. To do this, return to your console and type:

```
reboot
```

9. On a successful reboot, you can now check your new hostname and FQDN by typing the following commands and waiting for the response:

```
hostname --fqdn
```

10. To test if we can resolve domain names to IP addresses using our static DNS server addresses, use the following command:

```
ping -c 10 google.com
```

How it works...

A hostname is a unique label created to identify a machine on a network. It is restricted to alphanumeric-based characters, and making a change to your server's hostname can be achieved by using the `hostnamectl` command. A DNS server is used to translate domain names to IP addresses. There are several public DNS servers available; in a later recipe, we will build our own DNS service.

So, what have we learned from this experience?

In the first stage of the recipe, we changed the current hostname used by our server with the `hostnamectl` command. This command can set three different types of hostnames. Using the command with the `set-hostname` parameter will set the same name for all three hostnames: the high-level `pretty` hostname, which might include all kinds of special characters (for example, `Lennart's Laptop`), the static hostname which is used to initialize the kernel hostname at boot (for example `lennarts-laptop`), and the transient hostname, which is a default received from network configurations.

Following this, we set the FQDN of our server. A FQDN is the hostname along with a domain name after it. A domain name gets important when you are running a private DNS, or allowing external access to your server. Besides using a DNS server setting the FQDN can be achieved by updating the hosts file found at `/etc/hosts`.

This file is used by CentOS to map hostnames to an IP address, and it is often found to be incorrect on a new, un-configured, or recently installed server. For this reason, we first had to find out the IP address of the server using `ip addr list`.

An FQDN should consist of a short hostname and the domain name. Based on the example shown in this recipe, we set the FQDN for a server named `henry`, whose IP address is `192.168.1.100` and domain name is `henry.com`.

Saving this file would arguably complete this process. However, because the kernel makes a record of the hostname during the boot process, there is no choice but to reboot your server before you can use the changed settings.

Next, we opened the system's `resolv.conf` file, which keeps the IP addresses of the system's DNS servers. If your server does not use or have any DNS records, your system is not able to use domain names for network destinations in any program at all. In our example, we entered the public Google DNS server IP addresses, but you are allowed to use any DNS server you want or have to use (often in a cooperate environment, behind a firewall, you have to use internal DNS server infrastructures). On a successful reboot, we confirmed your new settings by using the `hostname` command, which can print out the hostname or the FQDN based on the parameters given.

So, in conclusion, you can say that this recipe has not only served to show you how to rename your server and resolve the network, but has also showed you the difference between a hostname and domain name:

As we have learned, a server is not only known by the use of a shorter, easier-to-remember, and quicker-to-type single-word-based host name, it also consists of three values separated with a period (for example jimi.henry.com). The relationship between these values may have seemed strange at first, especially where many people would have seen them as a single value, but by completing this recipe you have discovered that the domain name remains distinct from the hostname by virtue of being determined by the resolver subsystem, and it is only by putting them together that your server will yield the FQDN of the system as a whole.

There's more...

The hosts file consists of a list of IP addresses and corresponding hostnames, and if your network contains computers whose IP addresses are not listed in an existing DNS record, then in order to speed up your network it is often recommended that you add them to this file.

This can be achieved on any operating system, but to do this on CentOS, simply open the hosts file in your favorite text editor, as shown next:

```
vi /etc/hosts
```

Now, scroll down to the bottom of the file and add the following values by substituting the domain names and IP addresses shown here with something more appropriate to your own needs:

```
192.168.1.100    www.example1.lan
192.168.1.101    www.example2.lan
```

You can even use external address such as:

```
83.166.169.228  www.packtpub.com
```

This method provides you with the chance to create mappings between domain names and IP addresses without the need to use a DNS, and it can be applied to any workstation or server. The list is not restricted by size, and you can even employ this method to block access to certain websites by simply re-pointing all requests to visit a known website to a different IP address. For example, if the real address of `www.website.com` is `192.168.1.200` and you want to restrict access to it, then simply make the following changes to the hosts file on the computer that you want to block from access:

```
127.0.0.1      www.website.com
```

It isn't failsafe, but in this instance anyone trying to access `www.website.com` on this system will automatically be sent to `127.0.0.1`, which is your local network address, so this will just block access.

When you have finished, remember to save and close your file in the usual way before proceeding to enjoy the benefits of faster and safer domain name resolution across any available network.

Building a static network connection

In this recipe, we will learn how to configure a static IP address for a new or existing CentOS server.

While a dynamically assigned IP address or DHCP reservation may be fine for most desktop and laptop users, if you are setting up a server, it is often the case that you will require a static IP address. From web pages to e-mail, databases to file sharing, a static IP address will become a permanent location from which your server will deliver a range of applications and services, and it is the intention of this recipe to show you how easily it can be achieved.

Getting ready

To complete this recipe, you will require a working installation of the CentOS 7 operating system with root privileges and a console-based text editor of your choice.

How to do it...

For the purpose of this recipe, you will be able to find all the relevant files in the directory, `/etc/sysconfig/network-scripts/`. First, you need to find out the correct name of the network interface that you want to set as static. If you need to set more than one network interface as static, repeat this recipe for every device.

1. To do this, log in as root and type the following command to get a list of all of your system's network interfaces:

   ```
   ip addr list
   ```

2. If you have only one network card installed, it should be very easy to find out its name; just select the one not named `lo` (which is the loopback device). If you got more than one, having a look at the IP addresses of the different devices can help you choose the right one. In our example, the device is called `enp0s3`.

3. Next, make a backup of the network interface configuration file (change the `enp0s3` part accordingly, if your network interface is named differently):

```
cp /etc/sysconfig/network-scripts/ifcfg-enp0s3/etc/sysconfig/
network-scripts/ifcfg-enp0s3.BAK
```

4. When you are ready to proceed, open the following file in your favorite text editor by typing what is shown next:

```
vi /etc/sysconfig/network-scripts/ifcfg-enp0s3
```

5. Now, work down the file and apply the following changes:

```
NM_CONTROLLED="no"
BOOTPROTO=none
DEFROUTE=yes
PEERDNS=no
PEERROUTES=yes
IPV4_FAILURE_FATAL=yes
```

6. Now, add your IP information by customizing the values of XXX.XXX.XXX.XXX as required:

```
IPADDR=XXX.XXX.XXX.XXX
NETMASK= XXX.XXX.XXX.XXX
BROADCAST= XXX.XXX.XXX.XXX
```

7. We must now add a default gateway. Typically, this should be the address of your router. To do this, simply add a new line at the bottom of the file, as shown next, and customize the value as required:

```
GATEWAY=XXX.XXX.XXX.XXX
```

8. When ready, save and close the file before repeating this step for any remaining Ethernet devices that you want to make static. When doing this, remember to assign a different IP address to each device.

9. When finished, save and close this file before restarting your network service:

```
systemctl restart network
```

How it works...

In this recipe, you have seen the process associated with changing the state of your server's IP address from a dynamic value obtained from an external DHCP provider, to that of a static value assigned by you. This IP address will now form a unique network location from which you will be able to deliver a whole host of services and applications. It is a permanent modification, and yes, you could say that the process itself was relatively straightforward.

So, what have we learned from this experience?

Having started the recipe by identifying your network interface name of choice and creating a backup of the original Ethernet configuration files, we then opened the configuration file located at `/etc/sysconfig/network-scripts/ifcfg-XXX` (with `XXX` being the name of your interface, for example, `enp0s3`). As being static no longer requires the services of the network manager, we disabled `NM_CONTROLLED` by setting the value to `no`. Next, as we are in the process of moving to a static IP address, `BOOTPROTO` has been set to `none`, as we are no longer using DHCP. To complete our configuration changes, we then moved on to add our specific network values and set the IP address, the netmask, broadcast, and the default gateway address.

In order to assist the creation of a static IP address, the default gateway is a very important setting in as much as it allows the server to contact the wider world through a router.

When finished, we were asked to save and close the file before repeating this step for any remaining Ethernet devices. Having done this, we were then asked to restart the network service in order to complete this recipe and to enable our changes to take immediate effect.

Becoming a superuser

In this recipe, we will learn how to provide nominated users or groups with the ability to execute a variety of commands with elevated privileges.

On CentOS Linux, many files, folders, or commands can only be accessed or executed by a user called `root`, which is the name of the user who can control everything on a Linux system. Having one root user per system may suit your needs, but for those who want a greater degree of flexibility, a solid audit trail, and the ability to provide a limited array of administrative capabilities to a select number of trusted users, you have come to the right place. It is the purpose of this recipe to show you how to activate and configure the **sudo** (**superuser do**) command.

Getting ready

To complete this recipe, you will require a minimal installation of the CentOS 7 operating system with root privileges. It is assumed that your server maintains one or more users (other than root) who qualify for this escalation in powers. If you did not create a system user account during installation, please do so by first applying the recipe, *Managing users and their groups*, in *Chapter 3, Managing the System*.

How to do it...

To start this recipe, we will first test the `sudo` command with a non-privileged user.

1. To begin, log in to your system using a non-root user account, then type the following to verify that `sudo` is not enabled (use your user account's password when asked):

   ```
   sudo ls /var/log/audit
   ```

2. This will print the following error output with `<username>`, which is the user you are currently logged in with:

   ```
   <username> is not in the sudoers file.   This incident will be
   reported.
   ```

3. Now, log out the system user using the command:

   ```
   logout
   ```

4. Next, log in as root and use the following command to give the non-root user sudo power (change `<username>` appropriately):

   ```
   usermod -G wheel <username>
   ```

5. Now, you can test if `sudo` is working by logging out root again and re-logging in the user from step 1, and then trying again:

   ```
   sudo ls /var/log/audit
   ```

6. Congratulations, you've now set a normal user to have sudo powers and can view and execute files and directories restricted to the root user.

How it works...

Unlike some Linux distributions, CentOS does not provide sudo by default. Instead, you are typically allowed to access restricted parts of the system with the root user only. This offers a certain degree of security, but for a multi-user server there is little to no flexibility unless you simply provide these individuals with full administrative root access permissions. This is not advisable, and for this reason it was the purpose of this recipe to show you how to provide one or more users with the right to execute commands with elevated privileges.

So, what did we learn from this experience?

We started by logging in to the system with a normal user account having no root privileges or sudo powers. With this user, we then tried to list a directory that normally only the root user is allowed to see, so we applied the `sudo` command on it. It failed, giving us the error that we are not in the sudoers list.

The `sudo` command provides nominated users or groups with the ability to execute a command as if they were the root user. All actions are recorded (in a file called `/var/log/secure`), so there will be a trace of all the commands and arguments used.

We then logged in as the true root user and added a group called wheel to the system user that we wanted sudo rights for. This group is used as a special administration group and every member of it is granted sudo rights automatically.

From now on, the nominated user can implement sudo in order to execute any command with elevated privileges. To do this, the user would be required to type the word `sudo` before any command, for example, they could run the following command:

`sudo yum update`

They will be asked to confirm their user password (not the root password!), and after successful authentication the program will be executed as the user root.

Finally, we can say that there are three ways to become root on a CentOS Linux system:

First, to log in as the true user root to the system. Second, you can use the command, `su - root`, while any normal system user is logged in, giving the root user's password to switch to a root shell prompt permanently. Third, you can give a normal user sudo rights so that they can execute single commands using their own passwords as if they were the root user, while staying logged in as themselves.

> **sudo** (**superuser do**) should not be confused with the **su** (**substitute user**) command, which allows you to switch to another user permanently instead of executing only single commands as you would do being the root user.

The `sudo` command allows great flexibility for servers that have a lot of users, where one administrator is not enough to manage the whole system.

Customizing your system banners and messages

In this recipe, we will learn how to display a welcome message if a user successfully logs in to our CentOS 7 system using SSH or console, or opens a new terminal window in a graphical window manager. This is often used to show the user informative messages, or for legal reasons.

Getting ready

To complete this recipe, you will require a minimal installation of the CentOS 7 operating system with root privileges and a console-based text editor of your choice.

How to do it...

1. To begin, log in to your system using your root user account and create the following new file with your favorite text editor:

   ```
   vi /etc/motd
   ```

2. Next, we will put in the following content in this new file:

   ```
   ###################################################
   # This computer system is for authorized users only.
   # All activity is logged and regularly checked.
   # Individuals using this system without authority or
   # in excess of their authority are subject to
   # having all their services revoked...
   ###################################################
   ```

3. Save and close this file.

4. Congratulations, you have now set a banner message for whenever a user successfully logs in to the system using ssh or a console.

How it works...

For legal reasons, it is strongly recommended that computers display a banner before allowing users to log in; lawyers suggest that the offense of unauthorized access can only be committed if the offender knows at the time that the access he intends to obtain is unauthorized. Login banners are the best way to achieve this. Apart from this reason, you can provide the user with useful system information.

So, what did we learn from this experience?

We started this recipe by opening the file, /etc/motd, which stands for message of the day; this content will be displayed after a user logged in a console or ssh. Next, we put in that file a standard legal disclaimer and saved the file.

There's more...

As we have seen, the /etc/motd file displays static text after a user successfully logs in to the system. If you want to also display a message when an ssh connection is first established, you can use ssh banners. The banner behavior is disabled in the ssh daemon configuration file by default, which means that no message will be displayed if a user establishes an ssh connection. To enable this feature, log in as root on your server and open the /etc/ssh/sshd_config file using your favorite text editor, and put in the following content at the end of the file:

```
Banner /etc/ssh-banner
```

Then, create and open a new file called /etc/ssh-banner, and put in a new custom ssh greeting message.

Finally, restart your ssh daemon using the following line:

```
systemctl restart sshd.service
```

The next time someone establishes an ssh connection to your server, this new message will be printed out.

The motd file can only print static messages and some system information details, but it is impossible to generate real dynamic messages or use bash commands in it if a user successfully logs in.

Also, motd does not work in non-login shells, such as when you open a new terminal within a graphical window manager. In order to achieve this, we can create a custom script in the /etc/profile.d directory. All scripts in this directory get executed automatically if a user logs in to the system. First, we delete any content in the /etc/motd file, as we don't want to display two welcome banners. Then, we open the new file, /etc/profile.d/motd.sh, with our text editor and create a custom message, such as the following, where we can use bash commands and write little scripts (use the back ticks to run bash shell commands in this file):

```
#!/bin/bash
echo -e "
###############################
#
# Welcome to `hostname`, you are logged in as `whoami`
# This system is running `cat /etc/redhat-release`
```

```
# kernel is `uname -r`
# Uptime is `uptime | sed 's/.*up ([^,]*), .*/1/'`
# Mem total `cat /proc/meminfo | grep MemTotal | awk {'print $2'}` kB
###################################"
```

Priming the kernel

The Linux kernel is a program that constitutes the central core of the operating system. It can directly access the underlying hardware and make it available to the user to work with it using the shell.

In this recipe, we will learn how to prime the kernel by working with dynamically loaded kernel modules. Kernel modules are device driver files (or filesystem driver files) that add support for specific pieces of hardware so that we can access them.

You will not work very often with kernel modules as a system administrator, but having a basic understanding of them can be beneficial if you have a device driver problem or an unsupported piece of hardware.

Getting ready

To complete this recipe, you will require a minimal installation of the CentOS 7 operating system with root privileges.

How to do it...

1. To begin, log in to your system using your root user account, and type the following command in order to show the status of all Linux kernel modules currently loaded:

    ```
    lsmod
    ```

2. In the output, you will see all loaded device drivers (module); let's see if a cdrom and floppy module have been loaded:

    ```
    lsmod | grep "cdrom\|floppy"
    ```

3. On most servers, there will be the following output:

    ```
    cdrom               42556  1 sr_mod
    floppy              69417  0
    ```

4. Now, we want to show detailed information about the sr_mod cdrom module:

    ```
    modinfo sr_mod
    ```

5. Next, unload these two modules from the kernel (you can only do this if the module and hardware have been found and loaded on your system; otherwise skip this step):

```
modprobe -r -v sr_mod floppy
```

6. Check if the modules have been unloaded (output should be empty now):

```
lsmod | grep "cdrom\|floppy"
```

7. Now, to show a list of all kernel modules available on your system, use the following directory where you can look around:

```
ls /lib/modules/$(uname -r)/kernel
```

8. Let's pick a module from the subfolder `/lib/modules/$(uname -r)/kernel/drivers/` called `bluetooth` and verify that it is not loaded yet (output should be empty):

```
lsmod | grep btusb
```

9. Get more information about the module:

```
modinfo btusb
```

10. Finally, load this bluetooth USB module:

```
modprobe btusb
```

11. Verify again that it is loaded now:

```
lsmod | grep "btusb"
```

How it works...

Kernel modules are the drivers that your system's hardware needs to communicate with the kernel and operating system (also, they are needed to load and enable filesystems). They are loaded dynamically, which means that only the drivers or modules are loaded at runtime, which reflects your own custom specific hardware.

So, what did we learn from this experience?

We started using the `lsmod` command to view all the currently loaded kernel modules in our system. The output shows three columns: the module name, the amount of RAM the module occupies while loaded, and the number of processes this module is used by and a list of dependencies of other modules using it. Next, we checked if the `cdrom` and `floppy` modules have been loaded by the kernel yet. In the output, we saw that the `cdrom` module is dependent on the `sr_mod` module. So, next we used the `modinfo` command to get detailed information about it. Here, we learned that `sr_mod` is the SCSI `cdrom` driver.

Since we only need the floppy and cdrom drivers while we first installed the base system we can now disable those kernel modules and save us some memory. We unloaded the modules and their dependencies with the `modprobe -r` command and rechecked whether this was successful by using `lsmod` again.

Next, we browsed the standard kernel module directory (for example, `/lib/modules/$(uname -r)/kernel/drivers`). The `uname` substring command prints out the current kernel version so that it makes sure that we are always listing the current kernel modules after having installed more than one version of the kernel on our system.

This kernel module directory keeps all the available modules on your system structured and categorized using subdirectories. We navigated to `drivers/bluetooth` and picked the `btusb` module. Doing `modinfo` on the `btusb` module, we found out that it is the generic bluetooth USB driver. Finally, we decided that we needed this module, so we loaded it using the `modprobe` command again.

There's more...

It's important to say that loading and unloading kernel modules using the `modprobe` command is not persistent; this means that if you restart the system, all your changes to kernel modules will be gone. To load a kernel module at boot time create a new executable script file, `/etc/sysconfig/modules/<filename>.modules`, where `<filename>` is a name of your choice. There you put in `modprobe` execution commands just as you would on the normal command line. Here is an example of additionally loading the bluetooth driver on startup, for example `/etc/sysconfig/modules/btusb.modules`:

```
#!/bin/sh
if [ ! -c /dev/input/uinput ] ; then
exec /sbin/modprobe btusb >/dev/null 2>&1
fi
```

Finally, you need to make your new module file executable via the following line:

```
chmod +x /etc/sysconfig/modules/btusb.modules
```

Recheck your new module settings with `lsmod` after reboot.

To remove a kernel module at boot time for example `sr_mod`, we need to blacklist the module's name using the `rdblacklist` kernel boot option. We can set this option by appending it to the end of the `GRUB_CMDLINE_LINUX` directive in the GRUB2 configuration file `/etc/default/grub` so it will look like:

```
GRUB_CMDLINE_LINUX="rd.lvm.lv=centos/root rd.lvm.lv=centos/swap
crashkernel=auto rhgb quiet rdblacklist=sr_mod"
```

If you need to blacklist multiple modules, the `rdblacklist` option can be specified multiple times like `rdblacklist=sr_mod rdblacklist=nouveau`.

Next recreate the GRUB2 configuration using the `grub2-mkconfig` command (to learn more read the *Getting started and customizing the boot loader* recipe in *Chapter 1, Installing CentOS*).

```
grub2-mkconfig -o /boot/grub2/grub.cfg
```

Finally we also need to `blacklist` the module name using the blacklist directive in a `new.conf` file of your choice in the `/etc/modprobe.d/` directory for example:

```
echo "blacklist sr_mod" >> /etc/modprobe.d/blacklist.conf
```

3
Managing the System

In this chapter, we will cover the following topics:

- ▸ Knowing and managing background services
- ▸ Troubleshooting background services
- ▸ Tracking system resources with journald
- ▸ Configuring journald to make it persistent
- ▸ Managing users and their groups
- ▸ Scheduling tasks with cron
- ▸ Synchronizing files and doing more with rsync
- ▸ Maintaining backups and taking snapshots
- ▸ Monitoring important server infrastructure
- ▸ Taking control with Git and Subversion

Introduction

This chapter is a collection of recipes that provides for the need to maintain a performance-based server solution. From monitoring your free disk space, to working with system services and managing the synchronization of remote files, the purpose of this chapter is to show you how quickly and easily you can get to grips with the task of server maintenance.

Knowing and managing your background services

Linux system services are one of the most fundamental concepts of every Linux server. They are programs which run continuously in your system, waiting for external events to process something or do it all the time. Normally, when working with your server, a system user will not notice the existence of such a running service because it is running as a background process and is therefore not visible. There are many services running all the time on any Linux server. These can be a web server, database, FTP, SSH or printing, DHCP, or LDAP server to name a few. In this recipe, we will show you how to manage and work with them.

Getting ready

To complete this recipe, you will require a working installation of the CentOS 7 operating system with root privileges, a console-based text editor of your choice, and a connection to the Internet to facilitate the download of additional packages. Some commands shown here use *less* navigation in their output. Read the *Navigating text files with less* recipe from *Chapter 2, Configuring the System* to learn how to browse them.

How to do it...

systemctl is a program that we will use to manage all our background service tasks in a CentOS 7 system. Here, we will show you how to use it, taking the Apache web server service as an example in order to get familiar with it. For a full explanation of Apache, read *Chapter 12, Providing Web Services*:

1. First, we log in as root and install the Apache web server package:

    ```
    yum install httpd
    ```

2. Next we will check Apache's service status:

    ```
    systemctl status httpd.service
    ```

3. Start the webserver service in the background and print out it's status again:

    ```
    systemctl start httpd.service
    systemctl status httpd.service
    ```

4. Next, let's print out a list of all services currently running in the background of your system; in this list, you should identify the httpd service you just started:

    ```
    systemctl -t service -a --state running
    ```

5. Now, let's make a backup of the Apache configuration file:

    ```
    cp /etc/httpd/conf/httpd.conf /etc/httpd/conf/httpd.conf.BAK
    ```

6. Now, we will make some changes to the main Apache configuration file using sed:

```
sed -i 's/Options Indexes FollowSymLinks/Options -Indexes
+FollowSymLinks/g' /etc/httpd/conf/httpd.conf
```

7. Now, type the following command to stop and start the service and apply our changes:

```
systemctl stop httpd.service
systemctl start httpd.service
systemctl status httpd.service
```

8. Next, let's enable the httpd service to start automatically at boot time:

```
systemctl enable httpd.service
```

9. The last command will show how to restart a service:

```
systemctl restart httpd.service
```

How it works...

As we have seen, the systemctl utility can be used to take full control of your system's services. The systemctl is the control program for systemd, which is the system and service manager in CentOS 7 Linux. The systemctl command can be used for a variety of other tasks as well, but here we concentrate on managing services.

So, what have we learned from this experience?

We started this recipe by logging in as root and installed the Apache web server package as we want to use it for showing how to manage services in general using the systemctl program. Apache or the httpd.service, as it is called by systemd, is just an example we will use; other important services that might be running in a basic server environment could be sshd.service, mariadb.service, crond.service, and so on. Afterwards, we checked httpd's current status with the systemctl status command parameter. The output showed us two fields: **Loaded** and **Active**. The **Loaded** field tells us if it is currently loaded and if it will automatically be started at boot time; the **Active** field denotes whether the service is currently running or not. Next, we showed how to start a service using systemctl. The command's exact starting syntax for services is the systemctl start <name of the service>.service.

> By starting a service, the program gets detached from the terminal by forking off a new process that gets moved into the background where it runs as a non-interactive background process. This is sometimes called **daemon**.

Next, after we started the Apache webserver daemon, we then used systemctl's `status` parameter again to show how the status changes if we run it. The output shows us that it is currently loaded but disabled on reboot. We also see that it is running, along with the latest logging output from this service and other detailed information about the process. To get an overview of all status information for all services on the system, use `systemctl --type service --all`. A `systemctl` service must not be running all the time. Its state can also be stopped, degraded, maintained, and so on. Next, we used the following command to get a list of all currently running services on your system:

```
systemctl -t service -a --state running
```

As you can see here, we used the `-t` flag in order to filter only for type service units. As you may guess, `systemctl` can not only deal with service units, but also with a lot of other unit types. `systemd` units are resources `systemd` can manage using configuration files, and which encapsulate information about services, listening sockets, saved system state snapshots, mounting devices, and other objects that are relevant to the system. To get a list of all possible unit types, type `systemctl -t help`. These configuration unit files reside in special folders in the system, and the type they belong to can be read from the extension; all the service unit files have the file extension, `.service` (for example, device unit files have the extension, `.device`). There are two places where the system stores them. All the `systemd` unit files installed by the basic system during installation are in `/usr/lib/systemd/system`, all other services that come from installing packages such as Apache or for your own configurations should go to `/etc/systemd/system`. We can find our Apache service configuration file exactly at `/usr/lib/systemd/system/httpd.service`. Next, we showed the user how to stop a service, which is the opposite of starting it, using the syntax, `systemctl stop <name of the service>`. Finally, as a last step, we used systemctl's `restart` parameter, which just handles the stopping and starting of a service in one step with less typing. This is often useful if a service hangs and is unresponsive, and you quickly need to reset it to get it working. Before showing how to stop and restart a service, we did another important thing. While the Apache service was running, we changed its main service configuration file with the `sed` command, adding an `-Indexes` option that disables the directory web site file listings, and which is a common measure to increase the security of your web server. Since the Apache web server was already running and loading its configuration into memory during service startup, any changes to this file will never be recognized by the running service.

 Normally, to apply any configuration file change, running services need a full service restart, because configuration files will normally only be loaded during startup initialization.

Now, imagine that your web server is reachable from the Internet and at the moment there are a lot of people accessing your web pages or applications in parallel. If you restart the Apache normally, the web server will be inaccessible for a while (as long as it takes to restart the server) as the process will actually end and afterwards start all over again. All the current users would get HTML 404 error pages if they were to request something at that moment. Also, all the current session information would have gone; imagine you have an online web shop where people use shopping carts or logging in. All this information would also be gone. To avoid the disruption of important services such as the Apache web server, some of these services have a `reload` option (but not every service has this feature!) that we can apply instead of the `restart` parameter. This option just reloads and applies the service's configuration file, while the service itself stays online and does not get interrupted during execution. For Apache, you can use the following command-line: `systemctl reload httpd.service`. To get a list of all the services that have the reload functionality, use the following lines:

```
grep -l "ExecReload" /usr/lib/systemd/system/*.service /etc/systemd/
system/*.service
```

So, having completed this recipe, we can say that we now know how to work with the basic `systemctl` parameters to manage services. It can be a very powerful program and can be used for much more than only starting and stopping services. Also, in this recipe, we have used different names that all mean the same: system service, background process, or daemon.

There's more...

There is another important unit type called `target`. Targets are also unit files and there are quite a number of them already available in your system. To show them, use the following:

```
ls -a /usr/lib/systemd/system/*.target /etc/systemd/system/*.target
```

Simply said, targets are collections of unit files such as services or other targets. They can be used to create runlevel-like environments, which you may know from earlier CentOS versions. Runlevels define which services should be loaded at which system state. For example, there is a graphical state, or a rescue mode state, and so on. To see how the common runlevels correspond to our targets, run the following command, which shows us all the symbolic links between them:

```
ls -al /lib/systemd/system | grep runlevel
```

Targets can be dependent on other targets; to get a nice overview of target dependencies, we can run the following command to show all dependencies from the multi-user target to all the other targets (green means active and red means inactive):

```
systemctl list-dependencies multi-user.target
```

You can show the current target that we are in at the moment with:

```
systemctl get-default
```

You can also switch to another target:

```
systemctl set-default multi-user.target
```

Troubleshooting background services

Often, a big part of every system administrator's work is troubleshooting the server when something goes wrong. This is especially true for your system's services, as they are constantly running and processing information all the time. Services can be dependent on other services and on the server's system, and there will be situations in your administrator's life where the system services will fail or refuse to start. Here, in this recipe, we will show you how to troubleshoot them if something goes wrong.

Getting ready

To complete this recipe, you will require a working installation of the CentOS 7 operating system with root privileges and a console-based text editor of your choice; you should also have completed the *Knowing and managing your background services* recipe from this chapter, where we installed the Apache web server.

How to do it...

In order to show you how to troubleshoot services, we will introduce a random error in the Apache service's configuration file and then show you how to troubleshoot and fix it:

1. Log in as root and type the following command to append content to the httpd.conf:

    ```
    echo "THIS_IS_AN_ERRORLINE" >> /etc/httpd/conf/httpd.conf
    ```

2. Next, reload the httpd service and show its output:

    ```
    systemctl reload httpd.service
    systemctl status httpd.service -l
    ```

3. Let's revert this error line:

    ```
    sed -i 's/THIS_IS_AN_ERRORLINE//g' /etc/httpd/conf/httpd.conf
    ```

4. Now, restart the service again:

    ```
    systemctl reload httpd.service
    systemctl status httpd.service
    ```

How it works...

In this fairly short recipe, we showed you how an example service will behave if it contains errors, and what you can do to fix it to get you started. There are a lot of different scenarios where something can go wrong when services malfunction, and it can be a big part of a system administrator's job to solve those kinds of problem.

So, what have we learned from this experience?

We started this recipe by introducing a line of text in the main Apache configuration file, which does not contain any valid configuration syntax, and therefore the `httpd` service cannot interpret it. Then, we used the `systemctl reload` parameter to reload our server's configuration file. As said before, not all services have the reload option, so if your service of interest does not support this, use the `restart` parameter instead. Since Apache will try to reload the configuration file with our current changes, it will refuse to accept the new configuration because of the wrong syntax that we introduced. Since we are just reloading the configuration, the running Apache process will not be affected by this problem and will stay online using its original configuration. The `systemctl` parameter will print out the following error message, giving us a hint of what to do next:

```
Job for httpd.service failed. Take a look at systemctl status httpd.
service and journalctl -xe for details.
```

As suggested by the error output, the `systemctl` status parameter is a very powerful tool to see what's going on behind the scenes with this service, and to try and find out the reason for any failure (here you can also see that Apache is still running). If you start the `systemctl status` with the `-l` flag, it prints out an even longer version of the output, which can help you even more.

The output of this command shows us the exact reason for failing the configuration reload, so we can easily trace down the cause of the problem (the output has been truncated):

```
AH00526: Syntax error on line 354 of /etc/httpd/conf/httpd.conf:
Invalid command ERRORLINE, perhaps misspelled or defined by a module, is
not included in the server configuration.
```

This output is part of the complete `journald` log information. If you want to read more about it, please refer to the *Tracking system resources with journald* recipe in this chapter. So, with this very useful information from the output, we can easily spot the problem and redo the introduction of `ERRORLINE` using the `sed` command and reload the service again; this time everything will work fine.

So, in summary, we can say that the `systemctl status` command is a very comfortable command that can be tremendously helpful in finding out problems with your service. Most services are very sensitive to syntax errors, and sometimes it can be just a misplaced space character that caused the service to refuse to work. Therefore, system administrators must work precisely all the time.

Tracking system resources with journald

Log files contain system messages and output from services, the kernel, and all kinds of running applications. They can be very useful in many situations, for instance, to troubleshoot system problems and monitor services or other system resources, or doing security forensics after a breach of security. In this recipe, you will learn the basics of how to work with logging services using journald.

Getting ready

To complete this recipe, you will need a working installation of the CentOS 7 operating system with root privileges and a console-based text editor of your choice. Also, setting the time and date correctly is very crucial for the whole logging concept, so please apply the *Synchronizing the system clock with NTP and the chrony suite* recipe from *Chapter 2, Configuring the System* before using this recipe. Also, a basic knowledge of systemd and units can be advantageous. This is covered in the *Knowing and managing background services* recipe in this chapter. Journalctl uses *less* navigation to show output; please read the *Navigating text files with less* recipe from *Chapter 2, Configuring the System* if you don't know how to work with it.

How to do it...

On CentOS 7, we have a choice between two logging mechanisms called `rsyslog` and the `journald` log system, which is a component of the new `systemd` system manager, for viewing and managing logging information. Here, we will show you how to work with the `journalctl` command, which is the controlling client for the `journald` daemon:

1. To begin, log in as root and type the following command to view the whole journal log:

    `journalctl`

2. Next, we want to show only the messages within a specific time frame (change the date accordingly):

    `journalctl --since "2015-07-20 6:00:00" --until "2015-07-20 7:30:00"`

3. Afterwards, we want to filter the log system by all messages from the sshd service:

    `journalctl -u sshd.service --since "yesterday"`

4. Now, we want to show only messages with type error:

    `journalctl -p err -b`

5. To get the most verbose version of `journalctl`, use the `verbose` option:

    `journalctl -p err -b -o verbose`

6. To get a *current* view on the log output, use the following command (this is not *less* navigation—use the key combination *Ctrl+C* to exit this view):

```
journalctl -f
```

How it works...

In CentOS 7, we can use the new `journald` logging system, which is a part of the `systemd` system management. It is a centralized tool that will log just about everything on your system including all output from the early boot over kernel to services and all program messages. The main advantage over other logging mechanisms is that you don't have to configure logging for each of your services or other resources, because everything is already set up for all applications that are controlled and running through the centralized `systemd` system.

So, what have we learned from this experience?

We began our journey by running the `journalctl` command, which when applied without any parameters show us the complete journal log, which includes everything from starting your system and capturing the first boot log entries to the latest system messages in the order they appeared, appending new messages to the bottom (chronological order). If your system has been running for a while, it can contain hundreds of thousands of lines of logging data, and is very impractical to work with in this raw form.

This output is constantly captured by the `journald` daemon, but is not written to text files as other logging systems such as `rsyslog` do it. Instead, it uses a structured and indexed binary file, which stores a lot of additional meta information such as user Id, timestamp, and so on, and which makes it easy to transform into all kinds of different output formats. This can be very convenient if you want to further process journal information by another tool. As you cannot read binary files, you will need the client `journalctl` for it, which is used to query the `journald` database. Since it is almost impossible to parse through this sheer amount of data manually, we then take advantage of journalctl's rich filtering options. First, we used the `--since` and `--until` parameters to extract all log messages within a specific time frame. The syntax for specifying the time and date here is very flexible and understands phrases such as `yesterday` or `now`, but we stick with the simple date syntax, `YYYY-MM-DD HH:MM:SS`. Next, we used journalctl's `-u` parameter to filter log messages for a specific unit type. We used it to filter messages coming from the sshd daemon service. We added another filter using the `--since` parameter, which tightens the result of the `-u` unit filter even more, outputting only sshd service results that occurred yesterday. The next filter we applied was using the parameter string, `-p err -b`, which filters the log database by priority or log level. Every log message can have an associated priority that determines the importance of the message. To find out more about different log levels, refer to the manual using the command line `man 3 syslog` (if this manual is not available, install it by typing `yum install man-pages`). Our command will print out all log messages labeled as `error` or above, which includes: `error`, `critical`, `alert`, or `emergency`.

Next, we used the same command parameters but added `-o verbose`, which gives the most verbose output of logging information. Lastly we presented the `-f` parameter (for follow), which will give us a *live* view of the latest log messages and leaves this connection open, appending any new messages to the end of the output when they occur. This is often useful to see how the system reacts if you are currently testing out settings or starting/stopping services.

Summing up, one can say that, on CentOS 7, two logging systems do coexist: the older `rsyslog` and the newer `journald`, with the latter being your primary tool of choice for troubleshooting your system. But remember that on CentOS 7, `journald` is not a full replacement for `rsyslog` though. There are some `rsyslog` features that are missing in `journald`, and also there are lots of tools and scripts, such as log digesting tools or monitoring suites such as Nagios, that work exclusively with `rsyslog`.

System administrators often face a big challenge troubleshooting system errors or unexpected server behaviors. Often, it's not easy to find the single point of failure by searching through massive amounts of different log file texts while applying regular expression searches or Linux command line kung fu. Journald provides a very convenient alternative by providing a powerful and well-defined centralized querying system to get the log file analysis done quickly and efficiently!

Configuring journald to make it persistent

Journald's advantages over other logging systems such as `rsyslog` is that it is very efficient and logs just about everything on your system automatically without the need to configure anything, because it is a part of the `systemd` suite. The main disadvantage is that all `journald` log information will get lost after a system's restart. Journald logging can produce huge amounts of data and by default all logging information is only kept in memory, which is not very practicable if you need to access older log information or analyze causes of system crash reboots. Here, in this recipe, we show you how to configure `journald` to make it persistent.

Getting ready

To complete this recipe, you will require a minimal installation of the CentOS 7 operating system with root privileges and a console-based text editor of your choice.

How to do it...

To begin this recipe, we need to create a location that will hold our persistent journal database:

1. Log in as the root user and create the following directory:

    ```
    mkdir /var/log/journal
    ```

2. Next, add the new directory to `journald` to use it as a storage location and fix permissions:

```
systemd-tmpfiles --create --prefix /var/log/journal
```

3. Now, restart `journald`:

```
systemctl restart systemd-journald
```

4. Finally, to check whether the log survived the reboot, restart the computer and type the following:

```
journalctl --boot=-1
```

How it works...

We started this recipe by creating the new directory, `/var/log/journal`. By default, `journald` writes its log database to `/run/log/journal`, which is a directory only for runtime information, and its content does not survive system reboots. Afterwards, we used the `systemd-tmpfiles` command to set up our new directory for `journald`. Finally, we restarted the `journald` server daemon to apply our changes to the system. To test if persistence is working, restart your server and afterwards use `journalctl -boot=-1`. This will show us all journal information from the last boot. If persistence is not working, it will print out the following error; otherwise it will correctly show all journal messages before the last boot:

```
Failed to look up boot -1: Cannot assign requested address
```

In this fairly simple recipe, we have shown how to make `journald` persistent over system reboots. This is really useful if you need to review older log files from the past, which can sometimes help you find out problems, for example, the roots of past hardware failures.

Managing users and their groups

In this recipe, we will learn how to manage your system's users and groups on CentOS 7. Essential user and group managing skills are one of the most important CentOS system administrator fundamentals.

Getting ready

To complete this recipe, you will need a working installation of the CentOS 7 operating system with root privileges and a console-based text editor of your choice.

How to do it...

This recipe shows you how to manage users and groups by learning how to add, delete, and modify them:

1. To begin this recipe, we log in as root and type the following command to get a list of all the users known to the system: `cat /etc/passwd`.

2. Now, show the root user ID (**UID**) and group ID (**GID**):

    ```
    id root
    ```

3. Next, we will run the following command to add a new user to the system (exchange `your_new_username` with a username of your choice):

    ```
    useradd your_new_username
    ```

4. However, in order to complete this process, you will be expected to provide a suitable password. To do this, type the following command (change `your_new_username` with a username of choice) than enter a secure password when prompted:

    ```
    passwd your_new_username
    ```

     Passwords should not be less than six characters, but should not be longer than sixteen characters. They should consist of alphanumeric values, and for obvious reasons you must avoid the use of whitespaces. Do not use a dictionary-based word and refrain from using a known or obvious phrase.

5. Next, create a new group and give it a special name:

    ```
    groupadd your_new_group
    ```

6. Then, we add our new user to this new group:

    ```
    usermod -G your_new_group your_new_username
    ```

7. Finally, let's print the user ID and group IDs of our new user to see what has changed:

    ```
    id your_new_username
    ```

How it works...

The purpose of this recipe was to create a new user and group and show how to connect them together.

So, what did we learn from this experience?

First, we printed out the content of file /etc/passwd to show all the current users in the system. This list not only contains normal user-accounts that belong to real persons, but also accounts that are used to control and own a specific application or service. Then, we used the id command to display the unique user UID and GID for our existing user root. In Linux, every user can be identified by their UID and GID, and every file in the filesystem has specific permission settings that manage its access for the file owner, group owner, and the rest of the users. For each of those three groups, you can enable or disable read, write, and execute permissions using the command, chmod (use man chmod to learn more, and also check out man chown). The owner and group permissions correspond to a UID and GID that we can display for every file using ls -l.

Next, we issued the useradd command that required us to supply a suitable name for the new user, which in turn will enable the server to establish the new identity with a default set of values and criteria that includes a user ID, home directory, primary group (GID), and also set the default shell to bash. Completing this process is simply a matter of confirming a suitable password. To remove a user, there is the opposite command, userdel, which works similarly but can be given the option -f to remove the home directory instead of leave it on the system. Next, we used the groupadd command, which, as the name implies, will create a new group and associate a new unique GID to it. Afterwards, we made our user in question a member of the new group that we created before using the usermod -G command. As said before, each user has exactly one unique UID and GID. The first group is the primary group and is mandatory; however a user can belong to a number of different groups, which are then called secondary groups. The primary group is needed when creating a new file because it will set the GID and UID of the user creating it. To delete a group, we can use the groupdel command. Finally, we used the id command again on our new user to show its UID, primary GID, and the new secondary GID groups we added to it.

You are now able to fully control your user and groups with just a few commands: useradd, usermod, userdel, groupadd, groupmod, and groupdel.

Scheduling tasks with cron

In this recipe, we will investigate the role of server automation and the convenience of running specific tasks at predefined periods by introducing you to the time-based job scheduler known as cron. Cron allows for the automation of tasks by enabling the administrator to determine a predefined schedule based on any hour, any day, or any month. It is a standard component of the CentOS operating system, and it is the purpose of this recipe to introduce you to the concept of managing recurring tasks in order to take advantage of this invaluable tool and to make CentOS work for you.

Getting ready

To complete this recipe, you will require a minimal installation of the CentOS 7 operating system with root privileges, and a console-based text editor of your choice. The `crontab` program uses Vim for file editing. If you do not know how to work with Vim, go through the tutorial shown in the recipe *Introduction to Vim* in *Chapter 2, Configuring the System*.

How to do it...

The purpose of this recipe is to create a script that will write the time and date with a few words of your choice to a text file every five minutes. This may seem to be a relatively simple exercise, but the intention is to show you that, from such simplicity, cron can be used to do so much more that will make working with CentOS an absolute pleasure.

1. To begin this recipe, log in as root and create your first cron job by typing:

   ```
   crontab -e
   ```

2. We will now create a simple cron job that will write the date and time with the words `hello world` to a file located at `/root/cron-helloworld.txt` every five minutes. To do this, add the following line:

   ```
   */5 * * * * echo `date` "Hello world" >>$HOME/cron-
   helloworld.txt
   ```

3. When complete, simply save the file and exit the editor. The system will now respond with the following message:

   ```
   crontab: installing new crontab
   ```

4. The preceding message informs you that the server is now creating the new `cron` job and will automatically activate it. You can view the output of the script by reviewing the file found at `/root/cron-helloworld.txt` (you have to wait 5 minutes), or by monitoring the logfile found at `/var/log/cron` (use `tail -f /var/log/cron` and Ctrl+C to exit).

How it works...

Cron is the name of a program that enables CentOS users to execute commands or scripts automatically at a specified time and date. Cron's settings are kept in a user-specific file called `crontab`, and as we have seen in this recipe this file can be edited to create automated tasks as often as they are required.

So what did we learn from this experience?

The example used was very simple, but in many ways this was the purpose of this recipe. Crontab uses a daemon, `crond`, which runs constantly in the background and checks once a minute to see if any of the scheduled jobs need to be executed. If a task is found, then cron will execute it. To edit an existing `crontab` file or to create a new `crontab`, we use the `crontab -e` command. To view a list of current cron jobs, you can type `crontab -l`. Alternatively, to view a list of the current jobs for another user, you can type `crontab -u username -l`. Tasks or jobs are generally referred to as cron jobs, and by avoiding complication in our first script, it was the intention to show you that the nature of command construction was very simple. The formation of a cron job looks like this:

```
<minute> <hour> <day of the month> <month of the year> <day of the week>
<command>
```

Entries are separated by a single or tabbed space, and the allowed values are primarily numeric (that is, `0-59` for a minute, `0-23` for an hour, `1-31` for a day of the month, `1-12` for month of the year, and `0-7` for day of the week). However, in saying this, it is also true to say that there are more specific operators (`/` , `-`) and cron-specific shortcuts (that is, `@yearly`, `@daily`, `@hourly`, and `@weekly`) that do allow for additional controls. For example, where the `/` operator is used to step through specified units, it can be read as *every*, so in our recipe the use of `*/5` will run the task every five minutes while the use of `*/1` runs the task every minute. As an addition to this, you should be aware that the use of this syntax will align all commands on the hour. So, with this in mind, the most suitable template or starting point for anyone wanting to write their first `cron` job is to start with a series of five asterisks followed by the command, like this:

```
* * * * * /absolute/path/to/script.sh
```

Then, proceed to configure the minute, hour, day, month, and day-of-the-week values as desired. For example, if you want a particular PHP script to run at 8 P.M. (20:00 hrs) on every weekday (Monday-Friday), it may look like this:

```
0 20 * * 1-5 /full/path/to/your/php/script.php
```

So, with this in mind, and by completing this recipe, you can see how cron can be used to manage a database backup, run a scheduled system backup, provide support to websites by activating scripts at predefined intervals, or run various bash scripts and a whole lot more.

There's more...

To delete or disable a cron job, it is simply a matter of either removing the instruction from an individual user's cron file or by placing a hash (#) at the beginning of the line. Individual cron files can be found at `/var/spool/cron/<username>`, and the use of the hash will either disable the cron job or allow you to write comments. To completely remove a `crontab` file, you can also use `crontab -r`. For example, if you want to remove the cron job created in the main recipe, you can log in as root and begin by typing the command, `crontab -e`. At this point, you may either remove the entire line or comment it out, as shown here:

```
# */15 * * * * echo `date` "Hello world" >>$HOME/cron-helloworld.txt
```

Next, save the file. There are also some special cron directories in the filesystem for system-wide cron jobs that will, if you drop a script file in it, run it automatically at a certain time point. The folders are called `cron.daily`, `cron.hourly`, `cron.weekly`, and `cron.monthly` in the `/etc` directory, and their names refer to the time point that they are run. Just remove the script from the folder if you don't want to execute it anymore. Take a look at the *Monitoring important server infrastructure* recipe for an example.

Synchronizing files and doing more with rsync

`rsync` is a program that can be used to synchronize files and directories across a variety of local and remote locations. It can interact with multiple operating systems, work over SSH, provide incremental backups, execute commands on a remote machine, and replace the need for the `cp` and `scp` commands. The `rsync` program is an invaluable asset for any system administrator who intends to run a server or manage a network of computers, as it not only simplifies the process of making backups in general, but it can be used to action a complete backup solution. For this reason, it is the purpose of this recipe to offer a suitable starting point for a small utility that will quickly become your trusted friend.

Getting ready

To complete this recipe, you will require a working installation of the CentOS 7 operating system with root privileges, a console-based text editor of your choice, and a connection to the Internet in order to facilitate the download of additional packages.

How to do it...

During the course of this recipe, it will be assumed that you know the location of the source files and directories that you wish to synchronize, and that a suitable destination is available:

1. To begin this recipe, log in as root and install `rsync` by typing:

   ```
   yum install rsync
   ```

2. Now, create a target directory for our synchronization (change the folder name appropriately):

   ```
   mkdir ~/sync-target
   ```

3. To begin the synchronization process, simply repeat the following command by modifying the value used for `/path/to/source/files/` with something more applicable to your needs:

   ```
   rsync -avz --delete /path/to/source/files/  ~/sync-target
   ```

4. Having used the *Return* key to confirm the preceding instruction, your system will now respond with a live report of what is being copied. When this process has finished, you can then compare both directories to see that the contents are exactly the same. To do this, use the `diff` command (if both are the same, no output will be written):

   ```
   diff -r /path/to/source/files/ ~/sync-target
   ```

How it works...

In this recipe, we considered the use of `rsync` through the command line. Of course, this is only one of the many ways that this tool can be used, but by using this approach we were able to explore a handful of the features provided by this very valuable utility.

So, what did we learn from this experience?

Rsync is not intended to be complicated. It is a fast and efficient file synchronization tool that is designed to be versatile by giving you complete access to an array of features on the command line. It can be used to maintain an exact copy (or mirror) of the `source` directory on the same machine or on a completely different system, and it does this by copying all the files once and then only updating the files that have changed the next time you run it. This can save tremendous bandwidth and should be your primary tool when copying data over the network. The use of the phrase, `--delete`, is important, as it instructs `rsync` to delete files on the target that do not exist in the source, while the chosen flags imply that `rsync` should use `-a` archive mode in order to recursively copy files and directories while keeping all permissions and time-based information; `-v`)verbosity mode so you can see what is happening; and `-z` to compress the data during the file transfer in order to save bandwidth and reduce the amount of time required to complete the entire process.

As you can see, `rsync` is very flexible and has many options that go beyond the purpose of this recipe, but if you want to exclude certain files you could always extend the original instruction by invoking the `--exclude` flag. By doing this, you tell `rsync` to back up an entire directory but ensure that it does not include a predefined pattern of files and folders. For example, if you are copying files from your server to a USB device and you do not want to include large files (such as an `.iso` image) or ZIP files, then your command may look similar to this:

```
rsync --delete -avz --exclude="*.zip" --exclude="*.iso"  /path/to/source/
/path/to/external/disk/
```

On a final note, there is the subject of verbosity. Verbosity is very useful, but a tendency to use bytes as its primary unit of measurement can be a source of confusion. So, in order to change this, you can invoke `rsync` with the `-h` (or human readable) option, as shown next:

```
rsync -avzh --exclude="home/path/to/file.txt" /home/ /path/to/external/
disk/
```

Maintaining backups and taking snapshots

In this recipe, we will show you how to do data backups, on a regular basis, that will take snapshots of some of your system's directory using the `crond` daemon. This will run the `rsync` program at regular intervals to implement a fully automated backup solution.

Getting ready

To complete this recipe, you will require a working installation of the CentOS 7 operating system with root privileges and a console-based text editor of your choice. It is also advantageous if you have read the *Synchronizing files and doing more with rsync* and *Scheduling tasks with cron* recipes in this chapter to get a deeper understanding of used commands.

How to do it...

It's important to install the `rsync` program on your server before proceeding with this recipe.

1. First, log in as root and create a directory where our backups will land:

    ```
    mkdir /backups
    ```

2. Now, we will create the following shell script file and open it for editing:

    ```
    mkdir ~/bin;vi ~/bin/mybackup.sh
    ```

3. Put in the following content, replacing /backups in the environment variable DEST and SOURCE with the one you would like to backup as well as the recipient's EMAIL:

```
#!/bin/bash
SBJT="cron backup report for `hostname -s` from $(date
+%Y%m%d:%T)"
FROM=root@domain
EMAIL=johndoe@internet.com
SOURCE=/root
DEST=/backups
LFPATH=/tmp
LF=$LFPATH/$(date +%Y%m%d_%T)_logfile.log
rsync --delete --log-file=$LF -avzq $SOURCE $DEST
(echo "$SBJT"; echo; cat $LF ) | sendmail -f $FROM -t $EMAIL
```

4. Make the script executable:

```
chmod a+x /root/bin/mybackup.sh
```

5. Now, open crontab using:

```
crontab -e
```

6. Next, create the following entry by adding the following line to the end of the document, then save and close it:

```
30 20 * * * /root/bin/mybackup.sh
```

How it works...

In this recipe, we have created a full automatic backup solution for a single system directory, which will create a snapshot of the files at a certain time point. At the time the backup process is complete you will receive an e-mail informing you that a backup has been made with a brief review of the actions taken.

So what did we learn from this experience?

We started this recipe by creating a directory where our backup will be placed. Next we created the actual script and filled it with some commands. Line 1 defines the file as a bash script, lines 2-6 are variables you can modify and customize to fit your own needs. lines 7-8 create a path and name for the log file based on the date, and line 9 calls rsync which will synchronize all our source files to the target directory /backups. It uses a special --log-file parameter which writes all output to the given file. The final line (10) sends the content of this log file to an email address.

Remember, you should customize the values as required (that is, change the e-mail address used, select a source directory, and choose a destination directory, and so on.). Before it can be used and executed by `cron`, we made it executable. Finally, we added this script as a cron job to run on a daily schedule at 20:30 hours. However, as this may be some hours away, if you would like to test your script right now, you can execute it on the command line using the following:

```
/root/bin/mybackup.sh
```

In conclusion, it will go without saying that a backup should be located on an external drive or on a separate partition, but having completed this introduction I think you will agree that `rsync` is ideally positioned in such a way that it will enable any server administrator to develop their own policy with regard to maintaining an effective backup of important data.

Monitoring important server infrastructure

In this recipe, we will use a small script that will monitor the available filesystem's disk space periodically using cron, and if it exceeds a certain percentage threshold the script will send out a mail with a warning message.

Getting ready

To complete this recipe, you will require a working installation of the CentOS 7 operating system with root privileges and a console-based text editor of your choice. You should have read the *Scheduling tasks with cron* recipe to have a basic understanding of the principles behind the cron system.

How to do it...

1. To begin this recipe, log in as root and create the following file that will contain our monitoring script:

   ```
   vi /etc/cron.daily/monitor_disk_space.sh
   ```

2. Now, put in the following content:

   ```
   #!/bin/bash
   EMAIL="root@localhost"
   THRESHOLD=70
   df -H | grep -vE '^Filesystem|tmpfs|cdrom' | awk '{ print $5 " "
   $6 }' | while read output;
   do
     usep=$(echo $output | awk '{ print $1}' | cut -d'%' -f1  )
     partition=$(echo $output | awk '{ print $2 }' )
   ```

```
if [ $usep -ge $THRESHOLD ]; then

(echo "Subject: Alert: Free space low on `hostname -s`, $usep %
used on $partition"; echo) |

sendmail -t $EMAIL

fi

done
```

3. Now, save the file and make it executable:

```
chmod +x /etc/cron.daily/monitor_disk_space.sh
```

How it works...

We made this script executable and put it in the `/etc/cron.daily` directory, which is all we need to do to run this script automatically every day via the `crond` service.

This simple script showed us how easy it is to build monitoring scripts, and this can be a real alternative to installing and configuring big monitoring suites such as Nagios. You can use the shown script as a starting point to expand on, adding further resources that are important to monitor, such as CPU load, available RAM, and so on.

We used a script that executes the Linux command `df`, which is a tool to report file system disk space usage. From this command's output, the script then parsed the `USE%` column (with the Unix tools `awk` and `cut`), which gives us the total disk percentage used. This number will then be compared to a threshold the user can set by editing the script and changing the environment variable, `THRESHOLD`. If the extracted percentage number is higher than our threshold, there will be an email sent to the email address defined with the environment variable, `EMAIL` (change appropriately if needed).

Taking control with GIT and Subversion

Document revision control systems or version control systems, as they are sometimes called, are used for the management of changes to documents. These systems get more and more important these days as modern work often connects people from around the globe to collaborate and work together on all kinds of documents (for example, software source code) making it important to manage the file changes by different people using revisions. In this recipe, we will show you how to use modern version control systems such as GIT and Subversion to manage the versioning of config files.

Getting ready

To complete this recipe, you will require a working installation of the CentOS 7 operating system with root privileges, and a connection to the Internet in order to facilitate the download of additional packages.

How to do it...

Here in this recipe, we will put the complete main Linux configuration directory, /etc/, under version control of a Git repository to keep track of all our changes to configuration files:

1. To begin, log in as root, install Git, and configure it by providing an email address and username (please substitute your_username and your_email_address with real names):

```
yum install git
git config --global user.email  "your_email_address"
git config --global user.name "your_username"
```

2. Now, let's create a new repository in the /etc directory:

```
cd /etc/
git init
```

3. Now, after we have our new repository, let's add all the files in the /etc/ directory under version control:

```
git add *
```

4. To commit the files to the repository creating your first revision, type the following:

```
git commit -a -m "inital commit of the full /etc/ directory"
```

5. Now, let's change a file:

```
echo "FILE HAS CHANGED" >> yum.conf
```

6. Next, show the changes to your repository:

```
git status
```

7. Next, we will commit these changes and create a new revision of it:

```
git commit -a -m "changing yum.conf files"
```

8. Next, show all the commits so far:

```
git log --pretty=oneline --abbrev-commit
```

9. This will output the following commits on my system (the number hashes will be different on yours):

```
8069c4a changing yum.conf
5f0d50a inital commit of the full /etc directory
```

10. Based on the output from the earlier step, we will now show all the differences between the two revision numbers (change the number hashes on your system based on the output from the earlier step):

    `git diff 8069c4a 5f0d50a`

11. To complete this recipe, we will revert our changes to the original file revision (the initial commit):

    `git checkout 5f0d50a`

How it works

Here, in this recipe, we showed you how to use Git to manage changes to system config files in the `/etc` directory. This can be important, for example, if you are testing things out, so a lot of changes will be made to some configuration files and you will want to keep track of your changes, which is nice because you don't need to memorize every single step you have taken if you later have to revert the changes or go back to a specific revision, or compare different file versions.

So, what did we learn from this experience?

We started by installing Git and added a username and an e-mail address to its configuration, which is essential for using it later in the process. Then, we changed to the `/etc` directory and initialized (using the `init` parameter) a new empty Git project there, which is called repository and keeps track of all the files associated to it. This command will add a hidden `.git` directory to it, which will contain the complete file changes and revision information. Next, we added all the files (using the wildcard * operator) from this directory, including all sub-directories to the next revision. A revision is like a state the files are in at a given time point, and is identified by a unique hash ID such as `8069c4a`. Then, we actually created a new revision using the commit parameter and supplied a meaningful message using the `-m` parameter. After we set up the Git repository and added all the files to it, every change to the files gets watched in the `/etc` directory. Next, we changed the main YUM configuration file in our repository by adding a random string to the end of it using the echo `>>` command. If we now use git's `status` parameter again, we see in the output that the Git system has notified that this file has been changed. We can now create a new revision with the changed file by using git's `commit` parameter again, using another meaningful message here stating that `yum.conf` has been changed. We then used the git `log` command. This will show us all the committed revisions with their unique `md5` hash string IDs. With this ID, we can fuel the git `diff` command to see all the file changes between two revisions. To learn more about the output format, use `man git-diff-files` and read its section COMBINED DIFF FORMAT. In our last step, we used the checkout command to go to a specific file revision; here we reverted all our changes and went back to the original file state.

Git is a very powerful version management tool, and in this recipe we just scratched the surface of what can be done with it. To learn more about Git's wonderful techniques, such as branching, merging, pull requests, and so on, start with the Git tutorial pages by typing in `man gittutorial`.

There's more...

You can also use the program Subversion to bring your `/etc` directory under version control. Subversion is another common document revision control system whose main difference from Git is that it uses a centralized server to keep track of the file changes. Git is distributed, meaning that everybody working on a Git project will have the complete repository locally on their computer. Here, we will show you the exact steps necessary to use Subversion instead of Git for this purpose:

1. First, install Subversion and configure a new server directory for our `/etc` repository:

   ```
   yum install subversion
   mkdir -p /var/local/svn/etc-repos
   svnadmin create --fs-type fsfs /var/local/svn/etc-repos
   ```

2. Now, make an in-place import of the `/etc` filesystem to our new repository:

   ```
   svn mkdir file:///var/local/svn/etc-repos/etc
   -m "Make a directory in the repository to correspond to /etc"
   ```

3. Now, switch to the `/etc` directory and add all the files to a new revision:

   ```
   cd /etc
   svn checkout  file:///var/local/svn/etc-repos/etc ./
   svn add *
   ```

4. Now, create your first commit:

   ```
   svn commit -m "inital commit of the full /etc/ directory"
   ```

5. Next, change the `yum.conf` file:

   ```
   echo "FILE HAS CHANGED" >> yum.conf
   ```

6. Commit your changes to a new file revision:

   ```
   svn commit -m "changing yum.conf files"
   ```

7. Now, show the change log:

   ```
   svn log -r 1:HEAD
   ```

8. Show the file differences between our two commits (the first commit was the /etc import):

   ```
   svn diff -r 2:3
   ```

9. Finally, revert to the first revision of our yum.conf file:

   ```
   svn update -r 2 yum.conf
   ```

So, what have we learned from this experience?

We started the recipe by checking to see if any updates were available to our system using the `yum` command with the `check-update` option. In this way, YUM will now check a central repository to confirm if an update is applicable to our system. A repository is a remote directory or website that contains prepared software packages and utilities. YUM will use this facility to automatically locate and obtain the correct **Red Hat Package Manager** (**RPM**) and dependencies, and if an update is available, then YUM will respond accordingly with a full summary of what packages and dependencies are available. For this reason, YUM is a very useful tool, and without doubt its mechanism does serve to simplify the processes associated with package management, because it can talk to repositories and this saves us from having to find and install new applications or updates manually. If there are updates available, the output will show us exactly which packages are affected, then we can proceed to update the system by using YUM's `update` parameter. In this instance, the preceding command includes the `-y` flag. This is done in order to circumvent the need to agree with the transaction summary given, and to confirm that we have already agreed to make these updates after running the previous check. Otherwise, you would simply confirm the requests by using the *Y* key.

There's more...

You can also use the update parameter to update single packages instead of the whole system by providing the package name like so: `yum update package_name`. YUM will serve to ensure that all of the requirements for an application are met during installation, and it will automatically install the packages for any dependencies that are not already present on your system. However, and I am sure you will be pleased to hear this, if a new application has requirements that conflict with existing software, YUM will abort the process without making any changes to your system. If you want to automate the updating of your system using a specific time interval, you can install the `yum-cron` package, which can be highly customized but is outside the scope of this book. To start after installation, use `man yum-cron`.

Using YUM to search for packages

In this recipe, we will investigate the role of using YUM to find a package. YUM was developed to improve the installation of RPM software packages, and it is used to access a growing list of packages that provide a full range of services offered by your server. YUM is simple to use, but if you are not sure what a package is called, then your duties as the server administrator can become that much harder. To overcome this, YUM maintains an extensive range of discovery tools and it is the purpose of this recipe to show you how to use this functionality in order to search through the various repositories and find the package you need.

Getting ready

To complete this recipe, you will require a working installation of the CentOS 7 operating system with root privileges, a console-based text editor of your choice, and a connection to the Internet.

How to do it...

This recipe will show you how to find one or more packages by invoking YUM's searching options. To do this, you will need to log in as the root user and complete the following process:

1. To search for a single package, replace the `keyword` value with the appropriate phrase, string, or parameter, and type the following:

    ```
    yum search keyword
    ```

2. Wait for a summary of the search results, and when a list is generated, you can query any package shown by simply replacing `package_name` with the appropriate value:

    ```
    yum info package_name
    ```

3. If the preceding results prove satisfactory, and you want to view a list of dependencies associated with the package in question, type the following:

    ```
    yum deplist package_name
    ```

How it works...

Searching for packages with YUM can be achieved in the same way as you would search for anything on the **World Wide Web** (**WWW**). The types of words you can search for can be as specific or as general as you like. They can even consist of full or partial words; having found a package that you may be interested in, you will have noticed that this recipe has also served to show you how to discover additional information about the package in question.

So, what have we learned from this experience?

YUM maintains extensive search features and it allows you to query packages by keyword, package name, and pathname. For example, if you want to locate the correct package for compiling C, Objective-C, and C++ code, you can use the `yum search compiler` query. When using these search terms on the command line, there are a number of related results, and each package carries a brief description that enables us to use a simple process of elimination in order to select the most obvious or the most relevant value. With this in mind, you can then query YUM using the `info` parameter to find out more about certain packages. This option reveals the full package details together with a detailed description of what functionality the package is intended to provide. Generally speaking, you may not need to know any further details.

However, there may be circumstances in which you want to know how this package interacts with the server as a whole (especially if you are working with source installations or troubleshooting broken packages), so we can use YUM's `deplist` parameter that can give quite a detailed report; if you do happen to have any broken packages, you could simply use this output to detail what dependencies you may or may not need to install in order to fix an underlying issue. This command is particularly useful when debugging dependencies or when working with source-based installations.

There's more...

Sometimes, you may not want to search for a specific package, and instead you may prefer to display the contents of your repositories in a catalog-style format. Again, this is easy to do and YUM provides for this functionality with the following commands. If you would like to simply list all the packages available to you from the current repositories used by your system, type `yum list all`. However, because this list may be quite exhaustive, you may prefer to page through the results by using `yum list all | less`. In a similar fashion, if you would simply like to list all the software currently installed on your system, type `yum list installed | less`. If you would like to determine which packages provide for a specific file or feature, simply run the following command at any time by substituting `your_filename_here` with something more relevant to your own needs: `yum provides your_filename_here`.

Using YUM to install packages

In this recipe, we will investigate the role of YUM in installing new packages on your server. An important task for every server administrator is the installation of applications and services. There are several different ways to achieve this, but the most effective method involves the YUM package manager. YUM is able to search through any number of repositories, automatically resolve package dependencies, and specify the installation of one or more packages. YUM is a modern and definitive way to install your packages on your server, and it is the purpose of this recipe to show you how it is done.

Getting ready

To complete this recipe, you will require a working installation of the CentOS 7 operating system with root privileges, a console-based text editor of your choice, and a connection to the Internet in order to facilitate the download of additional packages. It's also good if you have already found some interesting packages to install, which can be learned by using the instructions from the *Using YUM to search for packages* recipe.

How to do it...

This recipe will show you how to install one or more packages by invoking the YUM installation option. To do this, you will need to log in as the root user and complete the following process:

1. To install a single package, replace the `package_name` value with the appropriate value and type the following:

   ```
   yum install package_name
   ```

2. Your system will now provide a transaction report that will require your approval. So, when prompted, simply respond by using the *Y* or *N* key and press the *Return* key to either accept or decline the transaction, as shown as follows:

   ```
   Is this ok [y/d/N]: y
   ```

3. If you have declined the transaction, then no further work is required and you will exit the package management routine. However, if you have confirmed the transaction, then watch the progress of your installation, and in the end it will show you a `Complete!` message.

4. Congratulations! You now have successfully installed your package of choice.

How it works...

All packages are stored in the RPM package file format, and it is the role of YUM to provide access to those files that are stored in various repositories on the Internet. YUM is the power behind the package management for CentOS and it really does make the installation process very easy, but what have we learned from this experience?

Having invoked the `install` command, YUM will conduct a search of the various repositories in order to find the relevant headers and metadata associated with the package in question. For example, if you wanted to install a package called `wget`, you would begin by issuing the `install` command like so: `yum install wget`. YUM will then locate the package and generate a transaction summary that will not only indicate the required disk size and expected installation size, but will also indicate any necessary dependencies required by the requested package. YUM will then check several different repositories (`base`, `extras`, and `updates`) and, having resolved the need for any necessary dependencies, YUM will be asking us to confirm the request before continuing with the installation process. So, as you can see, by using the *Y* key, we will be providing YUM with the permission to fulfill the request, which in turn will result in the download, verification, and installation of the package(s) concerned.

There's more...

There are times when you may wish to install more than one package at a time. To do this, simply invoke the same `install` command, but instead of naming a single package, simply identify the full list of packages you may require in such a way that it forms a long shopping list:

```
yum install package_name1 package_name2 package_name3
```

The number of packages you can install in this way is unlimited, but always leave a single space between each package name and keep the command on a single line. For very long installation instructions, line-wrapping may occur.

You do not need to list the packages in any particular order and the request will be processed in exactly the same way as it was in the original recipe, and again after listing the transaction summary, it will remain pending until it is confirmed or declined. Again, use the *Y* key to confirm your request so that the process completes.

Using YUM to remove packages

In this recipe, we will investigate the role of using YUM with the intention of removing packages from your server. During the lifetime of your server, it is possible that certain applications and services may no longer be required. In such situations, it is typical that you will want to remove such packages in order to optimize your working environment, and it is the purpose of this recipe to show you how this is done.

Getting ready

To complete this recipe, you will require a working installation of the CentOS 7 operating system with root privileges, a console-based text editor of your choice, and a connection to the Internet.

How to do it...

This recipe will show you how to remove one or more packages by invoking the `yum remove` option. To do this, you will need to log in as the root user and complete the following process:

1. To remove a single package, replace the `package_name` value with the appropriate value and type the following:

    ```
    yum remove package_name
    ```

2. Wait for the transaction summary and confirmation prompt to be displayed, and then press either the *Y* key to confirm, or the *N* key to decline the transaction, as shown next:

```
Is this ok [y/d/N]: y
```

3. If you have declined the transaction, then no further work is required and you will exit YUM. However, if you have confirmed the transaction, then simply watch the progress of package removal until it is confirmed and prints out a `Complete!` message.

How it works...

Applications that are no longer required can be removed with YUM. The process is very intuitive and similar to installing a new package, and it only requires you to confirm the name of the packages you want to remove.

So, what have we learned from this experience?

Having invoked the `remove` command, YUM will search your system to discover the relevant package; and by reading the package headers and metadata, it will also determine what dependencies this will affect. For example, if we wanted to remove a package called `wget`, we would begin by issuing the `remove` command like so: `yum remove wget`. YUM, in turn, would then locate the package details from your system and obtain a transaction summary that may include any necessary dependencies that are no longer required. The transaction printed out will remain pending until you instruct YUM to remove the package(s) concerned. When confirmed, YUM will complete the transaction, which in return will result in the removal of the package or packages. You should take extra care if the summary makes reference to any dependencies as these may be required by other RPMs. If you are concerned that certain dependencies should remain on the system, it is often a good idea to end the current transaction and simply de-activate or disable the software concerned. As with the `install` command, you can also remove multiple packages at a time, leaving a single space between the package names:

```
yum remove package_name1 package_name2 package_name3
```

Keeping YUM clean and tidy

In this recipe, we will investigate the role of YUM with regard to ensuring that the working cache remains current. As a part of its typical mode of operation, YUM will create a cache that consists of metadata and packages. These files are very useful, but over time, they will accumulate in size to such an extent that you may find that YUM is acting erratically or not as intended. The frequency of this happening can vary from system to system, but it generally implies that the YUM cache system requires your immediate attention. Such a situation can be quite frustrating, but it is the purpose of this recipe to provide a quick solution that will serve to assist you in cleaning the cache and restoring YUM to its original working state.

Getting ready

To complete this recipe, you will require a working installation of the CentOS 7 operating system with root privileges, a console-based text editor of your choice, and a connection to the Internet in order to facilitate the download of additional packages.

How to do it...

Before we begin, it is important to realize that, while we are troubleshooting a current problem, this same recipe can be run as often as required in order to keep YUM in an optimal working state:

1. We will begin this recipe by asking YUM to clean any cached package information. To do this, log in as root and type the following:

```
yum clean packages
```

2. Allow time for your system to respond and when finished, type the following command to remove any cached XML-based metadata:

```
yum clean metadata
```

3. Again, wait for YUM to respond and when ready, type the following command to remove any cached database files:

```
yum clean dbcache
```

4. Following this, you will want to clean all the files to confirm the preceding instructions and to ensure that unnecessary disk space is not used. To do this, type the following line:

```
yum clean all
```

5. Finally, you will want to rebuild the YUM cache by typing what is shown next:

```
yum makecache
```

How it works...

YUM is a very powerful tool that is known for its ability to resolve package dependencies and automate the process of package management, but as with all things, there are times when even the best utilities can get confused and may report errors or behave erratically. Fixing this issue is relatively simple and the approach outlined in this recipe will also serve to keep your package manager in a healthy running state for the life of your operating system.

So, what have we learned from this experience?

During its typical operation, YUM will create a cache of metadata and packages that can be found at `/var/cache/yum`. These files are essential, but as they grow in size, this cache will ultimately serve to slow down the overall use of this utility and may even cause some issues. To address this situation, we started by using the following command to clean the current package-based cache using YUM's `clean packages` parameter options. We then followed this by cleaning the metadata cache using the command `clean metadata`, which will remove any excess XML-based files. YUM uses a SQLite database as a part of its normal operation, so the next step was to remove any remaining database files using the `clean dbcache` parameters. The next step was to clean all files associated with enabled repositories in order to reclaim any unused disk space: `yum clean all`. Finally, we restored YUM to its normal working state by rebuilding the cache using the `makecache` option.

There's more...

On a typical server, YUM is a great tool that will solve the most complex problems related to package dependencies and package management. However, in instances where you have knowingly mixed incompatible repositories or have used incomplete sources, there is a risk that YUM will not be able to help.

Remember, in this situation, you should consider the following advice to be a temporary remedy only. A tendency to ignore any warnings provided by YUM will only lead to bigger problems later on.

If such instances occur, and if the error is RPM-based, as a temporary fix, you can skip broken packages by using the following command:

```
yum -y update --skip-broken
```

This command will allow YUM to continue working by bypassing any packages with errors, but as stated earlier this should be regarded as a temporary fix only. You should always be aware that a system with broken dependencies is not considered to be a healthy system. This situation is to be avoided at all costs, and under these circumstances fixing such errors should become your first priority.

Knowing your priorities

In this recipe, we will investigate the task of preparing YUM to manage additional repositories by installing a plugin known as **YUM priorities**. YUM has the ability to search, remove, install, retrieve, and update packages from various remote locations. Such features make YUM a powerful tool, but if you ever decide to add an additional third-party repository, there is a chance that conflicts will render the system unstable. Stability is one of the many advantages of using the CentOS operating system, and it is the purpose of this recipe to show you how this confidence can be maintained while simultaneously allowing for the addition of new repositories.

Getting ready

To complete this recipe, you will require a working installation of the CentOS 7 operating system with root privileges, a console-based text editor of your choice, and a connection to the Internet in order to facilitate the download of additional packages.

How to do it...

This recipe will show you how to prepare YUM in order to manage the process of using one or more third-party repositories by installing and configuring YUM priorities:

1. To begin this recipe, log in as root and type the following:

   ```
   yum install yum-plugin-priorities
   ```

2. Confirm the installation, and when complete type what is shown here:

   ```
   vi /etc/yum/pluginconf.d/priorities.conf
   ```

3. You should ensure that this file indicates that the plugin is enabled. It should show the instruction `enabled = 1`. It is not expected that you will need to change anything in this file, but if you have made any changes, simply save and close the file before proceeding.

4. We now need to establish a priority value for each repository. This is a numeric value in ascending order, where the highest priority is given the lowest number. To do this, open the following file as shown next:

   ```
   vi /etc/yum.repos.d/CentOS-Base.repo
   ```

5. Add the following line at the end of the `[base]` section:

   ```
   priority=1
   ```

6. Now, add the following line at the end of the `[updates]` section:

   ```
   priority=1
   ```

7. And finally, add the following line at the end of the `[extras]` section:

   ```
   priority=1
   ```

8. When complete, save and close the file before running a package update:

   ```
   yum update
   ```

How it works...

YUM priorities is a simple plugin that enables YUM to decide what repositories will assume the highest priority when installing and updating new packages. Using this plugin will reduce the chance of package confusion by ensuring that any particular package will always be installed or updated from the same repository. In this way, you can add an unlimited number of repositories and enable YUM to stay in control of package management.

So, what did we learn from this experience?

Enhancing YUM with this plugin was simply a matter of installing the `yum-plugin-priorities` package and ensuring that it was enabled in its configuration file. We then discovered that the priority is set in ascending order, where the lowest values are given precedence over all others. This, of course, serves to simplify the overall process, and for this reason, we ensured that the default repositories were given a value of `1` (`priority=1`). This will ensure that the default repositories maintain the highest priority, so when you do decide to add additional repositories you could assign them a priority value of 2, 3, 4... and 10, or more. On the other hand, it should be noted that we only set this value across three main sections: `[base]`, `[updates]`, and `[extras]`. In simple terms, this was only because the other sections are shown to be disabled. For example, you may have noticed that the `[centosplus]` section in `/etc/yum.repos.d/CentOS-Base.repo` include the following line: `enabled=0`, whereas the `[updates]` and `[extras]` sections show this value as `enabled=1`. Of course, if you intend to activate this repository, you will need to set a priority value for it, but for the purpose of this recipe such an action was not required. Finally, we ran a simple YUM package update in order to activate our revised settings.

So, as we can see, YUM priorities is an extremely flexible package that enables you to determine what repositories take priority when you want to expand your installation options. However, you should always be aware that YUM priorities may not be appropriate for your system, as you are giving it the power to decide what packages are to be ignored, what packages are installed, what packages are updated, and in what order and from which repository you will get them. For most users who tend not to stay away from the typical server functions, this may not be an immediate concern; you may even safely ignore this warning. But if stability and security are an overriding concern, and you do intend to use additional packages from external repositories, then you should give careful consideration to the use of this plugin or at least consider and research the integrity of the third-party repositories used.

Using a third-party repository

In this recipe, we will investigate the desire to take full advantage of the packages that are available to CentOS by installing both the EPEL and Remi repositories. CentOS is an enterprise-based operating system that prides itself on stability, and during the lifetime of your server, it is possible that not every piece of software you need can be found in the default repositories. It is also possible that you may require updated packages of current software, and for these reasons many server administrators choose to install both the EPEL and Remi repositories. These are not the only repositories available, but because they represent one of the most popular combinations, it is the purpose of this recipe to show you how both the EPEL and Remi repositories can be added to your system.

Getting ready

To complete this recipe, you will require a working installation of the CentOS 7 operating system with root privileges, a console-based text editor of your choice, and a connection to the Internet in order to facilitate the download of additional packages.

How to do it...

Before we start, it is assumed that you have followed the previous recipe that showed you how to install and activate YUM priorities.

1. To begin, log in as root and install the EPEL release repository using YUM:

   ```
   yum install epel-release
   ```

2. Next, from your home directory, type the following commands to download the remi release rpm package:

   ```
   curl -O http://rpms.famillecollet.com/enterprise/remi-release-7.
   rpm
   ```

    Please note that, while you are reading this, this URL may have changed; if so, please do some Internet research to find out if there is a new URL available.

3. The preceding file should now be located in your home folder. To proceed, type the following command:

   ```
   rpm -Uvh remi-release-7.rpm
   ```

4. After the installation is done, open the Remi repository file with your favorite text editor:

   ```
   vi /etc/yum.repos.d/remi.repo
   ```

5. Change `enabled=0` to `enabled=1` and add the line `priority=10` to the end of the [remi] section.

6. Now, open the EPEL repository file with your favorite text editor:

   vi /etc/yum.repos.d/epel.repo

7. Again, change `enabled=0` to `enabled=1` if not set automatically and add the line `priority=10` in the [epel] section.

8. To finish, update YUM as shown here:

   yum update

9. If updates are available, choose *Y* to proceed. Having completed the update process, you will now be able to download and install packages from both the Remi and EPEL repositories as an addition to those that are used by default.

How it works...

In order to use and enjoy the benefits of a third-party repository, you are required to install and enable it first using the YUM and RPM package manager.

So, what did we learn from this experience?

Having started the recipe, the task of installing both the Remi and EPEL repositories is a remarkably smooth process. While the installation of the EPEL repository using YUM is very safe to changes, the preceding URL for Remi is maintained at the discretion of the repository owners, so you should always ensure that they are the most current. However, having obtained the necessary repository setup file, it was then a matter of applying an RPM-based command in order to install all necessary repository files on your system. Having done this, we were then required to open the relevant configuration files of each of the installed repositories and enable them (by changing `enabled=0` to `enabled=1`) and setting a priority value (`priority=10`). While the former value will merely switch the repository on, the latter one will be used by YUM to correctly identify which repositories were the most appropriate when we called the `update` command. As it was discussed in the previous recipe regarding YUM priorities, the simple rule of thumb is based on remembering the phrase "the lower the number, the higher the priority." This, in itself (depending on your reasons), may not be a bad thing to do, but for the purpose of this recipe, it is shown that the default CentOS repositories should take priority over all others. Of course, you may disagree with this, and yes, there is nothing stopping you from applying the same priority rule to a third-party supplier, but I do caution you before diving in, and this is particularly the case if this is for a mission-critical production server. Remember, if all the priority values are the same, then YUM will attempt to download the latest version by default.

The reason for setting both Remi and EPEL to a higher value than the existing CentOS-based repositories is based on the need to consider security updates. Unless you have determined otherwise, it is always advised that the base files should come from CentOS first. This includes, but it is not limited to, Kernel updates, SELinux, and related packages. Third-party repositories should be used for additional packages that cannot be obtained from the original sources, or for access to particular updates that may not be available to the base release of CentOS. This may include packages such as Apache, MariaDB, or PHP. As a final footnote, you will have noticed that both Remi and EPEL repositories shared the same priority value. This is by design as these repositories are often viewed as partners. However, if you decide to begin mixing repositories, or use this recipe as a gateway to installing other repositories not mentioned here, then you should always do your research and evaluate every third-party on a case-by-case basis. The Remi and EPEL repositories are very popular, so if you do intend to add more third-party resources, read around the subject, choose your repositories carefully, and stay loyal.

There's more...

There are many other interesting repositories available for CentOS 7, such as ELRepo, which focuses on hardware-related packages such as filesystem drivers, graphics drivers, network drivers, sound drivers, and webcam or video drivers. Go to `http://elrepo.org` to learn how to install and access it.

Creating a YUM repository

If you maintain multiple CentOS servers in your local network and want to save Internet bandwidth or speed up the downloading of the same remote repository packages over and over again, or are within a very restrictive network environment where access to any remote CentOS repository is blocked for your clients, you might want to consider running your own YUM repository. Having your own repository is also an excellent solution if you want to rollout a few custom or unofficial RPM packages (for example in-house configuration files or programs) to your local crowd or if you just want to create an official CentOS 7 repository mirror site. Here in this recipe we will show you how to set up your own first YUM CentOS 7 repository and how to serve it to your local network.

Getting ready

To complete this recipe, you will require a working installation of the CentOS 7 operating system with root privileges, a console-based text editor of your choice, and a connection to the Internet to facilitate the download of additional packages. For this recipe to work, you will also need to place the CentOS 7 Everything DVD iso file image in your server's root home directory, if you haven't downloaded it yet, refer to a detailed description in the first recipe in *Chapter 1, Installing CentOS* (but download the latest `CentOS-7-x86_64-Everything-XXXX.iso` file instead of the minimal iso file). Also, we need a running Apache web server to share our YUM repository to our local network; please read the first recipe in *Chapter 12, Providing Web Services* in order to learn how to set it up.

How to do it...

To create our own YUM repository, we need the `createrepo` program, which is not installed on CentOS 7 by default. Let's begin our journey by installing it. In this example, we will use the IP address, `192.168.1.7`, for our YUM repository server:

1. Log in as root on your server and install the following package:

   `yum install createrepo`

2. Next, for every repository you want to share, create a subfolder beneath the Apache web root folder under `/var/www/html/repository/`, which will be publicly available when Apache is running; for example, to share the complete CentOS 7 `Everything` repository packages, you could use:

   `mkdir -p /var/www/html/repository/centos/7.1`

3. Now, put all your RPM package files of choice into the repository folders created here. In our example, we will put all RPM packages from the `Everything` iso image file into our new local repository location after we have mounted the content of the iso file to the filesystem:

   `mount ~/CentOS-7-x86_64-Everything-1503-01.iso /mnt/`

   `cp -r /mnt/Packages/* /var/www/html/repository/centos/7.1/`

4. Afterwards, we need to update the SELinux security contexts for all the new files copied into the Apache web root directory:

   `restorecon -v -R /var/www/html`

5. Now, for every repository we want to set up, run the following command:

   `createrepo --database /var/www/html/repository/centos/7.1`

6. Congratulations, you now have successfully created your first YUM repository, which can be accessed from any computer in the same network through the running Apache web server. In order to test it, log in as root to any other CentOS 7-based system that can ping our repository server and add our new repository to its YUM repository configuration directory:

```
vi /etc/yum.repos.d/myCentosMirror.repo
```

7. Add the following content to this empty file (change the `baseurl` appropriately to fit your own needs):

```
[myCentosMirror]
name=my CentOS 7.1 mirror
baseurl=http://192.168.1.7/repository/centos/7.1
gpgcheck=1
gpgkey=http://mirror.centos.org/centos/RPM-GPG-KEY-CentOS-7
```

8. Save and close the file, then test if your new repository is available (it should appear on the list) on your client:

```
yum repolist | grep myCentosMirror
```

9. Now, to test our new YUM repository, we can try the following command:

```
yum --disablerepo="*" --enablerepo="myCentosMirror" list available
```

How it works...

In this recipe, we have shown you how easy it is to install and set up a local YUM repository. However, we have only shown you how to create a mirror site of all the CentOS 7 Everything iso RPM packages, but you can repeat this process for creating YUM repositories of every kind of package that you want to share with your network.

So, what did we learn from this experience?

Setting up your own YUM repository was simply a matter of installing the `createrepo` package and copying all the RPM packages that you want to share into a subfolder of your choice beneath your Apache's document root directory (In our example, we had to mount the CentOS 7 Everything iso file to the filesystem, in order to access its included RPM package files that we want to share). As the Apache's document root directory is under the control of SELinux, afterwards we needed to set the security context for all the new RPM files in this directory to the `httpd_sys_content_t` type label; otherwise, no access through the web server would be possible. Finally, we needed to run the `createrepo` command on our new repository folder, which will create our new repository's metadata that is needed for any YUM client that wants to connect to the repository later to make queries to it.

Afterwards, to test our new repository, we created a new repository definition file on another CentOS 7 system that wants to use this new service and that must be in the same network as our YUM repository server. In this custom `.repo` configuration file, we put the correct URL path to the repository, enabled `gpg` checks, and took the standard CentOS 7 `gpgkey` so that our YUM client can proof the validity of the RPM packages official repository packages. Finally, we used the `yum` command with the `--disablerepo="*"` and `--enablerepo="myCentosMirror"` parameters, which will make sure to only use our new custom repository as a source. You can use these two parameters in combination with any other `yum` command such as `install`, `search`, `info`, `list`, and so on. This was just for testing; if you want to combine your new repository with the existing ones, please use YUM priorities for it (as shown in another recipe in this chapter).

There's more...

Now, before we announce our new centralized YUM repository to our network, we should first make an update of all the RPM packages that have changed since the release of the CentOS Everything iso. In order to do this, visit `http://www.centos.org` and choose a `rsync://` mirror link that is geographically near your current location. For example, if you are located in Germany one option could be `rsync://ftp.hosteurope.de/centos/` (for more detailed instructions on navigating the CentOS website, read the first recipe in *Chapter 1, Installing CentOS*). Also, before we can use the `rsync` protocol, we need to install the `rsync` package (`yum install rsync`), if not done already. Now, open the following empty script file `vi ~/update-myCentosMirror-repo.sh` file and put in the following content (replacing the `rsync://` location accordingly, if needed):

```
rsync -avz rsync://ftp.hosteurope.de/centos/7/os/x86_64/Packages/ /var/
www/html/repository/centos/7.1

restorecon -v -R /var/www/html
```

Now, make the file executable using `chmod +x ~/update-myCentosMirror-repo.sh`, and run it with `~/update-myCentosMirror-repo.sh`. This should update your repository to the latest version. Finally, to automate this process, let's create a cron job that will update our repository packages with the other mirror site every night at 2:30 am (open `crontab -e`):

```
30 2 * * * /root/update-myCentosMirror-repo.sh
```

Working with the RPM package manager

All software on a CentOS 7 system is distributed through RPM packages. Most of the time the YUM package manager is the first choice of any system administrator, performing software installation and maintenance, and is highly recommended whenever possible as it provides system integrity checks and has excellent package dependency resolution. In this recipe, we will show you an alternative way to manage your packages. We will be exploring the RPM package manager, which is a powerful tool used to build, install, query, verify, update, and erase individual RPM software packages. Though it is not as *intelligent* as YUM, as it cannot resolve package dependencies or work with repositories, it can be still relevant today since it provides very useful querying options that are not available in YUM, and it can be used to install single software packages manually.

Getting ready

To complete this recipe, you will require a working installation of the CentOS 7 operating system with root privileges, a console-based text editor of your choice, and a connection to the Internet in order to facilitate the download of additional RPM packages.

How to do it...

We start this recipe by downloading a `rpm` package from the Internet, which we will use to show you an example of how the `rpm` command works:

1. We will begin by logging in as root into the root's home directory and downloading the pipe view program from the EPEL repository, which cannot be found in the official CentOS repository:

   ```
   cd ~;curl -O http://dl.fedoraproject.org/pub/
   epel/7/x86_64/p/pv-1.4.6-1.el7.x86_64.rpm
   ```
   Please note that while you are reading this, the package URL may have changed.

2. After the download has been completed, we will install this package using the following `rpm` command:
   ```
   rpm -Uvh ~/pv-1.4.6-1.el7.x86_64.rpm
   ```

3. If the installation has finished, let's check if the installation of the package was successful by querying the RPM database:
   ```
   rpm -qa | grep "pv-"
   ```

4. You can also test the `pv` program directly (press *Ctrl+C* keys to quit):

   ```
   dd if=/dev/urandom | pv | dd of=/dev/null
   ```

5. We can now use the `rpm` command's rich querying options to show useful information of the installed package:

   ```
   rpm -qi pv
   rpm -ql pv
   rpm -qd pv
   ```

6. Finally, let's remove the package if you don't like or need it anymore:

   ```
   rpm -e pv
   ```

How it works...

Here, in this recipe, we introduced you to the RPM package manager, which is the original program to manage RPM packages. The RPM package is a packaging standard for the distribution of software, and contains useful metadata in the file to verify the authorship (for example, using signature verification with PGP) and integrity of the software included. The installation of packages containing binary programs instead of manually compiling and building them from scratch is much easier and more consistent, but RPM packages can also contain any type of file, such as source code or just documentation files. As said in the introduction, the `rpm` command has six different modes of operation: building, installing, uninstalling, updating, querying, and verifying rpm packages. Here, in this recipe, we showed you how to use the most important five operations (we don't show building RPM's).

So, what have we learned from this experience?

We started by logging in as root and downloading the `pv` (pipe viewer) rpm package example from the non-official EPEL CentOS repository (EPEL contains high-quality add-on packages, thoroughly checked and officially conformed; see the *Using a third-party repository* recipe to learn more about the EPEL repository) manually using `curl`, because it is not available in the official repository but can be a very useful tool.

> Although there are many RPM repositories and download sources on the Internet, for security and compatibility reasons, on productive systems you should consider installing only official CentOS 7 RPM packages from valid and reputable repositories and sources. In general, the packages contained are best tested and reviewed by many experts and users.

The downloaded package file's name can be read the following way, which follows the following non-mandatory naming convention for RHEL/CentOS packages:

```
pv-1.4.6-1.x86_64.rpm  = package name (pv)-version number
(1.4.6)-release(1)-CPU architecture (x86_64)
```

Next, we installed the downloaded `pv` package using the RPM package manager, which can be executed using the `rpm` command on the command line. We used it with the `-Uvh` command parameters together with the full name of the downloaded package rpm file.

> If using the rpm command for installing or upgrading rpm software packages, you should always use `-Uvh` with one exception; which are kernel packages. `-U` will remove old packages while updating, and this is not what you want if you install a new kernel. Use `-i` (for installing) here instead, as this will keep the old kernel files so that you can go back to an earlier version if you run into some problems.

`-U` is the parameter for installing or upgrading a package. If the package is not installed on the system, it will get installed; otherwise `rpm` tries to upgrade it if it the RPM package version is newer than the one installed. The `-v` parameter prints a more verbose output, while `-h` displays a nice progress bar. Installing the `pv` package when you have not enabled the EPEL repository on your system will get the following warning message:

```
pv-1.6.0-1.x86_64.rpm: Header V3 DSA/SHA1 Signature, key ID 3fc56f51:
NOKEY
```

RPM will automatically check the validity of the package's signature before installing to make sure that the package's content has not been modified since it has been signed. Also, it checks that an RPM package is trustworthy, as it should be signed by an official third-party authority vendor using an encrypted key. You can ignore this message, as packages from the EPEL repository are from a secure source. To permanently trust EPEL sources, you can install its `gpg` public key on your system using the following command and getting rid of all future signature warning messages:

```
rpm --import https://dl.fedoraproject.org/pub/epel/RPM-GPG-KEY-EPEL-7
```

Having successfully installed the package, we now have a nice command line tool called `pv` to show the progress of data going through a Unix pipe, which can be useful if you are transferring huge amounts of data through pipelines where you normally never know the current state of progress. Afterwards, we queried the RPM database that stores information about all installed packages on a CentOS 7 system, using the `rpm` command with the `-q` flag. Working on the RPM database, we must use the true package name (`pv`) instead of the filename (`pv-1.4.6-1.x86_64.rpm`) that we used when we installed the packages in the first place. The same is true when removing an installed package; please specify the package name and not the version number or full filename.

To get detailed information about the installed package, `pv`, we used `-qi` (i for information), with the `-ql` parameter; we showed the full filename and path of all files in the package. `-qd` showed all the files in the package containing documentation. To read about more querying options, type `man rpm` and look under the `PACKAGE QUERY OPTIONS` section.

In summary, we can say that there are situations in a system administrator's life where one needs to install a piece of software that is not distributed through an official repository (for example, non-open-source, cutting-edge program or beta versions, software that have a license disallowing the ability to put it into a repository such as Java, or software from independent developers), and where one will have to download individual RPM packages and install them manually. Under the hood, YUM also depends and uses the RPM package manager in the background, so you are also able to use the YUM program to install rpm files (`yum install <filename.rpm>`). However, when it comes to querying your downloaded rpm files or installed packages on your system, there are situations where it's better to use the older `rpm` command without having to install additional YUM-based software such as `yum-utils`.

The biggest weakness of RPM is that it does not support repositories and is missing a dependency management system. If you work with RPM alone to install all your software on a CentOS system, you will easily run into package dependency problems where you cannot install a specific package because it relies on some other packages. Often, when you try to install the dependent packages, you need other packages that they depend on and so on. This can be very tedious work and should always be avoided by using YUM instead.

There's more...

The `rpm` command can not only be used to query the rpm database for information about installed packages, you can also use it to query rpm files that you downloaded. For example, use the `-qlp` parameter to show all files in a local `rpm` package file:

```
rpm -qlp ~/pv-1.4.6-1.el7.x86_64.rpm
```

To get detailed information about the package from the `rpm` file, use the `-qip` parameter, as shown here:

```
rpm -qip ~/pv-1.4.6-1.el7.x86_64.rpm
```

If you want to install an RPM package that you have downloaded locally and that has dependencies, you can use the `yum localinstall` command. This will install the local package once supplied with its filename, and will try to resolve all the dependencies from remote sources, for example:

```
wget http://location/to/a/rpm/package_name.rpm
yum localinstall package_name.rpm
```

5
Administering the Filesystem

In this chapter, we will cover the following topics:

- ▸ Creating a virtual block device
- ▸ Formatting and mounting a filesystem
- ▸ Using disk quotas
- ▸ Maintaining a filesystem
- ▸ Extending the capacity of the filesystem

Introduction

This chapter is a collection of recipes that provides for the need to drive a CentOS-based server solution. From formatting and mounting disks to extending a logical volume and maintaining your filesystem and disk quotas, the purpose of this chapter is to show you how quickly and easily you can get to grips with the task of managing the needs of its users in today's most demanding environments.

Creating a virtual block device

In this recipe, we will create a virtual block device that we will use to simulate real devices and partitions so that we can test-drive concepts and commands used in all later recipes in this chapter. Working with real disks and partitions often involves the risk of losing important data or even having to re-install your complete system. A virtual block device is ideal to learn the techniques and try things out before switching to "production mode". Later, if you have gained enough experience and feel safe, you can easily replace it with "real" hardware devices, partitions, and logical volumes (which is a part of LVM; see the later recipe). All you need to do is substitute your virtual device with "real" block device names.

Getting ready

To complete this recipe, you will require a minimal installation of the CentOS 7 operating system with root access. To create a virtual block device, you should have at least one gigabyte of free hard disk space that we will use temporarily to create and make. You can delete this reserved space later (or it will be automatically deleted on reboot). It's just for testing.

How to do it...

1. To begin, log in as `root` and create an empty file with the exact size of 1 gigabyte:

   ```
   dd if=/dev/zero of=/tmp/test-image.dd bs=1M count=1000
   ```

2. Now, let's create a loop device from the file we just created:

   ```
   losetup -fP /tmp/test-image.dd
   ```

3. Next, print the generated loop device name:

   ```
   losetup -a
   ```

4. As this will be the first loop device created in the current system, the output will be as follows (`loop0` can be a different number if you have created a loop device before):

   ```
   /dev/loop0: [0035]:3714186 (/tmp/test-image.dd)
   ```

5. To get a list of all the block devices currently attached to the system, as well as important details, type the following:

   ```
   lsblk -io NAME,TYPE,SIZE,MOUNTPOINT,FSTYPE,MODEL
   ```

6. Now, let's create a new partition table of the type `gpt` on our new loop device (confirm the deletion of any data):

   ```
   parted /dev/loop0 mklabel gpt
   ```

7. Finally, create device maps from your loop device to make it more similar to real hard disk partitions:

```
kpartx -a /dev/loop0
```

How it works...

In this recipe, we have learned how to create a virtual block device that acts as a starting point for testing out how to create partitions, logical volumes, and filesystems in later recipes in this chapter.

So, what did we learn from this experience?

We started this recipe by creating a new empty file, which was one gigabyte in size, in the /tmp directory using the dd utility. dd is used to make exact copies of files (which is sometimes called cloning) and expects two parameters: an input file (the if parameter) and an output file (the of parameter). We used the zero device (/dev/zero) as our input file that returns an endless stream of bytes containing zero. We then limited the stream by defining a blocksize (bs) and count parameter. The bs defines the amount of data in bytes read at a time, while the count parameter counts how many repetitions of bs will be allowed. So, these arguments can be read as *stop the copying process when we reach a blocksize times count data received*. In our example, we used a blocksize of 1 *Megabyte times 1000 = 1 Gigabyte*. This zero byte data was written to our output file (of) called /tmp/test-image.dd.

After we created this empty file, we created a temporary **loop** device with it. A loop device is just a pseudo-device that makes it possible to use a file as a **block device**. Often, such a file is a CD ISO image, and using it as a loop device will make it accessible as if it were a normal hardware drive. Any device that allows reading or writing data in blocks can be called a block device; in order to get a list of all available block devices in your system, we used the lsblk command, and as you can see, this includes our loop device as well. Standard loop device names start with the number zero, as in /dev/loop0.

Afterwards, we created a new **partition table** on our loop device using the parted command. A partition table is a table maintained on a disk by the operating system describing the partitions on it, and it must be created before we can create them. We used the partition table type gpt, but you can also use the old msdos type here instead.

Normally, when creating a partition table on a virtual block device, we cannot access individual partitions or make filesystems for different partitions on it, because the partitions cannot be addressed individually. Here we used the kpartx command to create device mappings from partition tables, which allows us later to access single partitions for creating filesystems using the notation, /dev/loop0p1, for partition 1 on loop device 0 and /dev/loop0p2 for partition 2 on loop device 0.

Congratulations, you have now created a brand new virtual block device with a standard partition table, which can be used and accessed as if it were a normal disk device.

There's more...

If we want to remove a virtual block device, we first have to unmount it from the filesystem if it is currently mounted (for example, `umount /dev/loo0p1`). Next, we need to detach the virtual block device file from the loop device using the `-d` parameter like so: `losetup -d /dev/loop0`. Afterwards, we can delete the block file if we want to: `rm /tmp/test-image.dd`.

Formatting and mounting a filesystem

In this recipe, you will be introduced to the standard CentOS filesystems **XFS**, **Ext4**, and **Btrfs**. Filesystems form one of the most fundamental parts of any operating system and nearly everything depends on them. Here, you will learn how to create different types of standard filesystems available in CentOS 7, and how to link them to your system so that we can access them afterwards for reading and writing. These two techniques are called **formatting** and **mounting** filesystems; while you do not do this very often, it remains one of the most fundamental Linux system administrator tasks.

Getting ready

To complete this recipe, you will require a minimal installation of the CentOS 7 operating system with root access. We will also use virtual block devices instead of real disk devices because it's better to demonstrate the usage of creating filesystems and formatting disks using "dummy" devices, instead of erasing your real hard disk contents. Therefore, you should have applied the *Creating a virtual block device* recipe and created a 1 Gigabyte virtual block device, which will be named `/dev/loop0` in this example.

If you want to apply this recipe for real disk devices, all you have to do is replace `/dev/loop0` with your correct partition—for logical volumes (lv) for example, `/dev/mapper/myServer/data`, for a SATA device `/dev/sdX`, or for an IDE-based hard disk name `/dev/hdX` (where `X` is a character `a-z`).

How to do it...

In our example, this block device is labeled at `/dev/loop0`. Please note that, if you have created more than one block device, your number could be different, so please change the name accordingly:

1. First, let's log in as `root` and show information about all currently available block devices:

   ```
   lsblk -io NAME,TYPE,SIZE,MOUNTPOINT,FSTYPE,MODEL
   ```

2. Now, recheck that we have a valid partition table installed on the device:

   ```
   parted /dev/loop0 print
   ```

3. The preceding line should print out the following content: `Partition Table: gpt`. If this is not the case, let's create a new partition table (confirm the deletion of any data):

```
parted /dev/loop0 mklabel gpt
```

4. Now, we will create a new partition spanning the complete disk space with an `ext4` filesystem label (no filesystem will be installed yet; it's just a label):

```
parted -a optimal /dev/loop0 mkpart primary ext4 2048KiB 100%
```

5. Print the partition table again to show the new partition we just created:

```
parted /dev/loop0 print
```

6. Now, let's remove the partition:

```
parted /dev/loop0 rm 1
```

7. We can also create a btrfs-labeled partition:

```
parted -a optimal /dev/loop0 unit MB mkpart primary btrfs 2048KiB
100%
```

8. Afterwards, let's create an XFS-labeled partition spanning the whole disk:

```
parted /dev/loop0 rm 1
```

```
parted -a optimal /dev/loop0 mkpart primary xfs 2048KiB 100%
```

9. Now, show the block table again to see what we have changed:

```
lsblk -io NAME,TYPE,SIZE,MOUNTPOINT,FSTYPE,MODEL
```

10. As we have only defined the partition type *label*, we still don't have a valid filesystem on our partition; so, in the next step, we format our disk using the correct type. We use XFS in our example. Please change `mkfs -t <type>` if you use `ext4` or `btrfs` instead:

```
mkfs -t xfs /dev/loop0p1
```

11. Next, let's mount our virtual block device partition on the system, into the directory `/media/vbd-1`, and please change `-t <type>` if you use `ext4` or `btrfs` instead:

```
mkdir /media/vbd-1
```

```
mount -t xfs /dev/loop0p1   /media/vbd-1
```

12. Finally, test if we can read and write to the new filesystem:

```
echo "this is a test" > /media/vbd-1/testfile.txt
```

```
cat /media/vbd-1/testfile.txt
```

How it works...

Here, in this recipe, we showed the user how to create CentOS 7 standard partitions spanning the whole disk, and then we created some filesystems on them, which is called formatting, using different filesystem types. The standard filesystem available in CentOS 7 is XFS, but as we have learned in this recipe, there are lots of other ones available as well, including the popular ext4 and btrfs. XFS is a very robust and high-performing file system for large storage configurations; it is considered very mature and stable. Before CentOS 7, the standard file system was ext4, but it had some limitations and not the best performance when working with millions of files and is considered barely suitable for today's very large filesystems. btrfs is a relatively new filesystem and is included in CentOS 7, but at the time of writing it is still under development and should not be used for production systems. It is considered to be fully supported in later CentOS 7 minor releases and is likely to replace XFS as the standard CentOS filesystem type in the future, as it has a list of very promising features and enhancements, such as copy-on-write, which copies files each time you write to them, and which makes it possible to go back to former file versions.

So, what have we learned from this experience?

We started this recipe by using the `lsblk` command to print a list of all available block devices currently attached to the system. We used this command to check if our target block device that we want to use for installing partitions and filesystems on is available. In our example we will use the `/dev/loop0` device, please change this name if it's different on your system (as said before, you could also use a "real" disk block device, such as `/dev/sda`, but always be careful!). After confirming that we have our device ready, we used the `parted` command to check the partition table of the disk. A partition table is mandatory for any hard disk to keep track of the partition information on it. As you have seen, our primary tool for creating partition tables and partitions is *parted*, as it is the officially recommended CentOS 7 tool for these tasks, but there are other programs that do the same as well, such as `fdisk` or `gdisk`. If there is no partition table available, we must create one of type `gpt` using parted's `mklabel gpt` parameter.

Next, after we created the partition table, we put some partitions on it. Therefore, we issued parted's `mkpart` command with the `-a optimal primary ext4 2048KiB 100%` options.

 Be careful with the `parted` command all the time and recheck everything before executing, as most of its commands will completely destroy all the data currently stored on the disk.

This will create a new partition starting at 2,048 kilobytes (kb) until the end of the disk. We did not start at the very beginning of the disk (0%) as 2,048 kb is the start of the first sector on the disk to leave some space left to store some additional data. `-a optimal` aligns the partition to a multiple of the physical block size that will guarantee optimal performance. Next, we removed the partition again using the `rm` option and number 1, which refers to the first partition we just created. We recreated new partitions of type `btrfs` and finally `xfs`. After the disk is partitioned, we need an actual filesystem on it, as parted only labels the partition to a specific type, but does not do the actual formatting. To make the filesystem, we use the `mkfs` utility. You can either run it with the `-t` flag, as we did, or use a dot notation, such as `mkfs.xfs`, to specify the type you want to format it to. The `mkfs` command gives us a detailed output of what it has done, such as how many blocks have been written and so on.

Finally, after we have created the filesystem on our disk partition, we can use the `mount` command to make it available and work with it in our current system. `mount` either attaches or detaches a device's filesystem to our system's root filesystem. Therefore, we need to first create a directory to define where we want to attach it to. We use the directory, `/media/vbd-1`, as a parameter for the actual `mount` command with the syntax, `mount -t <file system type> <device> <dir>`. For almost all standard filesystems, you can skip the `-t` parameter as it will automatically detect the right type. To detach a filesystem from your system, you can use the `umount` command with the argument of the device you want to remove (you can also use the folder it's mounted to; both do work!). In our example, to unmount our loop device's first partition, type `umount /dev/loop0p1`.

After mounting our formatted partition device, we can access it like any other component beneath the root folder.

There's more...

In this recipe, we always use one partition spanning the complete available disk space. Often, you have more than one partition on a disk, so let's create this kind of layout instead. In this example, we create three 100 MB partitions on `/dev/loop0`:

1. First, let's delete our partition once again using the `rm` parameter so that we can add new ones:

   ```
   parted /dev/loop0 rm 1
   ```

2. Now, let's create three equal partitions:

   ```
   parted -a optimal /dev/loop0 unit MiB mkpart primary ext4 2048KiB
   100
   parted -a optimal /dev/loop0 unit MiB mkpart primary ext4 100 200
   parted -a optimal /dev/loop0 unit MiB mkpart primary ext4 300 400
   ```

3. Let's review our layout:

```
parted /dev/loop0 print
```

 Using the `gpt` partition table, we can create up to 128 primary partitions on any disk; when using the older `msdos` partition type, there is a maximum of four primary partitions. If you need more, you have to create extended partitions out of primary ones.

Using disk quotas

When administering a Linux multiuser system with many system users, it is wise to set some kind of restrictions or limits to the resources shared by the system. On a filesystem level, you can either restrict the available hard disk space or the total file number to a fixed size at a user, group, or directory level. The introduction of such rules can prevent people from "spamming" the system, filling up its free space, and generally your users will get more aware of the differentiation between important and unimportant data and will be more likely to keep their home directories tidy and clean. Here in this recipe, we will show you how to set up a **disk quota** limiting system for XFS filesystems, which puts restrictions on the amount of data your system's user accounts are allowed to store.

Getting ready

To complete this recipe, you will require a minimal installation of the CentOS 7 operating system with root access and a console-based text editor of your choice. For this recipe to work, and in order to set quotas, you will need at least one system user account next to your root account; if you don't have one yet, please refer to the recipe *Managing users and their groups* in *Chapter 3, Managing the System* to learn how to create one. Also, in the main recipe, it is expected that your CentOS 7 uses the XFS filesystem, which is standard on installation. Finally, your CentOS 7 installation needs to have been installed on a disk with at least 64 GB space, otherwise the installer will not create a *separate* logical /home volume, which is required in this recipe to make quotas work.

How to do it...

Here, we will learn how to set up a quota system for the XFS filesystem in two different ways: first, setting limits on the user and groups, and then on the directory (project) level. Disk quota systems have to be set on filesystem mount.

Enabling user and group quotas

1. To begin, log in as `root` and open the `fstab` file, which contains static mount information:

   ```
   vi /etc/fstab
   ```

2. Now, navigate the cursor to the line containing /home (with the *up* and *down* arrow keys) and move it to the word `defaults`, and then add the following text after `defaults`, separated by commas:

   ```
   ,uquota,gquota
   ```

3. The complete line will look like the following (your device name will be different, depending on your individual LVM name; here, it is `myserver`):

   ```
   /dev/mapper/myserver-home /home  XFS    defaults,uquota,gquota 0 0
   ```

4. Save and close the file, then remount the /home partition to activate the `quota` directive:

   ```
   umount /home;mount -a
   ```

5. Next, create a user quota on the total file size for a specific user named `john` (change appropriately to match a user available on your system):

   ```
   xfs_quota -x -c 'limit bsoft=768m bhard=1g john' /home/
   ```

6. Next, create a user quota for the total *amount* of files another user, `joe`, can have:

   ```
   xfs_quota -x -c 'limit isoft=1000 ihard=5000 joe' /home/
   ```

7. Let's create a file amount and size limit for everyone in the user group `devgrp` (the filesystem group `devgrp` must exist):

   ```
   xfs_quota -x -c 'limit -g bsoft=5g bhard=6g isoft=10000
   ihard=50000 devgrp' /home
   ```

8. Finally, show the whole quota report for the `home` volume:

   ```
   xfs_quota -x -c 'report -bi -h' /home
   ```

Enabling project (directory) quotas

In order to enable disk quotas for a single directory instead of user or group quotas, we have to add the project quota directive called `pquota` to the volume containing the directory. As we will use a directory called /srv/data for our project quota, we need to take the full underlying / root partition under quota control. For the root partition, we have to set quota flags as kernel boot options:

1. To begin with, open the following file as root after first making a backup of it:

   ```
   cp /etc/default/grub /etc/default/grub.BAK
   ```

   ```
   vi /etc/default/grub
   ```

2. Add the `rootflags=pquota` directive to the end of the line (add one whitespace character before it) starting with `GRUB_CMDLINE_LINUX=` before the closing double quote as shown here:

```
GRUB_CMDLINE_LINUX="rd.lvm.lv=centos/root rd.lvm.lv=centos/swap
crashkernel=auto rhgb quiet rootflags=pquota"
```

3. Save and close the file, and then rebuild the `grub` configuration with our new `boot` option:

```
grub2-mkconfig -o /boot/grub2/grub.cfg
```

4. Now, add the `pquota` flag to your root volume in `/etc/fstab` as well:

```
vi /etc/fstab
```

5. Navigate the cursor to the line containing the root mount point / and move it to the word `defaults`, and then add the following text, separated by a comma:

```
,prjquota
```

6. The complete line will look similar to the following:

```
/dev/mapper/myserver-root /          XFS     defaults,prjquota 0 0
```

7. Next, reboot your computer to apply your changes to the `root` volume:

```
reboot
```

8. After rebooting, make sure that the `root` volume has project quota enabled, which is defined as the `prjquota` flag in the volume's options (otherwise, if it is wrong and doesn't work, it will show as `noquota`):

```
cat /etc/mtab  | grep root
```

9. Next, let's create our target folder that we want to set quotas for:

```
mkdir /srv/data
```

10. We need to add a project name and an associated new, unique ID:

```
echo "myProject:1400" >> /etc/projid
```

11. Now, define that `/srv/data` will use quota rules from our project ID:

```
echo "1400:/srv/data" >> /etc/projects
```

12. Next, initialize the `project` quota for the `root` volume:

```
xfs_quota -xc 'project -s myProject' /
```

13. Finally, apply the following rule to create specific directory limits:

```
xfs_quota -x -c 'limit -p bsoft=1000m bhard=1200m myProject' /
```

14. Print out our quota rules for this device:

```
xfs_quota -x -c 'report -bi -h' /
```

How it works...

In this recipe, you learned how easy it is to set up a quota system on a user, group, or directory (project) level. Also, you have learned that there are two basic ways of defining quotas: either put a restriction on the *total file size* (called blocks), or a limit on the *number* of files (called inodes).

So, what have we learned from this experience?

We began this recipe by setting user and group quotas. As you have seen, a quota system can easily be enabled by adding associated directives to the partition of choice in the `/etc/fstab` file. Therefore, we began this recipe by opening this file and adding the special quota keywords for the XFS user, and group quotas to our `/home` partition. In order to apply these changes, we had to remount the filesystem using the `mount` command. As the quota system had been successfully started, we used the `xfs_quota -x -c` command line to set some quota limits on our enabled filesystem `/home`. `-x` enables expert mode while `-c` lets us run commands as arguments on the command line. When running `xfs_quota` without the `-c` option, you will get to an interactive prompt instead. First, we set some user limits for the users, `john` and `joe`. We did this by defining the following parameters with numbers: `bsoft, bhard, isoft, ihard`. As you can see, there are both soft and hard limits for file size (**blocks**) and file amount (**inodes**). Block quotas can be given in the typical metrics such as kilobyte (`k`), megabyte (`m`), and gigabyte (`g`), whereas an inode is a number. A soft limit is a threshold that, when crossed, prints out a warning message to the command line, whereas a hard limit will stop the user from adding any more data or files to the filesystem under quota protection. Afterwards, we set a group-based quota. If you use the `-g` flag, the limit will be defined for a group instead of the user. Using group rules can be very helpful to separate your users into different groups depending on the amount of files or total file size they should be allowed to have. Finally, we generated a report for all our current quota limits. The command we used there was `'report -bi -h'`, which generates reports for used filespace (`-b` for blocks) and the total amount of files (`-i` for inodes). `-h` specified that we want the output to be human-readable in megabytes or gigabytes.

To test that quotas work, let's create the following block and inode quotas for the user `jack`:

```
xfs_quota -x -c 'limit bhard=20m jack' /home/
xfs_quota -x -c 'limit ihard=1000 jack' /home/
```

Log in as the user `jack` (`su - jack`) and run the following command:

```
dd if=/dev/urandom of=~/test.dd bs=1M count=21
```

With this command, the user `john` will try to create a 21 megabyte size file, but when starting to write the twentieth megabyte, the following error message will appear:

```
dd: error writing '/home/jack/test.dd': Disk quota exceeded
```

Now, delete the `~/test.dd` file so that we can start another test. The same happens if you exceed your file amount limit. Test the following quota limit by trying to create 2,000 multiple files while the quota is limited to 1,000; do this by adding a lot of new files: `for i in {1..2000}; do touch ~/test$i.txt; done`. This results in the following error message:

```
touch: cannot touch '/home/jack/test1001.txt': Disk quota exceeded
```

To temporarily turn off user and group quota checking for a specific filesystem, you can run `xfs_quota -x -c 'off -u -g' /home/` (`-u` for user, `-g` for group) as `root` user. This is only temporary; to re-enable it, you need to remount the filesystem of interest, which is `umount /home;mount -a`. To remove a specific quota rule, just set its limit to zero, for example:

```
xfs_quota -x -c 'limit bhard=0 john' /home
```

Next, we set up quota on a *directory*, instead of the user/group level. This is a feature only XFS file systems are capable of; all other filesystems can only set quotas on a disk or partition level. Being able to control the disk usage of a directory hierarchy is useful if you do not otherwise want to set quota limits for a privileged user or groups. To activate directory quota, we first had to enable this as a kernel boot option because, by default, the root volume is flagged as `noquota`. Also, we added the `prjquota` directive in `/etc/fstab` to the root partition to make it work. If you want to learn more about kernel boot options, read the boot loader recipe in *Chapter 1, Installing CentOS*. To set file system flags for the root partition, we needed to reboot the system. After doing this, we made sure that the boot option has been set successfully by looking into the `mtab` file, which is a file that lists all currently mounted filesystems. Next, we set up a project name with an associated unique project ID (we randomly choose `1400`) in the `/etc/projid` file. In the next step, we applied this new project ID (`1400`) to a directory in the `/etc/projects` file called `/srv/data`. This system allows the application of specific project quota rules to many different directories. Afterwards, we initialized project quota for the root partition using the `project` option with the `xfs_quota` command, and then created a `limit` quota rule for this project name. All directories that are defined in the `/etc/projects` file under the corresponding project id are affected by this rule. This type of system can be used for fine-grain multiple folder quota rules. For every directory, you can set up a new project name or reuse a specific one, making this system very flexible.

In this recipe, we have created a block size hard limit of 1,200 megabytes for our project name, which is `myProject`. To test this quota, type the following:

```
dd if=/dev/zero of=/srv/data/dd.img bs=1M count=1201
```

This should stop `dd`, exactly after writing 1200 megabytes, with the following command line error message:

```
dd: error writing '/srv/data/dd.img': No space left on device
```

There's more...

As the name implies, the `xfs_quota` program shown in this recipe only works for XFS filesystems. If you want to use disk quotas on a user or group level for other file systems such as ext4 or btrfs, you have to install the `quota` package (`yum install quota`). Setting quotas works in a similar way to the steps shown in this recipe; please read the manual `man quota` to get you started.

Maintaining a filesystem

In this recipe, we will learn how to check the consistency and optionally repair CentOS 7 filesystems. Filesystem inconsistencies are rare events and filesystem checks normally are running automatically at boot time. But system administrators should also know how to run such tests manually, if they believe there is a problem with the filesystem.

Getting ready

To complete this recipe, you will require a working installation of the CentOS 7 operating system with root privileges. We will use virtual block devices instead of real disk devices because we *cannot* apply any file system check on a *mounted* disk. Therefore, you should have applied the *Formatting and mounting a filesystem* recipe and created a 1 gigabyte virtual block device with two partitions of half the total size: first, a partition with an XFS, and then another one with an ext4 filesystem. We will use the virtual block device named `/dev/loop0` in this example.

As said before, these can be easily exchanged with real disk names.

How to do it...

1. To begin with, log in as `root` and show information about the current block devices attached to the system:

    ```
    lsblk -io NAME,TYPE,SIZE,MOUNTPOINT,FSTYPE,MODEL
    ```

2. Here, you should see two partitions on the `loop0` device: `/dev/loop0p1` and `/dev/loop0p2`. If you see that they are currently mounted to the system, unmount them now:

    ```
    umount /dev/loop0p1
    umount /dev/loop0p2
    ```

3. Now, let's check the XFS filesystem which in our example is loop0p1 (change appropriately):

    ```
    xfs_repair -n /dev/loop0p1
    ```

4. For the second partition on the disk that is ext4, we will use the following line:

```
fsck -f /dev/loop0p2
```

How it works...

In this recipe, we have learned how easy it is to run a filesystem check on a XFS or ext4 filesystem. The most important lesson you should have learned here is that you always have to *unmount* your disk partitions before running any filesystem checks!

So, what did we learn from this experience?

Since we cannot run any filesystem checks on any mounted device, if you want to check your system's disks and partitions, often you have to run such checks in the *rescue* mode where your filesystems are not mounted (for example, you cannot unmount the root partition to check because it's needed by the system all the time, whereas, for a separate home partition, it would be possible).

For the XFS file system, we use the `xfs_repair` tool, and for all others we will use the `fsck` program with the `-f` parameter (force) to check our filesystem.

It is important to note that we always need to run `fsck` instead of the specific `fsck.<file system type>` (such as `fsck.ext4`, `fsck.btrfs`), because it auto-detects the right tool for you. This is necessary because if you run the wrong specific `fsck.<file system type>` tool on the wrong filesystem (let's say running `fsck.ext4` on a btrfs filesystem), it can completely destroy it!

There's more...

So far, we have only showed you how to *check* a filesystem using `xfs_repair` and `fsck`. If some errors occur during the "checking" run on an XFS filesystem, run `xfs_repair` without the `-n` option—for example, use `xfs_repair /dev/loop0p1`. On a non-XFS partition, such as ext4, you would run `fsck` with the `-a` option (a for auto repair)—for example, `fsck -a /dev/loop0p2`. For `fsck`, if you got a lot of errors, it's best to use `-y` as well so that you do not have to confirm every error fix.

Now, let's simulate what would happen if we got a corrupted XFS filesystem using our virtual block device (*never* do this on any real disk partition!):

1. First, mount the `/dev/loop0p1` partition to your root filesystem:

```
mkdir /media/vbd-1
mount -t xfs /dev/loop0p1  /media/vbd-1
```

2. Next, create a large number of files on this mounted filesystem—for example, `2000` files:

```
for i in {1..2000}; do dd if=/dev/urandom bs=16 count=1 of=/media/
vbd-1/file$i; done
```

3. Now, unmount the device and corrupt the filesystem using `dd`:

```
umount /dev/loop0p1

dd bs=512 count=10 seek=100 if=/dev/urandom of=/dev/loop0p1
```

4. Now, run a filesystem check:

```
xfs_repair -n /dev/loop0p1
```

5. This will most likely show you a list of corrupted files; in order to fix it, use the following line:

```
xfs_repair /dev/loop0p1
```

You can also simulate such a filesystem corruption on your ext4 virtual block device, and then repair it using `fsck -ay /dev/loop0p2`.

Extending the capacity of the filesystem

CentOS 7 uses the **Logical Volume Manager** (**LVM**) to organize the structure and available capacity of your partitions. It is a very dynamic and flexible system that can be extended or rearranged over time, and which is essential in today's most demanding and ever-changing environments. At the moment, buzzwords such as big data or cloud computing can be heard everywhere. Since massive amounts of data get produced all the time, storage requirements and disk space have to grow at the same steady pace. In this recipe, you will learn how to work with the LVM system and how to extend your physical drives, and also how to shrink and extend the capacity of your filesystems.

Getting ready

To complete this recipe, you will require a working installation of the CentOS 7 operating system with root privileges. We will use virtual block devices instead of real disk devices to show you from scratch how to set up a LVM first, and afterwards how to work with it. Please read the *Creating a virtual block device* recipe and create three 1 gigabyte virtual block devices with the GPT partition table, which will be labeled as /dev/loop0, /dev/loop1, and /dev/loop2 in this example.

Again, feel free to use real disk devices if you feel ready for it.

How to do it...

First, we will start by creating an LVM test environment similar to the standard CentOS 7 LVM structure, which is set up during the installation of every server system:

1. First, let's log in as `root` and show information about our virtual block devices:

   ```
   lsblk -io NAME,SIZE
   ```

2. Next, create new partitions spanning the whole disk on each of the three virtual block devices (without a filesystem label):

   ```
   parted -a optimal /dev/loop0 mkpart primary  2048KiB 100%
   parted -a optimal /dev/loop1 mkpart primary  2048KiB 100%
   parted -a optimal /dev/loop2 mkpart primary  2048KiB 100%
   ```

3. Now, let's create LVM *physical volumes* on each of the loop devices (type `yes` to remove the `gpt` label):

   ```
   pvcreate /dev/loop0p1
   pvcreate /dev/loop1p1
   pvcreate /dev/loop2p1
   ```

4. Next, show information about our physical volumes:

   ```
   pvdisplay
   ```

5. Next, we will create a new LVM volume group on our first physical volume:

   ```
   vgcreate myVG1 /dev/loop0p1
   ```

6. Now, show information about the created group:

   ```
   vgdisplay myVG1
   ```

7. Afterwards, let's create some logical volumes on our first volume group, which will be treated as virtual partitions in our Linux system:

   ```
   lvcreate -L 10m   -n swap myVG1
   lvcreate -L 100m -n home myVG1
   lvcreate -L 400m -n root myVG1
   ```

8. Next, show information about the logical volumes:

   ```
   lvdisplay myVG1
   ```

9. Now, display how much free space our underlying volume group has left, which becomes important if you want to expand some logical volumes (see the section `Free  PE / Size` in the output):

   ```
   vgdisplay myVG1
   ```

10. Afterwards, let's create the filesystems on those new logical volumes:

```
mkswap /dev/myVG1/swap
mkfs.xfs /dev/myVG1/home
mkfs.xfs /dev/myVG1/root
```

11. Now, after we have created our test LVM system (which is very similar to the real CentOS LVM standard layout, but with smaller sizes), let's start working with it.

12. First, let's shrink the `root` partition, which is currently `400` megabytes (`M`) in size, by `200` megabytes, and afterwards, let's increase the `home` partition by `500` megabytes (confirm the possible data loss):

```
lvresize -L -200m /dev/myVG1/root
lvresize -L +500m /dev/myVG1/home
```

13. Use `vgdisplay myVG1` again to see how the volume group's free space changes by running the previous commands (see `Free   PE / Size`).

14. Now, let's expand the XFS filesystem on the grown logical volume:

```
mkdir /media/home-test;mount /dev/myVG1/home /media/home-test
xfs_growfs /dev/myVG1/home
```

 It is very important not to use `resize2fs` for growing XFS filesystems, because it's incompatible and can corrupt them.

15. Now, let's say that after some time your data has grown again, and you need the home partition to be 1.5 gigabytes (`G`), but you only have 184.00 MiB left on the underlying volume group. First, we need to add our two prepared physical volumes from the beginning of this recipe to our volume group:

```
vgextend myVG1 /dev/loop1p1 /dev/loop2p1
vgdisplay myVG1
```

16. Afterwards, we have enough free space in our volume group (see `Free   PE / Size`) to expand our home logical volume (the volume must stay mounted):

```
lvresize -L +1500m /dev/myVG1/home
xfs_growfs /dev/myVG1/home
```

How it works...

Here, in this recipe, we have shown you how to work with the LVM for XFS partitions. It has been developed with the purpose of managing disk space on several hard disks dynamically. You can easily merge many physical hard disks together to make them appear as a single virtual hard disk to the system. This makes it a flexible and very scalable system in comparison to working with plain old static partitions. Traditional partitions are bound to, and cannot grow over, the total disk capacity they reside on, and their static partition layout cannot be changed easily. Also, we have introduced some important LVM technical terms that provide different abstraction layers to a hard disk, and which will be explained in this section so as to understand the concepts behind it: **physical volume (pv)**, **volume group (vg)**, and **logical volume (lv)**.

So, what did we learn from this experience?

We started this recipe by creating three virtual block devices of 1 gigabyte (G) each and then one partition spanning the whole device on each of them. Afterwards, we defined these single-partition devices as physical volumes (pv) using the `pvcreate` command. A pv is an LVM term that defines a storage unit in the LVM world. It must be defined on a partition, full drive, or loop device. A pv is just an abstraction of all the space available in the surrounding partition so that we can work with it on an LVM basis. Next, we created a volume group (vg) with the `vgcreate` command, where we also had to define a volume group name of our choice and put the first pv in it as a basic storage volume. As you can see, a vg is a container for at least one pv (we add more pv's later). Adding or removing pv's to or from a vg is the heart of the whole scalability concept of the LVM system. The pv's don't have to be all the same size, and it is possible to grow your vg over time by adding dozens of new physical drives all defined as pv. You can have more than one vg on your system, and you can identify them by the unique names you are giving to them. So, in summary, to extend the space of your vg, you have to create pv's out of physical drives, which you can then add to.

Finally, we created logical volumes (lv) on our vg, which can be seen and used like real physical partitions within a vg. Here, we created three lv's using the `lvcreate` command, by which we need to define the name of the vg (remember, there can be more than one vg on your system) that we want to put our target lv on, along with the size of the volume, as well as a name for it as the last parameter. You can add multiple lvs into a vg and you don't need to use the whole allocated space from the underlying free space of the vg. You can be very flexible with it. The best part is that your decision about your volumes' size and layout doesn't have to be fixed for all time; you can change them anytime later. It is a very dynamic system that can be extended and shrunk, deleted and created, without having to unmount the volume beforehand. But you have to remember that all lvs are bound to a vg, and it is not possible to create them without it or outside its spacial boundaries. If you need to extend an lv's space over the borders of the underlying vg, you have to extend the vg, as show in this recipe.

As you may have seen, for every LVM term, there is a "display" and "create" command, so it's easy to remember: `pvdisplay`, `vgdisplay`, `lvdisplay`, `pvcreate`, `vgcreate`, `lvcreate`.

After you have successfully created your lv's, you can work with them as you would with every other block device partition on your system. The only difference is that they reside in special device folders: `/dev/<vg name>/<lv name>` or `/dev/mapper/<vg name>/<lv name>`. For example, the home volume created in this example has the name `/dev/myVG1/home`. Finally, in order to use them as normal mount points, we created some test filesystems on them.

In the second part of this recipe, we showed you how to extend our vg and how to shrink and expand our lv's test system.

We started by using the `vgdisplay myVG1` command to show the currently available space on the vg. In the command output, we saw that our current volume group has a total of `996M` (VG Size), the allocated size from our lv's (swap, home, root) is `512M` (Alloc PE / Size), and the free size is `484M` (Free PE /Size). Next, we used the `lvresize` command to shrink and expand the logical volume's root and home. The `-L` parameter sets the new size of the volume, and with the + or - sign, the value is added to or subtracted from the actual size of the logical volume. Without it, the value is taken as an absolute one. Remember that we could only increase the home partition because the current volume layout does not occupy the complete vg's total space. After resizing, if we use the `vgdisplay` command again, we see that we now occupy more space in the vg; its free size has been decreased to `184M`. Since we expanded the home volume from `100M` to `500M` in total, we need to remember to expand its XFS filesystem too, since expanding a volume does not automatically expand its filesystem. Therefore, `400M` of the current volume are unallocated without any filesystem information. We used the command, `xfs_growfs`, which will, without defining a limit parameter, use the complete unallocated area for the XFS filesystem. If you want to resize any other filesystem type, such as ext4, you would use the `resize2fs` command instead.

Finally, we wanted to grow the home volume by `1.5G`, but we only have `184M` left on our vg to expand. This is where LVM really *shines*, because we can just add some more physical volumes to it (in the real world, you would just install new hard disks in your server and use them as pvs). We showed you how to *extend* the capacity of your vg by adding two 1G-sized pvs to it using the `vgextend` command. Afterwards, we used `vgdisplay` to see that our vg has now grown to 3G in total size, so finally we could extend our home lv as it would now fit into it. As a last step, we expanded the XFS file system once again to fill up the whole 2G home volume size.

Please remember, all the time, that if you use vg's with several physical hard disks, your data will be distributed among these. An LVM is not a RAID system and has no redundancy, so if one hard disk fails, your complete vg will fail too and your data will be lost! In order to deal with this problem, a proposed solution could be to use a physical RAID system for your hard disks and create an LVM on top of that.

6
Providing Security

In this chapter, we will cover the following topics:

- ▸ Locking down remote access and hardening SSH
- ▸ Installing and configuring fail2ban
- ▸ Working with a firewall
- ▸ Forging the firewall rules by example
- ▸ Generating self-signed certificates
- ▸ Using secure alternatives to FTP

Introduction

This chapter is a collection of recipes that provides a solid framework on which a server can be made secure in almost any environment. Security is the cornerstone of a good administrator, and this chapter illustrates how quickly and easily you can design and implement a series of checkpoints that will deliver the protection you need.

Locking down remote access and hardening SSH

In this recipe, we will learn how to provide additional security measures in order to harden the secure shell environment. The **Secure Shell** (**SSH**) is the basic toolkit that provides remote access to your server. The actual distance to the remote machine is negligible, but the shell environment enables you to perform maintenance, upgrades, the installation of packages and file transfers; you can also facilitate whatever action you need to carry out as the administrator in a secure environment. It is an important tool; as the gateway to your system, it is the purpose of this recipe to show you how to perform a few rudimentary configuration changes that will serve to protect your server from unwanted guests.

Getting ready

To complete this recipe, you will require a minimal installation of the CentOS 7 operating system with root privileges, a console-based text editor of your choice, and a connection to the Internet in order to download additional packages. It is assumed that your server already maintains at least one non-root-based administration account that can use the new features provided by this recipe.

How to do it...

The role of SSH will be vital if you are forced to administer your server from a remote location, and for this reason it is essential that a few basic steps are provided to keep it safe:

1. To begin, log in as `root` and create a backup of the original configuration file by typing the following command:

   `cp /etc/ssh/sshd_config /etc/ssh/sshd_config.bak`

2. Now, open the main `sshd` configuration file by typing the following:

   `vi /etc/ssh/sshd_config`

3. We shall begin by adjusting the time allowed to complete the login process, so scroll down and find the line that reads:

   `#LoginGraceTime 2m`

4. Uncomment this line and change its value to something more appropriate such as:

   `LoginGraceTime 30`

5. Now, scroll down a couple of more lines and find the line that reads as follows:

    `#PermitRootLogin yes`

6. Change this to the following:

    `PermitRootLogin no`

7. Find the following line:

    `X11Forwarding yes`

8. And change it to the following:

    `X11Forwarding no`

9. Save and close the file before restarting the SSH service, as shown here:

    `systemctl restart sshd`

10. At this stage, you may want to consider creating a new SSH session using the new settings before exiting the current session. This is to ensure that everything is working correctly and to avoid locking yourself out of the server accidentally. If you have difficulty starting a new SSH session, then simply return to the original session window and make the necessary adjustments (followed by a restart of the SSH service). However, if no difficulties have been encountered and you are on a successful secondary login, you may close the original shell environment by typing `exit`.

 Remember, having followed this recipe you should now find that root access to the shell is denied and you must log in using a standard user account. Any further work requiring root privilege will require the `su` or `sudo` command, depending on your preferences.

How it works...

SSH is a vital service that enables you to access your server remotely. A server administrator cannot work without it. In this recipe, you were shown how to make that service a little more secure.

So, what did we learn from this experience?

We began the recipe by creating a backup copy of our original main `sshd` configuration file. The next step was to open and edit it. The configuration file for SSH maintains a long list of settings that is ideal for most internal needs, but for a server in a production environment it is often advised that the default SSH configuration file will need changing to suit your particular needs. In this respect, the first step was to make a recommended change to the login grace time, `LoginGraceTime 30`. Instead of the default two minutes, the preceding value will allow only up to 30 seconds. This is the period of time where a user may be connected but will have not begun the authentication process; the lower the number, the fewer unauthenticated connections are kept open. Following this, we then removed the ability of a remote user to log in as the root user by using the `PermitRootLogin no` directive. In most cases, this is a must and a remote server should not allow a direct root login unless the server is in a controlled environment. The main reason behind this is to reduce the risk of getting hacked. The first thing every SSH hacker tries to crack is the password for the user root. If you disallow root login, an attacker needs to guess the user name as well, which is far more complex. The next setting simply disabled `X11Forwarding`. In situations like these, it is often a good idea to apply the phrase "if you do not use it, disable it". To complete the recipe, you were required to restart the SSH server in order to allow the changes to take immediate effect and start a new SSH session with the intention of making sure that the modifications did indeed work as expected. No system is ever safe, but having done this you can now relax, safe in the knowledge of having made the SSH server a little bit safer.

There's more...

There are a few more topics to cover to make your SSH server even more secure: we should change the SSH port number and show you how to limit SSH access to specific system users.

Changing the SSH port number of your server

Port 22 is the default port used by all SSH servers, and changing the port number used can go a small way to increase the overall security of your server. Again, open the main SSH daemon configuration file, `sshd_config`. Now, scroll down and locate the following line that reads:

```
#Port 22
```

Remove the leading # character (uncomment) and change the port number to another value by replacing XXXX with an appropriate port number:

```
Port XXXX
```

You must ensure that the new port number is not already in use, and when complete, save the file and close it. It is important to remember that any changes made here are reflected in your firewall configuration. So, we need to open the new port in firewalld as well. Set the new port via the environment variable `NEWPORT` (replace `XXXX` with your new SSH port), then execute the following `sed` command to change the SSH firewalld service file and reload the `firewalld` daemon afterwards (for details, read the firewall recipe in this chapter):

```
NEWPORT=XXXX

sed "s/port=\"22\"/port=\"$NEWPORT\"/g" /usr/lib/firewalld/services/
ssh.xml > /etc/firewalld/services/ssh.xml firewall-cmd --reload
```

Also, we have to tell SELinux (see *Chapter 14, Working with SELinux* to learn more about it) about the port change because it is restricted to port 22 by default. Make sure that the SELinux tools have been installed, then create a security label for our custom port, replacing `XXXX` with your changed port number:

```
yum install -y policycoreutils-python semanage port -a -t ssh_port_t -p
tcp XXXX
```

Finally restart the sshd service to apply our port change.

Limiting SSH access by user or group

By default, all valid users on the system are allowed to log in and enjoy the benefit of SSH. However, a more secure policy is to only allow a predetermined list of users or groups to log in. When `henry`, `james`, and `helen` represent valid SSH users on the system, in the `sshd_config` add this line to read as follows:

```
AllowUsers henry james helen
```

Alternatively, you can use the following method to enable any user that is a member of a valid administration group to log in. When admin represents a valid SSH group on the system, add this line to read as follows:

```
AllowGroups admin
```

When you have finished, save and close the file before restarting the SSH service.

Installing and configuring fail2ban

In this recipe, we will learn how to implement additional security measures for protecting the SSH server with a package called `fail2ban`. This is a tool that serves to protect a variety of services including SSH, FTP, SMTP, Apache, and many more against unwanted visitors. It works by reading log files for patterns based on failed login attempts and deals with the offending IP addresses accordingly. Of course, you may have already hardened your SSH server or another service on a direct application level, but it is the purpose of this recipe to show that, when faced with the possibility of Brute Force Attacks, an added layer of protection is always useful.

Getting ready

To complete this recipe, you will require a working installation of the CentOS 7 operating system with root privileges, a console-based text editor of your choice, and a connection to the Internet in order to download additional packages. In addition to this, it will be assumed that YUM is already configured to download packages from the EPEL repository (see *Chapter 4, Managing Packages with YUM*).

How to do it...

Fail2ban is not installed by default, and for this reason we will need to invoke the YUM package manager and download the necessary packages:

1. To begin this recipe, log in as root and type the following command:

   ```
   yum install fail2ban-firewalld fail2ban-systemd
   ```

2. Create a new configuration file in your favorite text editor, like so:

   ```
   vi /etc/fail2ban/jail.local
   ```

3. Put in the following content:

   ```
   [DEFAULT]
   findtime = 900
   [sshd]
   enabled = true
   ```

4. Now, append the following line that defines the ban period. It is calculated in seconds, so adjust the time period to reflect a more suitable value. In this case, we have chosen this to be one hour:

   ```
   bantime  = 3600
   ```

5. Then, append the maximum number of login attempts:

   ```
   maxretry = 5
   ```

6. If you are running SSH over a custom port other than 22, you need to tell this to fail2ban as well (replace XXXX with your port number of choice) otherwise skip this step:

   ```
   port=XXXX
   ```

7. Now, save and close the file in the usual way before proceeding to enable the fail2ban service at boot. To do this, type the following command:

   ```
   systemctl enable fail2ban
   ```

8. To complete this recipe, you should now start the service by typing:

   ```
   systemctl start fail2ban
   ```

How it works...

`fail2ban` is designed to monitor users who repeatedly fail to log in correctly on your server, and its main purpose is to mitigate attacks designed to crack passwords and steal user credentials. It works by continuously reading your system's log files, and if this contains a pattern indicating a number of failed attempts, then it will proceed to act against the offending IP address. We all know that servers do not exist in isolation, and by using this tool, within a few minutes, the server will be running with an additional blanket of protection.

So, what did we learn from this experience?

`fail2ban` is not available from the standard CentOS repositories, and for this reason your server will need to have access to the EPEL repository. The installation of the `fail2ban` packages was very simple; besides the main `fail2ban` package, we installed two other packages to integrate it into CentOS 7's new `systemd` and firewalld server technologies. Next, for our local customization, we created a new `jail.local` file. We started specifying the `findtime` parameter for all targets (specified within the `[DEFAULT]` section), which is the amount of time a user has when attempting to log in. This value is measured in seconds and implies that, if a user fails to log in within the maximum number of attempts during the designated period, then they are banned. Next, we enabled `fail2ban` for the `sshd` daemon by adding a `[sshd]` section. In this section, we introduced the `bantime` value, which represents the total number of seconds that a host will be blocked from accessing the server if they are found to be in violation of the rules. Based on this, you were then asked to determine the maximum number of login attempts before blocking. Also, if you have changed your service's standard listening port, you have to define the custom port using the `port` directive. To test your settings, try to authenticate a user using SSH and provide a wrong password five times. On the sixth occasion, you should not be able to get back to the login prompt for one hour!

Protecting the `sshd` service from Brute Force Attacks is just the first step to get you started, and there is much more to learn with `failban`. To troubleshoot the service, please look at its log file at `/var/log/fail2ban.log`. To get some ideas about what can be done with it, open the following example `failban` config file: `less /etc/fail2ban/jail.conf`.

Working with a firewall

A firewall is a program that monitors and controls your system's network interfaces' incoming and outgoing network traffic, and can restrict the transmission to only useful and non-harmful data into and out of a computer system or network. By default, CentOS is made available with an extremely powerful firewall, built right into the kernel, called **netfilter**. While, in older versions of CentOS, we used the famous iptables application to control it, in version 7, the new standard netfilter management program has changed to a service called `firewalld`, which is already installed and enabled on every CentOS 7 server by default.

It is a very powerful service to take full control over your server's firewall security, and is much easier to work with than iptables. Its main advantages are that it features a better structured and more logical approach to managing and configuring every aspect of a modern firewall solution. Therefore, it will be the foundation of your server's security, and for this reason it is the purpose of this recipe to get you started on the fundamentals of firewalld quickly.

Getting ready

To complete this recipe, you will require a minimal installation of the CentOS 7 operating system with root privileges and a console-based text editor of your choice.

How to do it...

As the `firewalld` service is running on every CentOS 7 server by default, we can start directly working with the service by logging in to your server using the `root` user.

1. Type the following commands to query zone-related information:

   ```
   firewall-cmd --get-zones | tr " " "\n"
   firewall-cmd --list-all-zones
   firewall-cmd --get-default-zone
   firewall-cmd --list-all
   ```

2. We can switch to a different firewall `default` zone by using the following line:

   ```
   firewall-cmd --set-default-zone=internal
   ```

3. Add a network interface to a `zone` temporarily:

   ```
   firewall-cmd --zone=work --add-interface=enp0s8
   ```

4. Now, add a service to a `zone` temporarily:

   ```
   firewall-cmd --zone=work --add-service=ftp
   ```

5. Test if adding the interface and service has been successful:

   ```
   firewall-cmd --zone=work --list-all
   ```

6. Now, add the service permanently:

   ```
   firewall-cmd --permanent --zone=work --add-service=ftp
   firewall-cmd --reload
   firewall-cmd --zone=work --list-all
   ```

7. Finally, let's create a new firewall zone by opening the following file:

   ```
   vi /etc/firewalld/zones/seccon.xml
   ```

8. Now put in the following content:

```
<?xml version="1.0" encoding="utf-8"?>
<zone>
  <short>security-congress</short>
  <description>For use at the security congress. </description>
  <service name="ssh"/>
</zone>
```

9. Save and close, then reload the `firewall` config so that we can see the new zone:

   `firewall-cmd --reload`

10. Finally, check that the new zone is available:

    `firewall-cmd --get-zones`

How it works...

In comparison to iptables, the new firewalld system hides away the creation of sophisticated networking rules and has a very easy syntax that is less error-prone. It can dynamically reload netfilter settings at runtime without having to restart the complete service and we can have more than one firewall configuration set per system, which makes it great for working in changing network environments, such as for mobile devices like laptops. In this recipe, we have given you an introduction to the two fundamental building blocks of firewalld: the **zone** and the **service**.

So, what did we learn from this experience?

We started this recipe using `firewall-cmd` to get information about available firewall zones on the system. Firewalld introduces the new concept of network or firewall zones, which assigns different levels of trust to your server's network interfaces and their associated connections. In CentOS 7, there already exist a number of predefined firewalld zones, and all of these (for example, `private`, `home`, `public`, and so on, with the exception of the `trusted` zone) will block any form of incoming network connection to the server unless they are explicitly allowed using special rules attached to the zone (these rules are called firewalld services, which we will see later). We queried zone information using `firewall-cmd` with `--get-zones` or (more detailed) with the `--list-all-zones` parameter. Each of these zones acts as a complete and full firewall that you can use, depending on your system's environment and location. For example, as the name implies, the `home` zone is for use if your computer is located in home areas. If this is selected, you mostly trust all other computers and services on the networks to not harm your computer, whereas the public zone is more for use in public areas such as public access points and so on. Here, you do not trust the other computers and services on the network to not harm you. On CentOS 7, the standard `default` zone configuration set after installation is the `public` zone, which we displayed using the command's `--get-default-zone` parameter, and in more detail using `--list-all`.

Simply put, firewalld zones are all about controlling incoming connections to the server. Limiting outgoing connections with firewalld is also possible but is outside the scope of this book.

Also, to get more technical information about all currently available zones, we used the firewall client's `--list-all-zones` parameter. In the command's output, you will notice that a zone can have some associated networking interfaces and a list of services belonging to it, which are special firewall rules applied to incoming network connections. You may also notice that, while listing details of all zones and their associated services by default, all firewalld zones are very restrictive and barely allow anything to connect to the server at all. Also, another very important concept can be seen in the command's output from the above. Our `public` zone is marked as `default` and `active`. While the `active` zone is the one that is directly associated with a network interface, the `default` zone can really get important if you have multiple network adapters available. Here, it acts as a standard minimum firewall protection and fallback strategy, in case you missed to assign some active zone for every interface. For systems with only one network interface setting, the `default` zone will set the `active` zone automatically as well. To set a `default` zone, we used the `--set-default-zone` parameter and, to mark a zone as active for an interface, we used `--add-interface`. Please note that, if you don't specify the `--zone` parameter, most `firewall-cmd` commands will use the `default` zone to apply settings. Firewalld is listening on every network interface in your system, and waiting for new network packets to arrive. In summary we can say that if there is a new packet coming into a specific interface, the next thing firewalld has to do is find out which zone is the correct one associated with our network interface (using its active or if not available its default configuration); after finding it, it will apply all the service rules against the network packets belonging to it.

Next, we showed you how to work with firewalld services. Simply put, firewalld services are rules that open and allow a certain connection within our firewall to our server. Using such service file definitions allows the reusability of the containing rules because they can be added or removed to any zone. Also, using the predefined firewalld services already available in your system, as opposed to manually finding out and opening protocols, ports, or port ranges using a complicated iptables syntax for your system services of interest, can make your administrative life much easier. We added the `ftp` service to the `work` zone by invoking `--add-service`. Afterwards, we printed out details of the work zone using `--list-all`. Firewalld is designed to have a separated runtime and permanent configuration. While any change to the runtime configuration has immediate effect but will be gone, the permanent configuration will survive reload or restart of the firewalld service. Some commands such as switching the default zone are writing the changes into both configurations which mean they are immediately applied at runtime and are persistent over service restart. Other configuration settings such as adding a service to a zone are only writing to the runtime configuration. If you restart firewalld, reload its configuration, or reboot your computer, these temporary changes will be lost. To make those temporary changes permanent, we can use the `--permanent` flag with the `firewall-cmd` program call to write it to the permanent configuration file as well.

Other than with the runtime options, here the changes are not effective immediately, but only after a service restart/reload or system reboot. Therefore, the most common approach to apply permanent settings for such runtime-only commands is to first apply the setting with the `--permanent` parameter, and afterwards reload the firewall's configuration file to actually activate them.

Finally, we showed you how to create your own zone, which is just a XML file you have to create in the `/etc/firewalld/zones/` directory, and where we specified a name, description, and all the services that you want to activate. If you change something in any firewall configuration file, don't forget to reload the firewall config afterwards.

To finish this recipe, we will revert our permanent changes made to the `work` zone and reload firewalld to reset all the non-permanent changes we applied in this recipe:

```
firewall-cmd --permanent --zone=work --remove-service=ftp
firewall-cmd --reload
```

There's more...

To troubleshoot blocking services, instead of turning off the firewall completely, you should just switch `zone` to `trusted`, which will open all the incoming ports to the firewall:

```
firewall-cmd --set-default-zone=trusted
```

Once you have finished your tests, just switch back to the zone that you were in before, for example:

```
firewall-cmd --set-default-zone=public
```

Forging the firewall rules by example

In this recipe, we want to show you how to create your own firewalld service definitions or how to change existing ones, which any CentOS 7 system administrator should know if the predefined service files don't fit your system's need.

Getting ready

To complete this recipe, you will require a minimal installation of the CentOS 7 operating system with `root` privileges and a console-based text editor of your choice. We will be changing the SSH service's port number in firewalld, so make sure that you have configured the new port as shown in the recipe *Locking down remote access and hardening SSH*. Here, in our example, we have changed the port to `2223`. Also, we will create a new firewalld service for a small Python-based web server that we will use to demonstrate the integration of new system service's into firewalld. It's advantageous to grasp the basics of firewalld by working through the *Working with a firewall* recipe before starting here.

How to do it...

Here in this recipe, we will show you how to change and how to create new firewalld service definitions. In this recipe, it is considered that we are in the default public zone.

To change an existing firewalld service (ssh)

1. First, log in as `root` and copy the `ssh` service to the right place to edit it:

   ```
   cp /usr/lib/firewalld/services/ssh.xml /etc/firewalld/services
   ```

2. Next, open the `ssh` service definition file:

   ```
   vi /etc/firewalld/services/ssh.xml
   ```

3. Change the port from `22` to `2223`, then save the file and close it:

   ```
   <port protocol="tcp" port="2223"/>
   ```

4. Finally, reload the firewall:

   ```
   firewall-cmd --reload
   ```

To create your own new service

Perform the following steps to create your own new service:

1. Open a new file:

   ```
   vi /etc/firewalld/services/python-webserver.xml
   ```

2. Put in the following service definition:

   ```
   <?xml version="1.0" encoding="utf-8"?>
   <service>
     <short>Python Webserver</short>
     <description>For pythons webservers</description>
     <port port="8000" protocol="tcp"/>
   </service>
   ```

3. Save and close the file, and then finally reload the firewall:

   ```
   firewall-cmd --reload
   ```

4. Now, add this new service to our `default` zone:

   ```
   firewall-cmd --add-service=python-webserver
   ```

5. Afterwards, run the following command to start a simple Python web server in the foreground on port `8000` (press the key combination *Ctrl* + *C* to stop it):

   ```
   python -m SimpleHTTPServer 8000
   ```

6. Congratulations! Your new web server sitting at port `8000` can now be reached from other computers in your network:

```
http://<ip address of your computer>:8000/
```

How it works...

Here in this recipe, we have shown how easy it is to customize or define new firewalld services if the predefined needs to be changed, or for new system services that are not defined at all. Service definition files are simple XML files where you define rules for a given system service or program. There are two distinct directories where our firewalld service files live: `/usr/lib/firewalld/services` for all predefined services available from the system installation, and `/etc/firewalld/services` for all custom and user-created services.

So, what did we learn from this experience?

We started this recipe by making a working copy of the SSH firewalld service file in the right place at `/etc/firewalld/services`. We could just copy the original file because all files in this directory will overload the default configuration files from `/usr/lib/firewalld/services`. In the next step, we then modified it by opening it and changing the default port from `22` to `2223`. We have to do this every time we change a system's service standard listening port to make the firewall aware that it should allow network traffic to flow through the changed port. As you can see when opening this file, service files are simple XML text files with some mandatory and some optional tags and attributes. They contain a list of one or more ports and protocols that defines exactly what firewalld should enable if the service is connected to a zone. There can be another important setting in the XML file: helper modules. For example, if you open the SAMBA service file at `/usr/lib/firewalld/services/samba.xml`, you will see the tag, `<module name="nf_conntrack_netbios_ns"/>`. These are special kernel netfilter helper modules that can be dynamically loaded into the underlying kernel-based firewall, and which are needed for some system services, such as Samba or FTP, which create dynamic connections on temporary TCP or UDP ports instead of using static ports. After reloading the firewall configuration, we should now be able to test the connection from another computer in our network using the altered port.

In the second part of this recipe, we created a brand-new service file for a new system service, which is a simple Python web server listening on port 8000 displaying a simple directory content listing. Therefore, we created a simple XML service file for the Python web server including the right port 8000, restarted the firewall, and afterwards added this new service to our default public zone so that we can actually open connections through this service. You should now be able to browse to our web server's start page using another computer in the same network. However, as we did not use the `--permanent` flag, if you restart the firewalld daemon, the `python-webserver` service will be gone from the `public` zone (or you can also use the parameter, `--remove-service=python-webserver`).

In summary, we can say that the recommended firewall choice in CentOS 7 is firewalld, as all important system services have already been set up to use it via predefined service rules. You should remember that Linux firewalls are a very complex topic that can easily fill up a whole book, and you can do a lot more with the `firewall-cmd` that cannot be covered here in this book.

There's more...

Often, you just want to quickly open a specific port to test out things before writing your own custom-made service definition. In order to do this, you can use the following command line, which will open port 2888 using the tcp protocol temporarily on the `default` zone:

```
firewall-cmd --add-port=2888/tcp
```

Once you have finished your tests, just reload the firewall configuration to remove and close the specific port again.

Generating self-signed certificates

In this recipe, we will learn how to create self-signed **Secure Sockets Layer** (**SSL**) certificates using the OpenSSL toolkit. SSL is a technology used to encrypt messages between two ends of a communication (for example, a server and client) so that a third-party cannot read the messages sent between them. Certificates are not used for encrypting the data, but they are very important in this communication process to ensure that the party you are communicating with is exactly the one you suppose it to be. Without them, impersonation attacks would be much more common.

Getting ready

To complete this recipe, you will require a working installation of the CentOS 7 operating system with root privileges and a console-based text editor of your choice.

 Generally speaking, if you are intending to use an SSL Certificate on a production server, you will probably want to purchase a SSL Certificate from a trusted Certificate Authority. There are many options open to you regarding what certificate best suits your requirements and your budget, but for the purpose of this recipe we will confine our discussion to a self-signed certificate that is more than adequate for any development server or internal network.

How to do it...

1. To begin, log in as `root` and go to the following directory so that we can use the Makefile to generate our intended certificates and keyfiles:

   `cd /etc/pki/tls/certs`

2. Now, to create a self-signed certificate with an embedded public key (both in the file, `server.crt`) along with its private key for the server (with the filename as `server.key`), type the following:

   `make server.crt`

3. You will then be asked for a password and will receive a series of questions, to which you should respond with the appropriate values. Complete all the required details by paying special attention to the common name value, which should reflect the domain name of the server or IP address that you are going to use this certificate for. For example, you may type:

   `mylocaldomainname.home`

4. To create a `pem` file that includes a self-signed certificate and a public and a private key in one file, and is valid for five years, type the following:

   `make server.pem DAYS=1825`

5. Now, let's create a key pair (a private key and self-signed certificate that includes the public key) for an Apache web server that we will need for enabling `https`, and which will be generated in `/etc/pki/tls/private/localhost.key` and `/etc/pki/tls/certs/localhost.crt` (use a secure password and repeat it in the second command):

   `make testcert`

6. To create a **Certificate Signing Request** (**CSR**) file instead of a self-signed certificate, use this:

   `make server.csr`

How it works...

Here in this recipe, we introduced you to the SSL technology that uses **public key cryptography (PKI)** (where two forms of keys exist: public and private). On the server, we store the private key and our clients get a public key. Every message sent from one end to the other is encrypted by the key belonging to one side and can only be decrypted by the corresponding key from the other. For example, a message encrypted with the server's private key can only be decrypted and read by the client's public key and vice versa. The public key is sent to the client through a certificate file, where it is part of the file. As said before, the public key is encrypting and decrypting the data and the certificate is not responsible for this, but rather for identifying a server against a client and making sure that you are actually connected to the same server you are trying to connect. If you want to set up secure services using SSL encryption in protocols such as FTPS, HTTPS, POP3S, IMAPS, LDAPS, SMTPS, and so on, you need a signed server certificate to work with. If you want to use these services for your business, and you want them to be trusted by the people who are using and working with them, for example, on the public Internet, your certificate should be signed from a official **certification authority (CA)**. Certificate prices are paid by subscription and can be very expensive. If you don't plan to offer your certificate or SSL-enabled services to a public audience, or you want to offer them only within a company's intranet or just want to test out things before buying, here you can also sign the certificate by yourselves (self-signed) with the OpenSSL toolkit.

> The only difference between a self-signed certificate and one coming from an official CA is that most programs using the certificate for communication will give you a warning that it does not know about the CA and that you should not trust it. After confirming the security risk, you can work with the service normally.

So, what did we learn from this experience?

We started this recipe by going to the standard location where all the system's certificates can be found in CentOS 7: `/etc/pki/tls/certs`. Here, we can find a Makefile, which is a helper script for conveniently generating public/private key pairs, SSL CSRs, and self-signed SSL test certificates. It works by hiding away from you complicated command line parameters for the OpenSSL program. It is very easy to use and will automatically recognize your target through the file extension of your file name parameter. So, it was a simple process to generate an SSL key pair by providing an output filename with the `.crt` extension. As said before, you will be asked for a password and a list of questions regarding the ownership of the certificate, with the most important question being the common name. This should reflect the domain name of the server you are planning to use this certificate for, because most programs, such as web browsers or email clients, will check the domain names to see if they are valid. The result of running this command was the certificate with its embedded public key in file `server.crt`, as well as the corresponding private key for the server called `server.key`.

Next, we created a `.pem` file and provided a `DAYS` parameter to make the certificate valid for five years instead of the default one year when you are running without it. A `pem` file is a container file that contains both parts of the key pair: the private keys and the self-signed certificate (with its embedded public key). This file format is sometimes required by some programs, such as `vsftpd`, to enable SSL encryption instead of providing the key-pair in two separated files. Next, we ran the Makefile target `testcert`, which generates a private key as well as public key, plus the certificate in the correct location, where the Apache web server is expecting them for setting up HTTPS. Please note that, if you need to repeat any Makefile run later, you need to delete the generated output files; for example, for Apache, you need to delete the following files before you can build the output files again:

```
rm /etc/pki/tls/certs/localhost.crt /etc/pki/tls/private/localhost.key
make testcert
```

Finally, we showed you how to generate a CSR file, which will be needed if you plan to purchase an SSL certificate from a trusted certificate authority.

There's more...

We did not cover all the possibilities that the Makefile script has to offer to generate certificates. If you run the command, `make`, without giving any target parameter, the program will print out a usage help text with all possible options.

As we have learned, the public and private keys are generated in pairs, and will encrypt and decrypt each partner's messages. You can verify that your key pairs are valid and belong together by comparing the output of the following (which must be exactly the same):

```
openssl x509 -noout -modulus -in server.crt | openssl md5
openssl rsa -noout -modulus -in server.key | openssl md5
```

Using secure alternatives to FTP

While using FTP is still popular to share data or to transfer files over the network, you must be aware that you are using a very unsecure network protocol that has no protection built into it out-of-the-box. This means that, during network transfer, your data is fully exposed to potential attackers. This is not what you want for transferring sensitive data, such as login credentials, at all. To avoid these potential risks, we will show you in this recipe how to use and set up two alternatives for securing FTP using FTPS (FTP over SSL or FTP/SSL) or SFTPS (SSH-enabled FTP).

Getting ready

To complete this recipe, you will require a minimal installation of the CentOS 7 operating system with root privileges and a console-based text editor of your choice. You should already have installed and configured a basic vsftpd server (see *Chapter 12, Providing Web Services* for how to do it). Also, for setting up SFTP, we will need to create some self-signed certificates; if you want to know the details behind it, please read the *Generating self-signed certificates* recipe in this chapter.

How to do it...

You have to choose beforehand if you want to use SFTP or FTPS. These two methods cannot be applied together, so you have to decide which option to choose first. If you switch between those methods, you need to restore the default configuration file state of `vsftpd.conf` or `sshd_config` first.

Securing your vsftpd server with SSL–FTPS

To secure your vsftpd server with SSL-FTPS perform the following steps:

1. Log in as `root` and go to the standard certificate location:

   ```
   cd /etc/pki/tls/certs
   ```

2. Now, let's create a SSL key pair consisting of the certificate and its embedded public key, as well as the private key in one file for our `ftp-server` configuration (remember that the `Common name` value should reflect the domain name of your FTP server):

   ```
   make ftp-server.pem
   ```

3. Change to a more secure file access rule:

   ```
   chmod 400 /etc/pki/tls/certs/ftp-server.pem
   ```

4. Now, before working on it, first make a backup of the `vsftpd.conf` file.

   ```
   cp /etc/vsftpd/vsftpd.conf /etc/vsftpd/vsftpd.conf.BAK
   ```

5. Now, enable SSL and add the key pair file that we just created to our `vsftpd` configuration:

   ```
   echo "rsa_cert_file=/etc/pki/tls/certs/ftp-server.pem
   ssl_enable=YES
   force_local_data_ssl=YES
   force_local_logins_ssl=YES
   pasv_min_port=40000
   pasv_max_port=40100" >> /etc/vsftpd/vsftpd.conf
   ```

6. Next, we need to add a new firewalld service file, so open the following:

```
vi /etc/firewalld/services/ftps.xml
```

7. Put in the following content:

```
<?xml version="1.0" encoding="utf-8"?>
<service>
  <description>enable FTPS ports</description>
  <port protocol="tcp" port="40000-40100"/>
  <port protocol="tcp" port="21"/>
  <module name="nf_conntrack_ftp"/>
</service>
```

8. Finally, reload the firewall, add the `ftps` service, and restart your `vsftpd` server:

```
firewall-cmd --reload; firewall-cmd --permanent --add-service=ftps;
firewall-cmd --reload

systemctl restart vsftpd
```

Securing your vsftpd server using SSH – SFTP

To secure your vsftpd server using SSL-SFTP perform the following steps:

1. First, create a group for all valid SFTP users:

```
groupadd sshftp
```

2. We will work on the `sshd` main config file, so please make a backup before making any changes:

```
cp /etc/ssh/sshd_config  /etc/ssh/sshd_config.BAK
```

3. Now, open the `sshd_config` file, go to the line containing the `Subsystem` directive, disable it (which means putting a # sign at the beginning of the line), and add the following line to read as shown:

```
#Subsystem           sftp     /usr/libexec/openssh/sftp-server
Subsystem sftp internal-sftp
```

4. Next, add the following lines to the end of the file to enable SFTP:

```
Match Group sshftp
ChrootDirectory /home
ForceCommand internal-sftp
```

5. Finally, restart the `sshd` daemon.

```
systemctl restart sshd
```

How it works...

Here in this recipe, you have learned how to make your file sharing more secure by switching from the standard FTP protocol to using FTP over SSL, or FTP over SSH. Regardless of which option you prefer, SSL is used to encrypt the data during transmitting, which helps you keep your privacy. Which variant you choose is up to you, but remember that SFTP is a bit easier to set up as you do not have to configure additional ports or certificates in your firewall, because everything runs over SSH and this should be enabled by default on most systems.

So, what did we learn from this experience?

We began the recipe by configuring FTPS. We went into a special directory called `/etc/pki/tls/certs`, where CentOS stores all its certificates. In it, there is a Makefile, which we used to create a `.pem` file that contains the public/private key pair and a self-signed certificate that we needed for our FTP server's configuration. Afterwards, we used chmod to ensure that only the root user can read this file. Then, we appended six lines of code to our main `vsftpd` configuration file (first, we made a backup of the original file); they are pretty self-explanatory: enable the SSL protocol, use the self-signed certificate, disallow any non-SSL communication, and use a static range of passive control ports. Also, we created a new firewall service that will open these passive control ports that are needed for FTPS.

Afterwards, we configured SFTP using a chroot jail. If setting up SFTP without it, every login user can view the root filesystem, which is very unsecure. Configuring SFTP is done completely in the main `sshd` config file. After making a backup of the original file, we changed the FTP subsystem to `internal-sftp`, which is a newer FTP server version, has better performance, and runs in the same process. Next, we added three lines to the `vsftpd` configuration file; only users in the `sshftp` group are using SFTP and are put into a chroot jail and can only view files up to their `home` directory. `ForceCommand` ignores all local settings by the users and enforces these rules here instead. To add new chrooted SFTP users, all you have to do is create a standard Linux user account and add them to the `sshftp` user group.

There's more...

If you want to test your enabled FTPS server, you need an FTP client that supports "FTP over TLS." You have to find and enable this option in your FTP client's settings. Under Linux, you can install the `lftp` client to test if you can connect to our FTPS server. First, install the `lftp` package (for example, `yum install lftp`). Then, configure the client using TLS:

```
echo "set ftp:ssl-auth TLS
set ftp:ssl-force true
set ftp:ssl-protect-list yes
set ftp:ssl-protect-data yes
set ftp:ssl-protect-fxp yes
set ssl:verify-certificate no" >~/.lftprc
```

Now, you can connect and test your FTPS server using the following:

```
lftp -u username <server name>
```

If you want to test your enabled SFTP server, you need the program called `sftp`:

```
sftp john@<server name or ip address> -p 22
```

You have to remember that all the changes to `sshd_config` will be reflected in SFTP as well. So, if you disabled root login or ran SSH over a different port than `22`, you have to take it into consideration when you try to log in to SFTP.

7
Building a Network

In this chapter, we will cover the following topics:

- ▸ Printing with CUPS
- ▸ Running a DHCP server
- ▸ Using WebDAV for file sharing
- ▸ Installing and configuring NFS
- ▸ Working with NFS
- ▸ Securely sharing resources with Samba

Introduction

This chapter is a collection of recipes that covers the many facets of today's working environment. From printing and file sharing across different types of office computer systems to keeping your computers online, this chapter provides the necessary details on how quickly you can use CentOS to implement the necessary tools that will maximize efficiencies within your networking environment.

Printing with CUPS

Print servers allow local printing devices to be connected to a network and be shared among several users and departments. There are many advantages using such a system, including the lack of a need to buy dedicated printer hardware for each user, room, or department. The **Common Unix Printing System** (**CUPS**) is the de-facto standard for print servers on Linux, as well as Unix distributions including OS X. It is built with a typical client/server architecture, where clients in the network send print jobs to the centralized print server that schedules these tasks, then delegates and executes the actual printing on a printer that is locally connected to our printer server or sends the print job remotely to the computer that has the physical connection to the requested printer or to a standalone network printer. If you set up your printers within the CUPS system, almost all Linux and OS X printing application on any client in your network will be automatically configured to use them out-of-the box, without the need to install additional drivers. Here, in this recipe, we will show you how to get started with the CUPS printing server system.

Getting ready

To complete this recipe, you will require a working installation of the CentOS 7 operating system with root privileges, a console-based text editor of your choice, and a connection to the Internet in order to download additional packages. In this recipe, we will use the network interface with the IP address, `192.168.1.8`, and the corresponding network address of `192.168.1.0/24` to serve the CUPS printer server to our network.

How to do it...

We begin this recipe by installing the CUPS printing server software, which is not available by default on a fresh CentOS 7 minimal system:

1. To do this, log in as `root` and install the following package:

   ```
   yum install cups
   ```

2. Next, create an SSL certificate for the CUPS server, which we will need for secure authentication to the CUPS web application (add a secure password when asked):

   ```
   cd /etc/pki/tls/certs
   make cups-server.key
   ```

3. Now, let's open the CUPS main configuration file to customize the server (backup first):

   ```
   cp /etc/cups/cupsd.conf /etc/cups/cupsd.conf.BAK
   vi /etc/cups/cupsd.conf
   ```

4. First, to make CUPS available on the entire network, find the following line: `Listen localhost:631`, than change it to:

```
Listen 631
```

5. Next, we want to configure access to all normal web pages of the web-based CUPS frontend. Search for the `<Location />` directive (don't confuse this with other directives such as `<Location /admin>`) and change the complete block by adding your network address. After changing, the complete block looks like this:

```
<Location />
 Order allow,deny
 Allow 192.168.1.0/24
</Location>
```

6. Next, set access permissions for the `/admin` and `/admin/conf` `Location` directives, granting access to the local server only:

```
<Location /admin>
    Order allow,deny
    Allow localhost
</Location>
<Location /admin/conf>
    AuthType Default
    Require user @SYSTEM
    Order allow,deny
    Allow localhost
</Location>
```

7. Finally, add our SSL certificate information to the end of the configuration file:

```
ServerCertificate /etc/pki/tls/certs/cups-server.crt
ServerKey /etc/pki/tls/certs/cups-server.key
```

8. Close and save the file, then restart the CUPS server and enable it on boot:

    `systemctl restart cups.service systemctl enable cups.service`

9. Now, we have to open the CUPS server ports in firewalld so that other computers in the network can connect to it:

    `firewall-cmd --permanent --add-service=ipp firewall-cmd --reload`

10. You can test the accessibility of your CUPS server from another computer in your `192.168.1.0/24` network by browsing to the following location (allow a security exception in the browser when asked):

    `https://<IP address of your CUPS server>:631`

11. To access the administration area within the CUPS frontend, you need to be on the same server as CUPS is running (on a CentOS 7 minimal installation, please install a window manager and browser), and then use the system user, `root`, with the appropriate password to login.

How it works...

In this recipe, we showed you how easy it is to install and set up a CUPS printing server.

So, what did we learn from this experience?

We began our journey by installing the CUPS server package on our server because it is not available on the CentOS 7 system by default. Afterwards, we generated a SSL key-pair, which we will need later in the process (to learn more, read the *Generating self-signed certificates* recipe in *Chapter 6, Providing Security*). It is used to allow the encrypted submission of your login credentials to the CUPS administration web frontend (over secure HTTPS connections). Next, we opened CUPS's main configuration file, /etc/cups/cupsd.conf, with the text editor of our choice. As you may notice, the configuration format is very similar to the Apache configuration file format. We started changing the Listen address by removing the localhost name, therefore allowing all clients from everywhere in your network (192.168.1.0/24) to access our CUPS server at port 631 instead of allowing only the local interface to connect to the printer server.

> By default, the CUPS server has Browsing On enabled, which will broadcast, every 30 seconds, an updated list of all printers that are being shared in the system to all client computers on the same subnet. If you want to broadcast to other subnets as well, use the BrowseRelay directive.

Next, we configured access to the CUPS web interface. This frontend can be used to conveniently browse all available printers on the network, or even install new printers or configure them if you log in with an administrator account. As there are different tasks in the user interface, there are three different directives that can be used to fine-grain its access. Access to all normal web pages can be set using the <Location /> directive, whereas all administration pages can be managed with <Location /admin> and more specifically to change the configuration within the <Location /admin/conf> tag. In each of these Location tags, we added different Allow directives, thus granting normal CUPS web pages (such as, browsing all available network printers) from your complete network (for example, 192.168.1.0/24) while accessing the special administration pages is restricted to the server that runs the CUPS service (localhost). Remember, if this is too restrictive for your environment, you can always adjust these Allow settings. Also, there are various other Location types available, such as one that is used for activating our service in additional subnets. Please read the CUPS configuration manual using man cupsd.conf. Next, we configured SSL encryption, thus activating secure https:// addresses for the web interface. Then, we started the CUPS server for the first time and enabled it to start automatically when the server boots up. Finally, we added the ipp firewalld service, thus allowing incoming CUPS client connections to the server.

There's more...

Now that we have successfully set up and configured our CUPS server, it's time to add some printers to it and print a test page. Here, we will show you how to add _two different_ types of printers to the system using the command line.

> Adding or configuring printers can also be done using the graphical web-based CUPS interface.

First, we will install a true _network_ printer that is already available in the same network (in our case, the `192.168.1.0/24` network) as our CUPS server and afterwards a locally connected printer (for example, via USB to our CUPS server or any other computer in the same network).

> Why should you want to install an already connected network printer to our CUPS server? CUPS can do much more than just printing: it is a centralized printer server, thus managing scheduling and queuing of printers and their jobs, serving printers in different subnets, and providing unified printing protocols and standards for convenient access on any Linux or Mac client.

How to add a network printer to the CUPS server

To start adding a network printer to our CUPS server, we will use the command `lpinfo -v` to list all the available printing devices or drivers known to the CUPS server. Normally, the CUPS server will automatically identify all locally (USB, parallel, serial, and so on) and remotely available (network protocols such as `socket`, `http`, `ipp`, `lpd`, and so on) printers from most common printing protocols without any problems. In our example, the following network printer has been successfully identified (the output has been truncated):

```
network dnssd://Photosmart%20C5100%20series%20%5BF8B652%5D._pdl-
datastream._tcp.local/
```

Next, we will install this printer on the CUPS server to put it under its control. First, we need to look for the correct printer driver. As we can see in the last output, it is an HP Photosmart C5100 series printer. So, let's search for the driver in the list of all currently installed drivers on our CUPS server:

```
lpinfo --make-and-model HP -m | grep Photosmart
```

The list does not contain our model C5100, so we have to install an additional HP driver package using:

```
yum install hplip
```

Now, if we issue our command again, we can find the correct driver:

```
lpinfo --make-and-model HP -m | grep Photosmart | grep c5100
```

For other printer models and manufacturers, there are other driver packages available as well, for example, the `gutenprint-cups` RPM package.

The correct driver for this printer will be shown as follows:

```
drv:///hp/hpcups.drv/hp-photosmart_c5100_series.ppd
```

Now, we have everything ready to install the printer using the following syntax:

```
lpadmin -p <printer-name> -v <device-uri> -m <model> -L <location> -E
```

In our example, we installed it using:

```
lpadmin -p hp-photosmart -v "dnssd://Photosmart%20C5100%20series%20
%5BF8B652%5D._pdl-datastream._tcp.local/" -m "drv:///hp/hpcups.drv/hp-
photosmart_c5100_series.ppd" -L room123 -E
```

Now, the printer should be under our CUPS server's control and should immediately be shared and seen in the entire network from any Linux or OS X computer (on a CentOS 7 minimal client, you will first need to install the `cups` package as well and enable incoming `ipp` connections using firewalld's `ipp-client` service before any shared network printer information from our CUPS server will become available).

You can later change the configuration of this printer by opening and changing the file at `/etc/cups/printers.conf`. To actually print a test page, you should now be able to access the printer using its name, `hp-photosmart`, from any client (on a CentOS 7 minimal client, you would need to install the package `cups-client`):

```
echo "Hello printing world" | lpr -P hp-photosmart  -H 192.168.1.8:631
```

How to share a local printer to the CUPS server

If you want to share a local printer physically connected to our CUPS server, just plug in the printer to the system (for example, via USB) and follow the previous recipe, *How to add a network printer to the CUPS server*. In the step `lpinfo -v`, you should see it appear as a `usb://` address, so you need to take this address and follow the rest of the steps.

If you want to connect and share a printer on your centralized CUPS server, which is physically connected to any other computer on your CUPS network, install the `cups` daemon on this other machine (follow all the steps in the main recipe) and then install the printer driver for it as shown here in this section. This will make sure that the local CUPS daemon will make the printer available on the network, as it would be on our centralized CUPS server. Now that it is available on the network, you can easily add it to our main CUPS server to enjoy all the benefits of a centralized printing server.

Here in this recipe, we have only scratched the surface and introduced you to the basics of setting up a CUPS server for your network. There is always more to learn, and you can build very complex CUPS server systems managing hundreds of printers in the corporate environment, which is outside the scope of this recipe.

Running a DHCP server

If a connection to a network needs to be made, every computer needs a correct **Internet Protocol (IP)** configuration installed on their system to communicate. Assigning IP client configurations automatically from a *central point* using the **Dynamic Host Control Protocol (DHCP)** can make the administrator's life easier and simplify the process of adding new machines to a network in comparison to the tedious work of manually setting up static IP information on each computer system in your network. In small home-based networks, people often use DHCP servers directly installed in silico on their Internet routers, but such devices often lack advanced features and have only a basic set of configuration options available. Most of the time, this is not sufficient for bigger networks or in the corporate environment, where you are more likely to find dedicated DCHP servers for more complex scenarios and better control. In this recipe, we will show you how to install and configure a DHCP server on a CentOS 7 system.

Getting ready

To complete this recipe, you will require a working installation of the CentOS 7 operating system with root privileges, a console-based text editor of your choice, and a connection to the Internet in order to facilitate the download of additional packages. It is expected that your DHCP server will be using a static IP address; if you do not have one, refer to the recipe *Building a static network connection* in *Chapter 2, Configuring the System*. If you plan to send DNS information to the clients through DHCP as well, you should have already applied the recipe *Installing and configuring a simple nameserver* in *Chapter 8, Working with FTP*.

How to do it...

Here in this example, we will configure a DHCP server for a static network interface serving a single network with all its available IP addresses to all the computers connected directly to it (they are all in the same subnet).

1. First, log in as `root` and type the following command in order to install the DHCP server packages:

   ```
   yum install dhcp
   ```

2. In our example, we will use a network interface with the name, `ifcfg-enp5s0f1`, to serve our DHCP requests. Next, we need to collect some very important network information, which we will use later for configuring the DHCP server (change the network interface name to fit your own needs):

```
cat /etc/sysconfig/network-scripts/ifcfg-enp5s0f1
```

3. From this output, we need the following information, so please write it down (most likely, your output will be different):

```
BOOTPROTO="static"
IPADDR="192.168.1.8"
NETMASK="255.255.255.0"
GATEWAY="192.168.1.254"
```

4. We also need the subnet network address, which can be calculated using the following line:

```
ipcalc -n 192.168.1.8/24
```

5. This will print the following output (write it down for later):

```
NETWORK=192.168.1.0
```

6. Now, we will open our main DHCP configuration file, after we make a backup of the original file:

```
cp /etc/dhcp/dhcpd.conf /etc/dhcp/dhcpd.conf.BAK
vi /etc/dhcp/dhcpd.conf
```

7. Append the following lines to the end of the file, taking into account your individual network interface's configuration from the preceding steps (`routers = GATEWAY`, `subnet = NETWORK`):

```
authoritative;
default-lease-time 28800;
max-lease-time 86400;
shared-network MyNetwork {
    option domain-name            "example.com";
    option domain-name-servers    8.8.8.8, 8.8.4.4;
    option routers                192.168.1.254;
    subnet 192.168.1.0 netmask 255.255.255.0 {
        range 192.168.1.10 192.168.1.160;
    }
}
```

8. Finally, start and enable the DHCP service:

```
systemctl start dhcpd
systemctl enable dhcpd
```

How it works...

Here in this recipe, we showed you how easy it is to set up a DHCP server for a single network. With this, every time a new machine gets added to the network, the computer gets the correct IP information automatically, which it needs in order to connect to the network without any further human action.

So, what did we learn from this experience?

We started this recipe by installing the DHCP server package because it does not come with CentOS 7 out-of-the-box. Since our DHCP daemon communicates with its clients to assign IP information over a network interface, in the next step we had to choose a network device that would be used for the service. In our example, we selected the device named enp5s0f1. By default, the DHCP server can manage all available IP addresses from the same subnet as the associated network interface. Remember that your primary DHCP server's network interface must be configured to get its own IP information statically and not through (another) DHCP server! Next, we used the cat command to print out all the interesting lines from our enp5s0f1 network interface configuration file, which we will need for configuring the DHCP server. Afterwards, we used the ipcalc tool to calculate the (subnet) network address for our DHCP server's network interface. Then, we opened the main DHCP server configuration, started configuring some *global* settings, and defined a new *shared network*. In the global settings, we first set our DHCP server to be authoriative, which means it is the only and main responsible DHCP server in the network. Next, we defined default-lease-time to 28800 seconds, which is eight hours, and the max-lease-time to 86400, which is 24 hours. The lease time is the amount of time the DHCP server "rents out" an IP address to a client before it has to sign up again on the DHCP server asking for an extension of the IP. If it is not requesting a renewal of an existing lease at that time, the IP address will be released from the client and put into the pool of free IP addresses again, ready to be served to new machines that want to connect to the network. The client can define the amount of time it wants to lease an IP address by itself. If no time frame has been supplied from the client to the DHCP server, the default lease time will be used.

All subnets that share the same physical network interface should be defined within a shared-network declaration, so we defined this area using square brackets. This is also called a scope. In our example, we only have one network, so we only need one shared-network scope. Within it, we first defined a domain-name option, which will be sent and can be used by clients as their base domain name. Next, we added the **domain name servers** (**DNS**) to our configuration. Sending DNS information to the client is not mandatory for the DHCP server but can be useful. The more information a client gets for a given network, the better, because fewer manual configuration steps have to be made.

 You can send out a lot of other useful information to the client (using DHCP) about the network he is connecting to: gateway, time, WINS, and so on.

Here in our example, we used the official Google DNS servers; if you have already set up your own DNS server (see *Chapter 8, Working with FTP*), you could also use these addresses here. Next, we specified a `routers` option, which is another useful piece of information that will be sent out to the clients as well. Afterwards, we specified the most important part of any DHCP server: the `subnet` scope. Here, we defined our network ranges for assigning IP addresses for clients. We need to provide the subnet network address, its submask, and then the starting and ending IP address range that we want to allow to clients. In our example, we allow host IP addresses from `192.168.1.10`, `192.168.1.11`, `192.168.1.12` ... to `192.168.1.160`. If you have more than one subnet, you can use multiple `subnet` scope directives (called a multihomed DHCP server).

Next, we started the DHCP server and enabled it on boot. Your clients should now be able to get IP addresses dynamically from our new system.

In summary, we have only showed you some very basic DHCP server configuration options to get you started, and there are many more settings available, letting you build very complex DHCP server solutions. To get a better overview of its possibilities, please have a look at the example configuration file provided with the DHCP server documentation at `less /usr/share/doc/dhcp-4*/dhcpd.conf.example`.

There's more...

In the main recipe, we configured our basic DHCP server to be able to send complete IP network information to our clients so that they should be able to join our network. To use this server, you need to enable DHCP addressing on your client's network interfaces. On CentOS clients, please do not forget to use `BOOTPROTO=dhcp` and remove all static entries such as `IPADDR` in the appropriate network-scripts `ifcfg` file (read the recipe, *Building a static network connection* in *Chapter 2, Configuring the System* to get you started on network-scripts files). Then, to make a DHCP request, restart the network using `systemctl restart network` or try to do a reboot of the client system (with the `ONBOOT=yes` option). Confirm with `ip addr list`.

Using WebDAV for file sharing

The **Web-based Distributed Authoring and Versioning** (**WebDAV**) open standard can be used for sharing files over the network. It is a popular protocol to conveniently access remote data as an *online hard disk*. There are a lot of online storage and e-mail providers who offer online space through WebDAV accounts. Most graphical Linux or Windows systems can access WebDAV servers in their file managers out-of-the-box. For other operating systems, there are also free options available. Another big advantage is that WebDAV is running over normal HTTP or HTTPS ports, so you can be sure that it will work in almost any environment, even behind restricted firewalls.

Here, we will show you how to install and configure WebDAV as an alternative for the FTP protocol for your file sharing needs. We will use HTTPS as our communication protocol for secure connections.

Getting ready

To complete this recipe, you will require a working installation of the CentOS 7 operating system with root privileges and a console-based text editor of your choice. You will need a working Apache web server with SSL encryption enabled and reachable in your network; see *Chapter 11, Providing Mail Services* for how to install the HTTP daemon, and especially the recipe *Setting up HTTPS with SSL*. Also, some experience working with the Apache config file format is advantageous.

How to do it...

1. Create a location for sharing your data and for a WebDAV lock file:

    ```
    mkdir -p /srv/webdav /etc/httpd/var/davlock
    ```

2. Since WebDAV is running as an Apache module over HTTPS, we have to set proper permissions to the standard `httpd` user:

    ```
    chown apache:apache /srv/webdav /etc/httpd/var/davlock
    chmod 770 /srv/webdav
    ```

3. Now, create and open the following Apache WebDAV configuration file:

    ```
    vi /etc/httpd/conf.d/webdav.conf
    ```

4. Put in the following content:

    ```
    DavLockDB "/etc/httpd/var/davlock"
    Alias /webdav /srv/webdav
    <Location /webdav>
        DAV On
        SSLRequireSSL
        Options None
        AuthType Basic
        AuthName webdav
        AuthUserFile /etc/httpd/conf/dav_passwords
        Require valid-user
    </Location>
    ```

5. Save and close the file. Now, to add a new WebDAV user named `john` (enter a new password for the user as prompted):

    ```
    htpasswd -c /etc/httpd/conf/dav_passwords john
    ```

6. Finally, restart the Apache2 web server:

```
systemctl restart httpd
```

7. To test if we can connect to our WebDAV server, you can use a graphical user interface (most Linux file managers support WebDAV browsing) from any client in your network, or we can mount the drive using the command line.

8. Log in on any client machine as `root` in the same network as our WebDAV server (on CentOS, you need the `davfs2` filesystem driver package to be installed from the EPEL repository, and the usage of file locks must be disabled as the current version is not capable of working with file locks), enter the password for our DAV user account named `john`, and confirm the self-signed certificate when asked:

```
yum install davfs2

echo "use_locks 0" >> /etc/davfs2/davfs2.conf

mkdir /mnt/webdav

mount -t davfs https://<WebDAV Server IP>/webdav /mnt/webdav
```

9. Now, to see if we can write to the new network storage type:

```
touch /mnt/webdav/testfile.txt
```

10. If you've got connection problems, check the firewall settings on your WebDAV server for the services `http` and `https`, as well as on your client.

How it works...

Here in this recipe, we showed you how easy it is to set up a WebDAV server for easy file sharing.

So, what did we learn from this experience?

We started our journey by creating two directories: one, where all the shared files of our WebDAV server will live, and one for creating a lock file database for the WebDAV server process. The latter is needed so that users can *block* access to documents to avoid collisions with others if files are currently modified by them. As WebDAV runs as a native Apache module (`mod_dav`) that is already enabled by default in CentOS 7, all we need to do is create a new Apache virtual host configuration file, where we can set up all our WebDAV settings. First, we have to link our WebDAV host to the full path of the lock database that is used to track user locks. Next, we defined an alias for our WebDAV sharing folder, which we then configured using a `Location` directive. This will be activated if someone is using specific HTTP methods on the `/webdav` path URL. Within this area, we specified that this URL will be a DAV-enabled share, enabled SSL encryption for it, and specified basic user-based password authentication. The user account's passwords will be stored in a user account database called `/etc/httpd/conf/dav_passwords`. To create valid accounts in this database file, we then used the Apache2 `htpasswd` utility on the command line. Finally, we restarted the service to apply our changes.

For testing, we used the `davfs` filesystem driver, which you need to install on CentOS 7 using the `davfs2` package from the EPEL repository. There are many other options available, such as the `cadaver` WebDAV command-line client (also from the EPEL repository); alternatively, you can access it directly using integrated WebDAV support in a graphical user interface such as GNOME, KDE, or Xfce.

Installing and configuring NFS

The **Network File System** (**NFS**) protocol enables remote access to filesystems over a network connection. It is based on a client-server architecture, allowing a centralized server to share files with other computers. A client can attach those exported shares in their own file system to access it conveniently, as they will be located on a local storage. While Samba and AFP are more common distributed filesystems on Windows and OS X, NFS is now the de-facto standard and a key element of any Linux server system. Here in this recipe, we will show you how easy it is to set up an NFS server for file sharing over the network.

Getting ready

To complete this recipe, you will require a working installation of the CentOS 7 operating system with root privileges, a console-based text editor of your choice, and a connection to the Internet in order to facilitate the download of additional packages. It is expected that your NFS server and all the clients will be able to ping each other and are connected to each other by a static IP address (see the recipe, *Building a static network connection*, in *Chapter 2, Configuring the System*). In our example, the NFS server is running with IP `192.168.1.10` and two clients with the IPs `192.168.1.11` and `192.168.1.12` and the network's domain name `example.com`.

How to do it...

In this particular section, we are going to learn how to install and configure the NFS server, and create and export a share on a client.

Installing and configuring the NFS server

NFSv4 is not installed by default, and for this reason we will begin by downloading and installing the required packages:

1. To do this, log in as `root` on the server that you want to run the NFS daemon on and type the following command in order to install the required packages:

    ```
    yum install nfs-utils
    ```

2. For NFSv4 to work, we need the *same base* domain for all clients and the NFS server. So, let's define sub-domain names for our NFS server and the clients, if you haven't set up a domain name using DNS (see *Chapter 9, Working with Domains*), we will set up a new hostname for our computers in the `/etc/hosts` file:

```
echo "192.168.1.10 myServer.example.com" >> /etc/hosts
echo "192.168.1.11 myClient1.example.com" >> /etc/hosts
echo "192.168.1.12 myClient2.example.com" >> /etc/hosts
```

3. Now, open the `/etc/idmapd.conf` file and put in the base domain name (not the full domain name) of your NFS server; search for the line that reads `#Domain = local.domain.edu`, and replace it with the following:

```
Domain = example.com
```

4. Next, we need to open some firewall ports for the server to have proper NFS access:

```
for s in {nfs,mountd,rpc-bind}; do firewall-cmd --permanent --add-service $s; done; firewall-cmd --reload
```

5. Finally, let's start the NFS server service and enable it on reboot:

```
systemctl start rpcbind nfs-server systemctl enable rpcbind nfs-server systemctl status nfs-server
```

Creating an export share

Now that our NFS server is configured and up-and-running, it's time to create some file shares that we can export to our clients:

1. First, let's create a folder for our shares and change its permissions:

```
mkdir /srv/nfs-data
```

2. Create a new group with a specific GID and associate it with the export, and then change permissions:

```
groupadd -g 50000 nfs-share;chown root:nfs-share /srv -R;chmod 775 /srv -R
```

3. Open the following file:

```
vi /etc/exports
```

4. Now, enter the following text, but be very focussed while typing:

```
/srv/nfs-data *(ro) 192.168.1.11(rw) 192.168.1.12(rw) /home *.example.com(rw)
```

5. Save and close the file, then re-export all entries from `/etc/exports` using the following:

```
exportfs -ra
```

How it works...

On CentOS 7, you can install version 4 of the NFS, which has some enhancements over former versions, such as more flexible authentication options and being fully backward compatible with older NFS versions. Here, we showed you how easy it is to install and configure the NFS server and create some shared exports for our clients to use.

So, what did we learn from this experience?

We started this recipe by installing the `nfs-utils` package, since the NFS server functionality is not available on CentOS 7 by default. Next, we configured our server's domain name using the `/etc/hosts` file, as in our example, no DNS server of our own has been configured. If you have set up a DNS server, you should follow a similar domain name schema as shown here, because this is very important for NFSv4 to work, as all clients and the server should be in the same base domain. In our example, we specified that they are all sub-domains of `example.com`: `myClient1.example.com`, `myClient2.example.com`, and `myServer.example.com`. This is a means of securing the sharing of data, as the NFS server will only allow access to files from a client to a server if the domain names match (in our example, both server and client are part of the `example.com` domain). Next, we put this base domain in the `idmapd.conf` file, which takes care of mapping user names and group IDs to NFSv4 IDs. Afterwards, we enabled the `nfs`, `mountd`, and `rpc-bind` firewalld services in our firewalld instance, which are all needed for full support and communication between our clients and server. To finish our base configuration, we started the `rpcbind` and NFS servers and enabled them on boot.

After the NFS server was successfully set up, we added some export to it, to actually allow clients to access some shared folders from the server. Therefore, we created a special directory in the filesystem, which will keep all our shared files. We associated this sharing folder, `/srv/nfs-data`, with a new group, `nfs-share`, and gave it read/write/execute permissions. For practical reasons we will control Linux file permissions for our export on a group level. The name is unimportant but its group identifier (GID) has to be set to a static value (for example, `50000`). This new GID must be the same on the server as well as on every client for every user who wants to have write permissions because NFS transfers any access permissions between server and client on a user (UID) or GID level over the network. The whole sharing magic then happens in the `/etc/exports` file. It contains a table; in it you specify all the important information about your shared folders and their access securities for the clients. Every line in this file is equivalent to one shared folder in your system, and a whitespaced list of all the hosts allowed to access them together with their accessing options in brackets. As you can see, there are different possibilities to define your target clients using IP addresses or hostnames. For hostnames, you can use wildcards such as * and ? to keep the file more compact and allow for multiple machines at once, but you can also define export options for each single host name. Explaining all the options is outside the scope of this book; if you need more help, read the exports manual, which can be found using `man exports`.

For example, the line, `/srv/nfs-data *(ro) 192.168.1.11(rw) 192.168.1.12(rw)`, defines that we want to export the content of the folder `/srv/nfs-data` to all hostnames (because of the `*` symbol); read-only (`ro`) means that every client can read the content of the folder but not write in it. For clients with the IP address `192.168.1`, ending with `11` and `12`, we allow reading and writing (`rw`). The second line defines that we are exporting the `/home` directory to all clients in the subdomain of `*.example.com` with read/write capacity. Whenever you make a change to the `/etc/exports` file, run the `exportfs -r` command to apply your changes to the NFS server.

Finally, we can say that NFSv4 in CentOS 7 is very easy to set up and start. It's the perfect solution for sharing files between Linux systems, or for centralized home directories.

Working with NFS

Before a client computer can use file system exports shared by an NFS server, it has to be configured to correctly access this system. Here in this recipe, we will show you how to set things up and work with NFS on the client machine.

Getting ready

To complete this recipe, you will require a working installation of the CentOS 7 operating system with root privileges, a console-based text editor of your choice, and a connection to the Internet in order to facilitate the download of additional packages. It is expected that you have already followed the *Installing and configuring NFS* recipe and have set up an NFS server, such as in this example. It is expected that all the clients can ping each other and are connected to the NFS server, and will be using a static IP address (see the recipe, *Building a static network connection*, in *Chapter 2, Configuring the System*). In our example, the NFS server is running with the IP `192.168.1.10` and two clients with the IPs `192.168.1.11` and `192.168.1.12`.

How to do it...

On our client systems, we also need the same NFS software package, and a similar configuration to the one on the server, in order to establish a communication between them:

1. To begin, log in on your client as `root`, and apply the exact same steps as in the *Installing and configuring NFS* recipe until the end of step 3. Skip step 4 because no firewalld service must be opened. Then, instead of step 5, use the following commands, which will not start and enable the `nfs-server`, but only the `rpcbind` service instead:

    ```
    systemctl start rpcbind
    systemctl enable rpcbind
    ```

2. Stop there and do not apply anything else from the original recipe. To test the connection to our NFS server, use the following command:

```
showmount -e myServer.example.com
```

3. Now, to test if attaching the NFS exports works you can do so manually using a new user, `john`. This needs to be added to the `nfs-share` group first in the following way so that we can write on our share:

```
groupadd -g 50000 nfs-share;useradd john;passwd john;usermod -G
nfs-share john
```

```
mount -t nfs4 myServer.example.com:/srv/nfs-data /mnt
```

```
su - john;touch /mnt/testfile.txt
```

4. If the creation of the file in the shared directory works, you can put the import in the `fstab` file so that it will be automatically mounted on system boot:

```
vi /etc/fstab
```

5. Append the following line:

```
myServer.example.com:/srv/nfs-data   /mnt nfs defaults 0 0
```

6. Finally, to remount everything from `fstab`, type the following:

```
mount -a
```

How it works...

In this recipe, we showed you how easy it is to use some shared file system exports from an existing NFSv4 server.

So, what did we learn from this experience?

As you have seen, to set up an NFS client, you need a very similar setup to the one on the NFS server itself, with the exception of starting the rpcbind service instead of nfs-server (which, as the name implies, is only needed for the server side). The rpcbind service is a port mapper and is used for **Remote Procedure Calls** (**RPC**), which is a communication standard needed for NFS to work. Another very crucial step in the configuration that you should remember was setting up the domain name in the /etc/idmapd.conf file. We will have to use the *same* base domain name as on the server (example.com) in order to make the NFSv4 communication between server and client work. After having started and enabled the rpcbind service, we could then mount the NFS share to a local directory, either using the mount command (with -t type nfs4) directly, or via the fstab file. Remember, that every system user who wants proper read/write/execute permissions to a share needs the *same* permissions on the NFS server; in our example we manage correct permissions on an identical GID level. We used the default options to mount the share; if you need different or advanced options, please refer to man fstab. In order to apply changes to the fstab file, perform mount -a to remount everything from that file.

Securely sharing resources with Samba

Samba is a software package that enables you to share files, printers, and other common resources across a network. It is an invaluable tool for any working environment. One of the most common ways to share file resources across a heterogeneous network (meaning different computer systems such as Windows and Linux) is to install and configure Samba as a standalone file server to provide basic file-sharing services through *user level security* with the use of the system user's home directories. Standalone servers are configured to provide local authentication and access control to all the resources they maintain. All in all, every administrator knows that Samba remains a very popular open source distribution, and it is the purpose of this recipe to show you how to deliver an instant approach to file sharing that provides the seamless integration of any number of users on any type of modern computer across your entire working environment.

Getting ready

To complete this recipe, you will require a working installation of the CentOS 7 operating system with root privileges, a console-based text editor of your choice, and a connection to the Internet in order to facilitate the download of additional packages. It is expected that your server will use a static IP address.

How to do it...

Samba is not installed by default, and for this reason we will begin by downloading and installing the required packages.

1. To do this, log in as `root` and type the following command in order to install the required packages:

   ```
   yum install samba samba-client samba-common
   ```

2. Having done this, the first step is to rename the original configuration file:

   ```
   mv /etc/samba/smb.conf /etc/samba/smb.conf.BAK
   ```

3. Now, create a new configuration file in your preferred text editor by typing the following:

   ```
   vi /etc/samba/smb.conf
   ```

4. Begin building your new configuration by adding the following lines, replacing the values shown with values that better represent your own needs:

   ```
   [global]
   unix charset = UTF-8
   ```

```
dos charset = CP932
workgroup = <WORKGROUP_NAME>
server string = <MY_SERVERS_NAME>
netbios name = <MY_SERVERS_NAME>
dns proxy = no
wins support = no
interfaces = 127.0.0.0/8 XXX.XXX.XXX.XXX/24 <NETWORK_NAME>
bind interfaces only = no
log file = /var/log/samba/log.%m
max log size = 1000
syslog only = no
syslog = 0
panic action = /usr/share/samba/panic-action %d
```

WORKGROUP_NAME is the name of the Windows workgroup. Use the standard Windows name WORKGROUP if you don't have this value. MY_SERVERS_NAME refers to the name of your server. In most situations, this could be in the form of FILESERVER or SERVER1 and so on. XXX.XXX.XXX.XXX/XX refers to the primary network address that your Samba service is operating at, for example, 192.168.1.0/24. NETWORK_NAME refers to the name of your Ethernet interface. This could be enp0s8.

5. We will now configure Samba as a standalone server. To do this, simply continue to add the following lines to your main configuration file:

```
security = user
encrypt passwords = true
passdb backend = tdbsam
obey pam restrictions = yes
unix password sync = yes
passwd program = /usr/bin/passwd %u
passwd chat = *Enter\snew\s*\spassword:* %n\n *Retype\snew\s*\
spassword:* %n\n *password\supdated\ssuccessfully* .
pam password change = yes
map to guest = bad user
usershare allow guests = no
```

6. For the purpose of this recipe, we do not intend to configure Samba as a domain master or master browser. To do this, add the following lines:

```
domain master = no
local master = no
preferred master = no
os level = 8
```

7. We will now add support for home directory sharing by enabling valid users to access their home directories. This feature will support the appropriate read/write permissions and all folders will remain private from other users. To do this, add the following new lines:

```
[homes]
        comment = Home Directories
        browseable = no
        writable = yes
        valid users = %S
        create mask =0755
        directory mask =0755
```

8. Save and close the file. To test the syntax of the Samba configuration file we just created, use the following:

```
testparm
```

9. Now, add an existing system user, john, to the Samba user management system (this is for testing later; change it appropriately to a user name on your system):

```
smbpasswd -a john
```

10. Now, save the file and close it; back on the command line, open the ports in the firewall:

```
firewall-cmd --permanent --add-service=samba && firewall-cmd
--reload
```

11. Configure SELinux to use the Samba home directory:

```
setsebool -P samba_enable_home_dirs on
```

12. Now, ensure that the samba and nmb services will start up during the boot process and start them right away:

```
systemctl enable smb && systemctl enable nmb systemctl start smb
&& systemctl start nmb
```

How it works...

It was the purpose of this recipe to install Samba and configure its file sharing services, thus providing full connectivity across all modern computer systems in your network.

So, what did we learn from this experience?

Having installed the necessary packages, we renamed the originally installed configuration file to have a backup in place if anything broke later, and then we began setting up Samba from scratch, starting with an empty smb.conf configuration file. Having opened this new file, we began with the global configuration options; the first step was to declare compatibility with Unicode-based character sets. You will need to be aware that the values can vary as a result of your circumstances and network. Read more at man smb.conf.

Having done this, we then proceeded to confirm the name of our workgroup and server, disable WINS, establish a Samba log file, and register the network interface. Then, we elected the following standalone options by choosing a user-based security option, password encryption, and a `tdbsam` database backend. The preferred mode of security is user-level security, and using this approach implies that each share can be assigned to a specific user. Therefore, when a user requests a connection for a share, Samba authenticates this request by validating the given username and password with the authorized users in the configuration file and the Samba database. Next, we added the `master` information. In the case of a mixed operating system environment, a known conflict will result when a single client attempts to become the master browser. This situation may not disrupt the file-sharing service as a whole, but it will give rise to a potential issue being recorded by the Samba log files. So by configuring the samba server to not assert itself as the master browser, you will be able to reduce the chance of such issues being reported. So, having completed these steps, the recipe then considered the main task of enabling the `homes` directory file-sharing. Of course, you can experiment with the options shown, but this simple set of instructions not only ensures that valid users will be able to access their home directory with the relevant read/write permissions, but also, by setting the `browseable` flag to `no`, you will be able to hide the home directory from public view and achieve a greater degree of privacy for the user concerned. In our setup, Samba works with your Linux system users, but you should remember that any existing or new user is not added automatically to Samba and must be added manually using `smbpasswd -a`.

So, having saved your new configuration file, we tested its correctness using the `testparm` program and opened the Samba related incoming ports in firewalld using the `samba` service. The next step was to ensure that Samba and its related processes would be made available during the boot process using `systemctl`. Samba requires two primary processes in order to work correctly: `smbd` and `nmbd`. Beginning with `smbd`, it is the role of this service to provide file-sharing, printing services, user authentication, and resource locking to Windows-based clients using the SMB (or CIFS) protocol. At the same time, it is the role of the `nmbd` service to listen, understand, and reply to the NetBIOS name service's requests.

Samba often includes another service call named `winbindd`, but it has been largely ignored because the intention to provide a **Windows Internet Naming Service** (**WINS**)-based service or Active Directory authentication requires additional consideration, which is beyond the scope of this recipe.

Consequently, our final task was to start both the Samba service (`smb`) and the associated NetBIOS service (`nmb`).

You now know how incredibly simple Samba is to install, configure, and maintain. There is always more to learn, and yet this simple introduction has served to illustrate Samba's relative ease of use and the simplicity of its syntax. It has delivered a solution that has the ability to support a wide variety of different needs and a range of different computer systems, one that will fulfill your file-sharing requirements for many years to come.

There's more...

You can test our Samba server configuration from any client in your network that can ping the server. If it is a windows-based client, open the **Windows Explorer** address bar and use the following syntax: `\\<ip address of the Samba server>\<linux username>`. For example, we use `\\192.168.1.10\john` (on successfully connecting to it, you need to enter your Samba username's password). On any Linux client system, (the package, `samba-client`, needs to be installed on CentOS 7) to list all the available shares of an NFS server, use the following line:

```
smbclient -L <hostname or IP address of NFS server> -U <username>
```

In our example, we would use the following:

```
smbclient -L 192.168.1.10 -U john
```

To test, mount a share (this requires the `cifs-utils` package on CentOS 7) with the following syntax:

```
mount -t cifs  //<ip address of the Samba server>/<linux username> <local
mount point> -o  "username=<linux username>"
```

In our example, we would use the following:

```
mkdir /mnt/samba-share
```

```
mount -t cifs //192.168.1.10/john  /mnt/samba-share -o "username=john"
```

You can also put this import in the `/etc/fstab` file for permanent mounting using the following syntax:

```
//<server>/<share> <mount point> cifs <list of options>  0  0
```

for example:

For example, add the following line to the file:

```
//192.168.1.10/john /mnt/samba-share cifs username=john,password=xyz  0  0
```

If you don't want to use passwords in plaintext in this file, read the section about credentials using `man mount.cifs`, then create a credentials file and protect it with `chmod 600` in your home directory so that no other person can read it.

Here in this chapter, we showed you how to configure Samba as a standalone server and enable home directories, and how to connect to it from a client to get you started. But Samba can do so much more! It can provide printing services or act as a complete domain controller. If you want to learn more, feel free to visit `https://www.packtpub.com/` to learn more about other available material.

8

Working with FTP

In this chapter, we will cover the following topics:

- ▶ Installing and configuring the FTP service
- ▶ Working with virtual FTP users
- ▶ Customizing the FTP service
- ▶ Troubleshooting users and file transfers

Introduction

This chapter is a collection of recipes that provides the steps to unmask one of the most fundamental services in the Linux world and also provides the necessary starting point required to install, configure, and deliver the file transfer protocol without hesitation.

Installing and configuring the FTP service

While there are several modern and very secure network file sharing technologies, the good old **File Transfer Protocol** (**FTP**) remains one of the most widely used and popular protocols to share and transfer files between computers. There are a number of different FTP servers available in the Linux world. In this recipe, you will learn how to install and configure **very secure FTP daemon** (**vsftpd**), which is a well-known FTP server solution that supports a wide range of features and enables you to upload and distribute large files across a local network and the Internet. Here, we will show how to install the vsftpd daemon and provide some basic settings with the main goal being to increase the security of the daemon.

After working on this recipe, you are advised to use SSL/TLS encryption to further strengthen your FTP server (refer *Chapter 6, Providing Security*).

Getting ready

To complete this recipe, you will require a working installation of the CentOS 7 operating system with root privileges, a console-based text editor of your choice, and a connection to the Internet in order to facilitate the downloading of additional packages. It is expected that your server will be using a static IP address and that it maintains one or more system user accounts.

How to do it...

vsftpd is not installed by default. For this reason, we must begin this recipe by installing the relevant packages and associated dependencies:

1. To do this, log in as root and type the following command:

   ```
   yum install vsftpd
   ```

2. After we have created a backup copy of it, open the main configuration file in your favorite text editor as follows:

   ```
   cp /etc/vsftpd/vsftpd.conf /etc/vsftpd/vsftpd.conf.BAK
   vi /etc/vsftpd/vsftpd.conf
   ```

3. To disable anonymous users, scroll down and find the following line: anonymous_enable=YES, and then change this as follows:

   ```
   anonymous_enable=NO
   ```

4. Uncomment (remove # at beginning of the line) the following lines to enable the chroot environment for more security:

   ```
   chroot_local_user=YES
   chroot_list_enable=YES
   ```

5. Next, scroll down to the bottom of the file and add the following line:

   ```
   use_localtime=YES
   ```

6. Finally, add the following line to enable local users to write to their home directories:

   ```
   allow_writeable_chroot=YES
   ```

7. Save and close the file. Then create the following empty file:

   ```
   touch /etc/vsftpd/chroot_list
   ```

8. Next, configure the firewall to allow incoming FTP connections to the server on port 21:

```
firewall-cmd --permanent --add-service=ftp
firewall-cmd --reload
```

9. Now, we allow SELinux to use the FTP home directory feature:

```
setsebool -P ftp_home_dir on
```

10. Enable `vsftpd` at boot:

```
systemctl enable vsftpd
```

11. To complete this recipe, type the following command to start the FTP service:

```
systemctl start vsftpd
```

12. Now, we can test the connection from any client computer in the same network that our FTP server is in. This computer needs a FTP client installed (if its a CentOS computer, install one using `yum install ftp`). Log in to this computer with any account and by typing in the following command that replaces `<IPADDRESS>` with the IP address of the server running your `vsftpd` service:

```
ftp <IPADDRESS>
```

13. On successful connection to the server, the FTP client program will ask you for a username and password. Here, enter a known system user (other than root) from the FTP server. If the login was successful, you will get a `230 login successful` message and a `ftp>` prompt. Now to end our test, type the following FTP command to show all the files in your current `ftp` directory and check whether you have write-access on the remote server:

```
ls
mkdir test-dir
rmdir test-dir
```

14. Type the following command to end your FTP session:

```
exit
```

How it works...

vsftpd is widely recognized as a fast, lightweight, and reliable FTP server. The purpose of this recipe was to show you how to build a basic FTP service that is optimized to provide excellent performance for any number of valid system users.

So what did we learn from this experience?

We began the recipe by installing the necessary YUM package called `vsftpd`. We then opened the main configuration file located at `/etc/vsftpd/vsftpd.conf`, after we made a backup copy of it. Next, we disabled anonymous FTP access and thereby secured our FTP service against unknown users. We then restricted users to their home directory by enabling a `chroot` jail.

> The `chroot` jail represents an essential security feature; once this is done, all the users will be restricted to access the files in their own home directory only.

We then required `vsftpd` to use local time for our server. Afterwards, we fixed the write permissions for our chrooted FTP users by enabling the `allow_writeable_chroot` option. Having saved our work, we created a new empty `/etc/vsftpd/chroot_list` file, which will hold all the user names that can leave their chroot jails. We have to create this file; otherwise, `vsftpd` will not let us log in to the system. However, you should remember that you must leave it empty all the time because chroot jails are an important protection mechanism for your FTP server.

Next, we added the standard FTP protocol's port 21 to our firewall configuration to allow incoming connections. Then, we reloaded the firewall to apply these changes. After this, we activated our FTP home directories by setting the appropriate SELinux boolean variable `ftp_home_dir` to `true`. This will make the directories valid for SELinux. Please read *Chapter 14, Working with SELinux* to learn more about SELinux. Next, we enabled `vsftpd` on boot and started the service within `systemd`. At this point, `vsftpd` will now be operational and it can be tested with any regular FTP-based desktop software. Users can log in using a valid system username and password by connecting to the server's name, domain, or IP address (depending on the server's configuration).

The purpose of this recipe was to show you that `vsftpd` is not a difficult package to install and configure. There is always more to do but, by following this simple introduction, we have quickly enabled our server to run a standard FTP service.

There's more...

Having installed and configured a basic FTP service, you may wonder how to direct users to a specific folder within their home directory. To do this, open the main configuration file in an editor of your choice using `/etc/vsftpd/vsftpd.conf`.

Scroll down to the bottom of the file and add the following line by replacing the `<users_local_folder_name>` value with something more applicable to your own needs:

```
local_root=<users_local_folder_name>
```

For example, if this FTP server is mainly for accessing and uploading content for an user's private web pages hosted on the same server, you may configure Apache to use the user's home directories in a folder called /home/<username>/public_html. For this reason, you may add the following reference at the bottom of your vsftpd configuration file:

```
local_root=public_html
```

When finished, save and close the configuration file before restarting the vsftpd service. When testing this new feature make sure that the local_root location exists in the home directory of the user you want to login (for example, ~/public_html).

Working with virtual FTP users

In this recipe, you will learn how to implement virtual users in order to break away from the restriction of using local system user accounts. During the lifetime of your server, there may be occasions when you wish to enable FTP authentication for a user that does not have a local system account. You may also want to consider implementing a solution that allows a particular individual to maintain more than one account in order to allow access to different locations on your server. This type of configuration implies a certain degree of flexibility afforded by the use of virtual users. Since you are not using a local system account, it can be argued that this approach gives improved security.

Getting ready

To complete this recipe, you will require a working installation of the CentOS 7 operating system with root privileges and a console-based text editor of your choice. It is expected that your server will be using a static IP address and that vsftpd is already installed with a chroot jail and is currently running. This recipe needs the policycoreutils-python package installed.

How to do it...

1. The first step is to login as root on our vsftpd server and create a plain text file called virtual-users.txt that maintains a list of usernames and passwords of the virtual users. To do this, type the following command:

    ```
    vi /tmp/virtual-users.txt
    ```

2. Now add your usernames and corresponding passwords in the following way:

    ```
    virtual-username1
    password1
    virtual-username2
    password2
    virtual-username3
    password3
    ```

Repeat this process as required for every user you need but, for obvious reasons, maintain a good password policy and do not use the same virtual-username more than once.

3. When you have finished, simply save and close the file in the usual way. Then, proceed to build the database file by typing the following command:

```
db_load -T -t hash -f /tmp/virtual-users.txt /etc/vsftpd/virtual-
users.db
```

4. Having done this, we will now create the PAM file that will use this database to validate the virtual users. To do this, type the following command:

```
vi /etc/pam.d/vsftpd-virtual
```

5. Now add the following lines:

```
auth required pam_userdb.so db=/etc/vsftpd/virtual-users

account required pam_userdb.so db=/etc/vsftpd/virtual-users
```

6. When you have finished, save and close the file in the usual way. Open the main vsftpd configuration file in your favorite text editor as follows:

```
vi /etc/vsftpd/vsftpd.conf
```

7. Now, in the opened file, search for the line pam_service_name=vsftpd and disable it by adding a # sign at the beginning of the line so that it reads as follows:

```
#pam_service_name=vsftpd
```

8. Scroll down to the bottom of the file and add the following lines by customizing the value for local_root to suit your own specific needs—this will be the base directory in which all your virtual users will *live* in (for example, we will use /srv/virtualusers/$USER as shown here):

```
virtual_use_local_privs=YES

guest_enable=YES

pam_service_name=vsftpd-virtual

user_sub_token=$USER

local_root=/srv/virtualusers/$USER

hide_ids=YES
```

9. Now create a subfolder for each virtual user you defined in a previous step in your /tmp/virtual-users.txt file within the directory that you stated with the local_root directive. Remember to delegate the ownership of this folder to the FTP user. To keep up with our /srv/virtualusers example, we will use the following commands to do this in an automatic way (again, customize the /srv/virtualusers directory if needed):

```
for u in `sed -n 1~2p /tmp/virtual-users.txt`;
do
mkdir -p /srv/virtualusers/$u
chown ftp: /srv/virtualusers/$u
done
```

10. Now we need to inform SELinux to allow read/write access to our custom `local_root` directory outside of the typical `/home` directory:

```
setsebool -P allow_ftpd_full_access on
semanage fcontext -a -t public_content_rw_t "/srv/virtualusers(/.*)?"
restorecon -R -v /srv/virtualusers
```

11. Next, restart the FTP service as follows:

```
systemctl restart vsftpd
```

12. For security reasons, remove the plain text file now and protect the generated database file with this:

```
rm /tmp/virtual-users.txt
chmod 600 /etc/vsftpd/virtual-users.db
```

How it works...

Having followed the previous recipe, you will be now able to invite an unlimited number of virtual users to access your FTP service. The configuration of this feature was very simple; your overall security has been improved and all access is restricted to a defined `local_root` directory of your choice. Please note that this usage of virtual users will disable your system users' login to the FTP server from the first recipe.

So what did we learn from this experience?

We began this recipe by creating a new temporary text file that will contain all our usernames with the corresponding passwords in plain text. We then added all the required usernames and passwords one after another sequentially separated by newlines. Having done this for each of our virtual users, we then saved and closed the file before proceeding to run the `db_load` command that is installed on CentOS 7 by default. This can be used to generate a BerkeleyDB database out of our text file, which will be used for the FTP user authentication later in this process. Having completed this step, our next task was to create a Pluggable Authentication Modules (PAM) file at `/etc/pam.d/vsftpd-virtual`. This reads the previous database file to provide authentication from it for our `vsftpd` service using a typical PAM configuration file syntax (for more, see `man pam.d`). Then, we opened, modified, and added new configuration directives to the main `vsftpd` configuration file at `/etc/vsftpd/vsftpd.conf` in order to make `vsftpd` aware of our virtual users' authentication via PAM.

The most important setting was the `local_root` directive that defines the base location where all your user directories will be placed for your virtual users. Don't forget to put the `$USER` string at the end of your path. You were then prompted to create the relevant virtual hosting folder for every virtual user you have defined in the text file before.

Since virtual users are not real system users, we had to assign the FTP system user to take full ownership of the files for our new FTP users. We used a bash `for` loop to automate the process for all our users defined in the temporary `/tmp/virtual-users.txt` file. Next, we set the proper SELinux boolean to allow virtual users access to the system and also the right context on our `/srv/virtualusers` directory. Applying all these changes was simply a matter of restarting the `vsftpd` service using the `systemctl` command.

Afterwards, we removed the temporary user text file because it contains our passwords in plain text. We protected the access to the BerkleyDB database file by removing all access other than root. If you update, add, or remove FTP users on a regular basis, it's better to not delete this temporary plain text `/tmp/virtual-users.txt` file but rather put it in a safe place such as the `/root` directory. Then, you should also protect this using `chmod 600`. Then, you can rerun the `db_load` command whenever you make a change to this file to keep your users up-to-date. If you need to add new users at a later point, you have to create new virtual user folders for them as well (Please rerun the commands from step 9). Run the `restorecon -R -v /srv/virtualusers` command afterwards.

You can now test your new virtual user accounts by logging in to the FTP server using your newly created accounts from this recipe.

Customizing the FTP service

In this recipe, you will learn how to customize your `vsftpd` installation. `vsftpd` has a lot of configuration parameters, and here we will show how to create a custom welcome banner, change the server's default-time out, limit user connections, and ban users from the service.

Getting ready

To complete this recipe, you will require a working installation of the CentOS 7 operating system with root privileges and a console-based text editor of your choice. It is expected that your server will be using a static IP address and that `vsftpd` is already installed with a chroot jail and is currently running.

How to do it...

1. To begin with, log in as root and open the main `vsftpd` configuration file:

```
vi /etc/vsftpd/vsftpd.conf
```

2. First provide an alternative welcome message, uncomment the following line, and alter the message as required. For example, you could use this:

```
ftpd_banner=Welcome to my new FTP server
```

3. To change the default FTP time-outs, uncomment these lines and substitute the numeric values as required:

```
idle_session_timeout=600
```

```
data_connection_timeout=120
```

4. Now, we will limit the connections: the data transfer rate in bytes per second, the number of clients, and the maximum parallel connections per IP address. Add the following lines to the end of the file:

```
local_max_rate=1000000
```

```
max_clients=50
```

```
max_per_ip=2
```

5. Next, save and close the file. To ban a specific user, you can use the following commands while replacing the username with an appropriate system user value that fits your needs:

```
echo "username" >> /etc/vsftpd/user_list
```

6. Now to apply the changes, restart the FTP service:

```
systemctl restart vsftpd
```

How it works...

In this recipe, we have shown some of the most important vsftpd settings. Covering all the configuration parameters here is outside the scope of this recipe. To learn more about it, read through the entire main vsftpd configuration file at /etc/vsftpd/vsftpd.conf, as it contains a lot of useful comments; alternatively, you can read the man vsftpd.conf manual.

So what did we learn from this experience?

We began by opening the main vsftpd configuration file and then activated and customized the welcome banner using the ftpd_banner directive. On the next successful login, your users should see your new message. Next, when dealing with a large number of users, you may want to consider changing the values for a default timeout and limit the connections in order to improve the efficiency of your FTP service.

First, we changed our server's timeout numbers. An `idle_session_timeout` of `600` seconds will logout the user if he is inactive (not executing FTP commands) for 10 minutes, while a `data_connection_timeout` of `120` seconds will kill the connections when a client data transfer is stalled (not progressing) for 20 minutes. Then we changed the connection limits. A `local_max_rate` of `1000000` bytes per second will limit the data transfer rate of a single user to roughly one megabyte per second. A `max_clients` value of `50` will tell the FTP server to only allow 50 parallel users to the system, while a `max_per_ip` of `2` allows only two connections per IP address.

Then we saved and closed the file. Finally, we showed how to ban users from using our FTP service. If you wanted to ban a specific user from using the FTP service as a whole, the user's name should be added to the `/etc/vsftpd/user_list` file. If you ever need to re-enable the user at any time, simply reverse the previous process by removing the user concerned from `/etc/vsftpd/user_list`.

Troubleshooting users and file transfers

Analyzing log files is the most important technique for troubleshooting all kinds of problems or improving services on Linux. In this recipe, you will learn how to configure and enable vsftpd's extensive logging features in order to help system administrators when problems arise, or simply to monitor usage with this service.

Getting ready

To complete this recipe, you will require a working installation of the CentOS 7 operating system with root privileges and a console-based text editor of your choice. It is expected that your server will be using a static IP address and that `vsftpd` is already installed with a chroot jail and is currently running.

How to do it...

1. To do this, log in as root and type the following command to open the main configuration file in your favorite text editor:

    ```
    vi /etc/vsftpd/vsftpd.conf
    ```

2. Now, add the following lines to the end of the configuration file to enable verbose logging features:

    ```
    dual_log_enable=YES

    log_ftp_protocol=YES
    ```

3. Finally, restart the `vsftpd` daemon to apply the changes:

    ```
    systemctl restart vsftpd
    ```

How it works...

In this recipe, we have shown how to enable two separate logging mechanism: first, the `xferlog` log file that will log detailed information about user uploads and downloads, then the `vsftpd` log file that contains every FTP protocol transaction between the client and the server outputting the most detailed logging information possible for `vsftpd`.

So what did we learn from this experience?

In this recipe, we opened the main `vsftpd` configuration file and added two directives to the end of the file. First, `dual_log_enable` will make sure both the `xferlog` and `vsftpd` log files will be used for logging. Afterwards, we increased the verbosity of the `vsftpd` log file by enabling `log_ftp_protocol`.

After restarting the service, the two log files, `/var/log/xferlog` and `/var/log/vsftdp.log`, will be created and filled with useful FTP activity information. Now, before we open the files, let's create some FTP user activity. Log in with any FTP user on the server using the `ftp` command-line tool and issue the following FTP command at the `ftp>` prompt to upload a random file from the client to the server:

put ~/.bash_profile bash_profile_test

Now, back on the server, inspect the `/var/log/xferlog` file to see detailed information about the uploaded file and open `/var/log/vsftpd.log` for all other user activities (such as login time or other FTP commands that users issued).

Please note that both the log files only keep track of user and FTP activity and are not meant to debug problems with the `vsftpd` service such as configuration file errors. Use the `systemctl status vsftpd -l` or `journalctl -xn`, to debug general problems with the service.

9
Working with Domains

In this chapter, we will cover:

- ▶ Installing and configuring a caching-only nameserver
- ▶ Setting up an authoritative-only nameserver
- ▶ Creating an integrated nameserver solution
- ▶ Populating the domain
- ▶ Building a secondary (slave) DNS server

Introduction

This chapter is a collection of recipes that attempt to demystify a technology that remains the key component in making everything work in the networking world. From e-mail to web pages and remote logins to online chats, this chapter provides the necessary details on how quickly you can use CentOS to deliver a domain name service that will power your working environment.

Installing and configuring a caching-only nameserver

Every network communication between computers can only be made through the use of unique IP addresses to identify the exact endpoints of the communication. For the human brain, numbers are always harder to remember and work with than assigning names to *things*. Therefore, IT pioneers started in the early 70s to invent systems for translating names to physical network addresses using files and later simple databases. In modern computer networks and on the Internet, the relationship between the name of a computer and an IP address is defined in the **Domain Name System** (**DNS**) database. It is a worldwide distributed system and provides domain name to IP address resolution and also the reverse, that is IP address to domain name resolution. DNS is a big subject, and it is the purpose of this recipe to provide the perfect starting point by showing you how to install and setup your own caching-only and forwarding nameserver. Here we will use *Unbound*, which is a highly secure and fast recursive and caching DNS server solution, and therefore our preferred choice. But you need to remember that Unbound cannot be used as a fully authoritative DNS server (which means that it provides its own domain name resolution records) we will use the popular BIND server for this in a later recipe. A caching-only DNS server will serve to forward all the name resolution queries to a remote DNS server. Such a system has the intention of speeding up general access to the Internet by caching the results of any domain resolution request made. When a caching DNS server tracks down the answer to a client's query, it returns the answer to the client. However, it also stores the answer in its cache for a specific period of time. The cache can then be used as a source for subsequent requests in order to speed up the total round-trip time.

Getting ready

To complete this recipe, you will require a working installation of the CentOS 7 operating system with root privileges, a static IP address, and a console-based text editor of your choice. An Internet connection will be required to download additional packages. In this example, our DNS server runs in a private network with the network address `192.168.1.0/24`.

How to do it...

In this recipe, we will first configure a *caching-only* and then a *forwarding only* DNS server.

Configuring a caching-only Unbound DNS server

In this section, we will consider the role of Unbound as a caching-only nameserver, handling recursive DNS requests to the other remote DNS servers and caching the query for a certain time period to improve the response time when the server is asked for the same name resolution again:

1. To begin, log in as root and install the required packages by typing:

   ```
   yum install unbound bind-utils
   ```

2. Now make a copy of the unbound configuration file so we can revert our changes later, and then open it in your favorite text editor:

   ```
   cp /etc/unbound/unbound.conf /etc/unbound/unbound.conf.BAK
   vi /etc/unbound/unbound.conf
   ```

3. Scroll down to find the following line: # interface: 0.0.0.0 Remove the # sign to uncomment it (activate it), so it reads as follows:

   ```
   interface: 0.0.0.0
   ```

4. Next, scroll down to find the line # access-control: 127.0.0.0/8 allow. Uncomment the line to activate it and change the network address to fit your needs:

   ```
   access-control: 192.168.1.0/24 allow
   ```

5. Save and close the file, and then create an RSA keypair with certificates for secure DNSSEC support before you check the correctness of the changed configuration file:

   ```
   unbound-control-setup && unbound-checkconf
   ```

6. Next, open the DNS service in your firewalld configuration on your server because we want to be able to use our new DNS service from other clients in the network for querying as well:

   ```
   firewall-cmd --permanent --add-service dns && firewall-cmd --reload
   ```

7. Now ensure the service will be available at boot and start it afterwards:

   ```
   systemctl enable unbound && systemctl start unbound
   ```

8. To test if we can reach our Unbound DNS server and make queries, execute the following command from the same server running our Unbound DNS service locally, which should give back the IP address of www.packtpub.com:

   ```
   nslookup www.packtpub.com 127.0.0.1
   ```

9. For a more detailed view of the request you can also run locally on the DNS server:

   ```
   unbound-host -d www.packtpub.com
   ```

10. From any other client in the network (needs `bind-utils` installed), you can query any public domain name using our new DNS server as well. For example, if our DNS server has the IP `192.168.1.7`:

    `nslookup www.packtpub.com 192.168.1.7`

11. Finally, let us use our new nameserver on the server itself. To do this, open the following file with your favorite text editor after you have made a backup copy:

    `cp /etc/resolv.conf /etc/resolv.conf.BAK; vi /etc/resolv.conf`

12. Remove all the current nameserver references and replace them with the following:

    `nameserver 127.0.0.1`

> If you have set some DNS server information in your network-scripts interface (for example, when configuring a static IP address, see *Chapter 2, Configuring the System*), you will want to review the `/etc/sysconfig/network-scripts/ifcfg-XXX` file and modify the current DNS reference to read as `DNS1=127.0.0.1` as well.

Configuring a forwarding only DNS server

Now after we have successfully configured our first caching BIND DNS server, here we will show you how to transform it into a forwarding DNS server which will reduce the total bandwidth for resolving hostnames in comparison to the caching-only solution:

1. Open BIND's main configuration file again:

   `vi /etc/unbound/unbound.conf`

2. Add the following lines to the end of the file:

   ```
   forward-zone:
         name: "."
         forward-addr: 8.8.8.8
   ```

3. Next, check the correctness of your new configuration file and restart the service:

   `unbound-checkconf && systemctl restart unbound`

4. Finally, test your new forwarding DNS server using the tests from the preceding caching DNS server section.

How it works...

In this recipe, we have installed a caching-only Unbound DNS server with the basic aim of improving the responsiveness of our overall network by caching the answers to any name-based queries. Using such a process will shorten the waiting time on any subsequent visit to the same location. It is a feature that is particularly useful in saving bandwidth if you happen to be managing a large, busy, or slow network. It does not have its own domain name resolution feature but uses its default root domain's DNS servers in order to perform this task (to learn more about the root domain, see later). Also, as we have seen, you can easily transform your caching nameserver into a pure forwarding system as well. While a caching DNS server makes recursive requests to *several* associated DNS servers and constructs the complete name resolution result from those multiple requests, a forwarding DNS *delegates* the complete recursive DNS search to another resolving DNS server which executes the complete search instead. This saves even more bandwidth for our DNS server because only *single* network requests to communicate with the remote resolving server are made instead of *multiple* when using the caching-only DNS service.

So what did we learn from this experience?

We started this recipe by installing the necessary packages. This included the main DNS server program called Unbound and a reference to `bind-utils`, a small package that enables you to run many different DNS related network tasks, such as `dig`, `nslookup`, and `host`. The next step was to begin making the necessary configuration changes by editing Unbound's main configuration after we made a simple backup of the original file. Since after installation the default DNS server is completely restricted to doing everything *locally* only, our main purpose was to adjust the server to make connections from the outside possible. We began this process by allowing the DNS server to listen to all the available network interfaces using the `interface` directive and afterwards defined who on the network was allowed to make requests to our DNS server by setting `allow-query` to our local network. This means we allowed anyone in our subnetwork to make DNS resolution requests to our server.

At this point we created the RSA keypair with the `unbound-control-setup` tool, which is needed for the `unbound-checkconf` command to work. The generated keys and certificate are important if we want to use **Unbound's DNS Security Extensions** (**DNSSEC**) features which help protect DNS data by providing authentication of origin using digital signatures (configuring DNSSEC is outside the scope of this chapter. To learn more, consult the Unbound configuration manual: `man unbound.conf`). Afterwards, we used the `unbound-checkconf` command, which was necessary to confirm that Unbound's configuration file was syntactically correct. If the output of the command is empty, there are no errors in the file. We then proceeded by adding the predefined `dns` firewalld service to our default firewall, thus allowing the other computer systems in our local network to access the DNS server using port `53`. Finally, we activated Unbound at boot time and started the service.

Of course, to complete this recipe we then tested if our new DNS server worked as expected in resolving domain names to IP addresses. We ran a simple `nslookup` query locally on the server and also from the other computers in the same network to see if our new DNS service was reachable from the outside. When using `nslookup` without any additional parameters, the program will use the default DNS server resolver known to the system (on CentOS 7 this is defined in `/etc/resolv.conf`) to resolve our host names, so we added another parameter addressing our alternative DNS server we want to query instead (`127.0.0.1`). For successful testing, the output must contain the resolved IP address of the `www.packtpub.com` server. On the DNS server you could also use the `unbound-host -d` command to get a more technical view of the DNS query within the Unbound service.

After we successfully finished these tests, we updated the current nameserver resolver information on our DNS server with our new DNS service running on localhost.

There's more...

Now we want to see how BIND will perform for caching DNS information. To do this, on your DNS server simply select a target website you have not visited before and use the `dig` command. For example:

```
dig www.wikipedia.org
```

Having run this test, you may see a query time that results in something like the following:

```
;; Query time: 223 msec
```

Now repeat this exercise by retesting the same URL. Depending on your networking environment, this may produce the following result:

```
;; Query time: 0 msec
```

Now do it again for another website. On every repeat of the preceding command, you should not only see a reduced query time but also experience a faster response time in delivering the output. This same result will be evident in the browser refresh rate, and as a result we can say that this simple exercise has not only introduced you to Unbound but it will ultimately serve to improve the speed of your local network when surfing the World Wide Web.

Setting up an authoritative-only DNS server

In this recipe, we will learn how to create an *authoritative-only* DNS server, which can give answers to queries about domains under their control themselves instead of redirecting the query to other DNS servers (such as our caching-only DNS server from the previous recipe). We will create a DNS server to resolve all our own hostnames and services in our own private local network.

As said before, while Unbound should be your first choice when needing a caching-only DNS server as it is the most secure DNS server solution available, it has only limited authoritative capabilities which often is not enough for professional DNS server usage. Here, instead of name lookup of our local servers, we will use the popular authoritative BIND DNS server package and configure a new DNS zone to provide highly customizable name resolution. Technically speaking, we will be writing both a *forward* and *reverse zone* file for our domain. Zone files are text files that contain the actual domain name to IP address mappings or the other way around, that is, IP address mappings to domain name mappings. While most queries to any DNS server will be the translation of names to IP addresses, the reverse part is also important to set up if you need the correct domain name for any given IP address. We will configure BIND to be authoritative-only, which means that the server will only answer queries it is authoritative for (has the matching records in its zones), so if the DNS server cannot resolve a requested domain, it will stop the request and not contact other DNS servers using recursive requests to fetch and construct the correct answer.

Getting ready

To complete this recipe, you will require a working installation of the CentOS 7 operating system with root privileges, a static IP address, and a console-based text editor of your choice. An Internet connection will be required to download additional packages. In this example, our DNS server runs in the private network with the network address `192.168.1.0/24`. Our DNS server should manage a local private domain we decide to be `centos7.home` (in the form `domain.toplevel-domain`). The IP address of the new DNS server will be `192.168.1.7` and should get the hostname `ns1`, leading to the Fully Qualified Domain Name (FQDN) `ns1.centos7.home`. (Refer to the *Setting your hostname and resolving the network* recipe in *Chapter 2, Configuring the System* to learn more about FQDNs). Our configured zone will have an administrative e-mail address with the name `admin@centos7.home`, and for simplicity, all the other computers in this network will get hostnames such as `client1`, `client2`, `client3`, and so on. We will also have some mail, web, and FTP servers in our own network, each running on separate dedicated servers. We will be using the port `8053` for our BIND service as we already have Unbound running on the same server using the default DNS port `53`.

How to do it...

For security reasons, we will allow BIND to resolve internal LAN names only (authoritative-only) and only allow localhost to make DNS queries; no other clients in our network can connect to it:

1. To begin with, log in as root on your Unbound DNS server and install the required BIND package and enable the DNS server on boot:

```
yum install bind && systemctl enable named
```

2. The actual name of the DNS server in the BIND package is called `named`, so let's open its main configuration file to make some adjustments after creating a backup copy of it first:

   `cp /etc/named.conf /etc/named.conf.BAK; vi /etc/named.conf`

3. First find the line `listen-on port 53 { 127.0.0.1; };` and then change the port number to the custom `port 8053`, so it reads as follows:

   ```
   listen-on port 8053 { 127.0.0.1; };
   ```

4. Next, find the line `listen-on-v6 port 53 { ::1; }` and change it to:

   ```
   listen-on-v6 port 8053 { none; };
   ```

5. Next, since we are configuring an authoritative-only server, we will disable contacting other remote DNS servers, find the line that reads `recursion yes;` and change it to:

   ```
   recursion no;
   ```

6. Save and close the file, and then validate the syntax of our config changes (no output means no errors!):

   `named-checkconf`

7. Now tell SELinux about the changed named DNS port (this needs package `policycoreutils-python`):

   `semanage port -a -t dns_port_t -p tcp 8053`

8. Now type the following command in order to create your forward zone file. Name the file after the domain whose resource records it will contain:

   `vi /var/named/<domain>.<top-level domain>.db`

9. In our example, for our `centos7.home domain`, this will be:

   `vi /var/named/centos7.home.db`

10. Now simply add the following lines (be careful not to forget typing the tailing dots in the domain names). We will start with the **Start of Authority** (**SOA**) block:

    ```
    $TTL 3h
    @ IN SOA ns1.centos7.home. admin.centos7.home. (
     2015082400        ; Serial yyyymmddnn
     3h                ; Refresh After 3 hours
     1h                ; Retry Retry after 1 hour
     1w                ; Expire after 1 week
     1h)               ; Minimum negative caching
    ```

11. Afterwards, add the rest of the file's content:

```
; add your name servers here for your domain
        IN     NS      ns1.centos7.home.
; add your mail server here for the domain
        IN     MX      10    mailhost.centos7.home.
; now follows the actual domain name to IP
; address mappings:

; first add all referenced hostnames from above
ns1        IN     A       192.168.1.7
mailhost   IN     A       192.168.1.8
; add all accessible domain to ip mappings here
router     IN     A       192.168.1.0
www        IN     A       192.168.1.9
ftp        IN     A       192.168.1.10
; add all the private clients on the Lan here
client1    IN     A       192.168.1.11
client2    IN     A       192.168.1.12
client3    IN     A       192.168.1.13
; finally we can define some aliases for
; existing domain name mappings
webserver  IN     CNAME   www
johnny     IN     CNAME   client2
```

12. When you have finished, simply save and close the file before proceeding to create the reverse zone file for our private subnetwork used by our domain (the C-Class are the first three numbers (octets) which are separated by dots: XXX.XXX.XXX. For example, for the 192.168.1.0/24 subnet the C-Class is 192.168.1:

vi /var/named/db.<C-Class of our search IP in reverse order>

13. In our example, a reverse zone file resolving our centos7.home's 192.168.1 C-Class subnet will be:

vi /var/named/db.1.168.192

14. First put in the exact same SOA as in step 10, and then append the following content to the end of the file:

```
;add your name servers for your domain
          IN     NS      ns1.centos7.home.
; here add the actual IP octet to
; subdomain mappings:
7       IN     PTR     ns1.centos7.home.
8       IN     PTR     mailhost.centos7.home.
9       IN     PTR     www.centos7.home.
```

```
10      IN      PTR     ftp.centos7.home.
11      IN      PTR     client1.centos7.home.
12      IN      PTR     client2.centos7.home.
13      IN      PTR     client3.centos7.home.
```

15. Save and close the file, and then add our new zone pair to the named configuration. To do this, open `named.conf` again:

    vi /etc/named.conf

16. Now locate the line including "`/etc/named.rfc1912.zones`";. Immediately following this line, create a space for your work and add the appropriate zone statement to enable your *reverse* zone, as follows (substitute `XXX.XXX.XXX` with the reversed C-Class of your reverse zone file name, in our example `1.168.192`):

```
zone "XXX.XXX.XXX.in-addr.arpa." IN {
  type master;
  file "/var/named/db.XXX.XXX.XXX";
  update-policy local;
};
```

17. Having done this, you can now proceed to add a zone statement for your forward zone right afterwards, as follows (replacing `<domain>.<top-level domain>.db` with your forward zone file name, in our example `centos7.home`):

```
zone "<domain>.<top-level domain>." IN {
  type master;
  file "/var/named/<domain>.<top-level domain>.db";
  update-policy local;
};
```

18. When you have finished, simply save and close the file, and then restart the `bind` service using:

```
named-checkconf && systemctl restart named
```

How it works...

All DNS servers are configured to perform caching functions, but where a caching-only server is restricted in its ability to answer queries from remote DNS servers only, an authoritative nameserver is a DNS server that maintains the master zone for a particular record.

So what have we learned from this experience?

The purpose of this recipe was to setup an authoritative-only BIND DNS server and provide a new zone for it. A DNS zone defines all the available resources (hostnames and services) under a single domain. Any DNS zone should always consist of both a forward and reverse zone file. To understand zone configurations, we need to discuss DNS hierarchy first. For example, take a DNS domain from the example in this recipe `client1.centos7.home`. Every computer in our private network has a hostname (for example, `client1` or `www`) and is a member of a domain. A domain consists of the **Second-level Domain** (**SLD**) (for example, `centos7`) and a **Top-level Domain** name (**TLD**) (for example, `home`, `org`, `com`, and so on). On top of that TLD is the root domain (written `.` dot) which often is neglected when working with other programs or configurations. However, when working or defining FQDN in zone configurations, it is very important to never forget to add this dot `.` after the TLD. For example, a DNS domain for our `client1` computer would be `client1.centos7.home.`, whereas an FQDN for the `/etc/hosts` file is often written in the format `client1.centos7.home` (technically this is incorrect but most of the time sufficient). The root domain is very important because it contains the root DNS servers which will be queried first if an authoritative DNS server cannot find an existing entry for a requested domain in its own records (zones) or cache. But we have DNS servers in all the other domain hierarchies as well and this is how a DNS server makes its recursive requests. A root DNS server, as any other DNS server, resolves all its subdomains (defined in its zone files) which are the TLDs. These TLDs themselves can resolve all the SLDs (also defined in their zone files). The second-level domains resolve all their hostnames (which are special subdomains as they refer to individual computer or services on your network). So any DNS request traverses through the different DNS server hierarchies from the root DNS over the TLD DNS to the SLD DNS server. The root and the TLD DNS servers cannot fully resolve full domain DNS queries such as `www.centos7.home` and instead will resolve the correct address of the next DNS hierarchy. This system ensures that the root DNS will always find the correct TLD DNS server address and the TLD DNS server will always send the request to the right SLD DNS which has the correct zone file and is finally able to answer the requested DNS query.

So what did we learn from this experience?

As we have learned, a zone file is a simple text file that consists of directives and resource records and can look quite complicated as it contains a lot of two-letter abbreviations. Remember, you need to set up a zone file pair (forward and reverse) on a base domain level (for example, `centos7.home`) for all the hostnames and services running under it (for example, `www`, `host1`, `api`, and so on). After installing the `named` DNS server (which is part of the **Berkeley Internet Name Domain** (**BIND**) package), we made a copy of the original main configuration file and changed the default listening port from 53 to 8053 (as unbound is already listening on port 53) but kept it listening to localhost only, and disabled IPv6 to keep compatibility with the other major DNS servers (as IPv6 support is still limited on the Internet). Also, here we disabled recursion because our BIND DNS server had to be authoritative-only, which means that it is not allowed to forward DNS requests to other remote DNS servers when it could not resolve the query from its own zone records.

Then we began creating and customizing our own forward DNS zone file with the filename convention `/var/named/<domain>.<top-level domain>.db`. This file is opened with the `$TTL` control statement, which stands for **Time to Live** and which provides other nameservers with a time value that determines how long they can cache the records from this zone. This directive, as many others, is defined using seconds as the default time unit, but you can also use other units using BIND specific short forms to indicate minutes (`m`), hours (`h`), days (`d`), and weeks (`w`), as we did in our example (`3h`). Following this, we then provided a **Start of Authority** (**SOA**) record. This record contains specific information about the zone as a whole. This begins with the zone name (`@`), a specification of the zone class (`IN`), the FQDN of this nameserver in the format `hostname.domain.TLD.`, and an e-mail address of the zone administrator. This latter value is typically in the form `hostmaster.hostname.domain.TLD.` and it is formed by replacing the typical `@` symbol with a dot (`.`). Having done this, it was then a matter of opening the brackets to assign the zone's serial number, refresh value, retry value, expire value, and negative caching `time-to-live` value. These directives can be summarized as follows:

- The `serial-number` value is a numeric value, typically taking the form of the date in reverse (`YYYYMMDD`) with an additional value (`VV`), which is incremented every time the zone file is modified or updated, in order to indicate that it is time for the named service to reload the zone. The value `VV` typically starts at `00`, and the next time you modify this file, simply increment it to `01`, `02`, `03`, and so on.

- The `time-to-refresh` value determines how frequently the secondary or slave nameservers will ask the primary nameserver if any changes have been made to the zone.

- The `time-to-retry` value determines how frequently the secondary or slave nameservers should check the primary server after the serial number has failed. If a failure has occurred during the time frame specified by the `time-to-expire` value elapses, the secondary nameservers will stop responding as an authority for requests.

- The `minimum-TTL` value determines how long the other nameservers can cache negative responses.

Having completed this section and having closed the corresponding bracket, we then proceeded to add the authoritative nameserver information (`NS`) with the `IN NS <FQDN of the nameserver>` definition. Typically speaking, you will have at least two, if not three, nameservers (put each nameserver's FQDN in a new `IN NS` line). However, it is possible to set only one nameserver, which is particularly useful if you are running the server in an office or a home environment and would like to enjoy the benefit of local name resolution, such as `.home`, `.lan`, or `.dev`. The next stage then required us to include a reference for the **Mail eXchanger** (**MX**) records in order for us to specify a mail server for the zone. The format is `IN MX <priority> <FQDN of your mailserver>`. The priority becomes important if you define more than one mail server (each in its separate `IN MX` line)—the lower the number, the higher the priority. In this respect, a secondary mail server should have a higher value.

> In the SOA, NS and MX lines we already referenced hostnames which aren't defined as an IP mapping yet (A record). We could do this because the zone file is not processed sequentially. But do not forget to create corresponding A lines for each hostname later.

Depending on your needs, you may also intend to use your name server as your mail server (then you would write instead MX 10 ns1.centos7.home.), although you may have another server dedicated to that role as shown in the example.

Following this, it was then a matter of creating the appropriate A records (A for address) and assigning the appropriate IP address to the values shown. This is the heart of any domain name resolution requests to the server. An A record is used for linking an FQDN to an IP address, but much of the preceding settings will be based on your exact needs. Here you can define all the local host names you want to map in your network. As we have already used and referenced some domain names before in the zone file such as the nameserver or mailserver we would begin with these. Afterwards, we defined all the hostnames to IP address mappings for all public available and afterwards our internal clients. Remember that when using the A records you can have multiple mappings of the same IP address to different hostnames. For example, if you do not have dedicated servers for every service in your network but rather one server running all your DNS, mail, web, and ftp services, you can write the following lines instead:

```
ns1         IN A 192.168.1.7
mailhost    IN A 192.168.1.7
www         IN A 192.168.1.7
ftp         IN A 192.168.1.7
```

You can also use a canonical name (CNAME) record for this task, which is used to assign an alias to an existing A record. Arguably, the CNAME value make your DNS data easier to manage by pointing back to an A record. So if you ever consider the need to change the IP address of the A record, all your CNAME records pointed to that record automatically. However, and as this recipe has tried to show, the alternative solution is to have multiple A records, which implies the need for multiple updates in order to change the IP address.

At this stage of the recipe, we then turned our attention towards the reverse DNS zone. As with the forward zone file, the reverse zone files also have a special naming convention /var/named/db.<C-Class of our search IP in reverse order>. Naming your reverse zone file like db.1.168.192 can look strange first but makes sense when you look at how reverse lookup works. It starts from the highest node (in our example 192, which corresponds to the root domain in the forward zone file) and traverses its way down from it. As you see, the content we put in this file has some similarities between the directives and the resources used in the forward zone file. However, it is important to remember that reverse DNS is wholly separate and distinct from forward DNS.

The reverse DNS zone is designed to assist in the conversion of an IP address to a domain name. This can be done by using the **Pointer Resource Record** (**PTR**) which assigns unique IP addresses to one or more host names. For this reason, you must ensure that a unique PTR record exists for every A record. Every reverse zone file collects IP to hostname translations for a complete Class C address range (the first three dotted numbers, for example, 192.168.1). The last octets of such an IP range are all the hostnames which can be defined within such a file. Remember, the IP address value for the first column in a PTR record should only show this last octet. For example, the line 9 IN PTR www.centos7.home. in the reverse zone file db.1.168.192 will be able to resolve any reverse IP address requests of 192.168.1.9 to the domain value www.centos7.home.

Having created our forward and reverse zone files in this recipe, we then completed the configuration of the named service by adding our new zones to our BIND server in order to start our own domain name service resolving local domain names of our network. In these new appended forward and reverse zone definition blocks, we defined that we are the master zone holder and also specified update-policy local; because this is needed if we want to use the nsupdate command to update our zones dynamically from the localhost (see later). You may add unlimited zone pairs, but remember that each forward or reverse zone definition must be given a single zone entry in curly brackets.

In summary, we can say that forward and reverse zone files are defined on a single base domain name basis, one base domain gets one forward zone file. For reverse zone files, it's a bit different because we are working with IP addresses. We create one zone file based on the Class C address range of the network address of our domain and here the last octet is called the hostname, for which we define our mappings in such a specific file.

BIND is a big subject and there is a lot more to learn as this recipe has only served to introduce you to the subject. In most cases, you may even find that your initial learning period will become known as a process of trial and error, but it will improve. Remember, practice makes perfect and if you do create additional forward zones, always reference them in the reverse zone file.

There's more...

Having created and added your zones to your BIND server, you are now able to test your configuration. To do this, you can use the host, dig or nslookup command to resolve internal hostnames from localhost only. For example, for testing forward DNS resolution we can use the dig command by specifying that our DNS server is running on localhost with port 8053: dig -p 8053 @127.0.0.1 client2.centos7.home. This should finish DNS lookup successfully and return the following line (output is truncated):

```
;; ANSWER SECTION:
client2.centos7.home.   10800   IN   A   192.168.1.12
```

For reverse lookup, you will use an IP address instead (in this instance, the IP address used should correspond to a domain for which you have configured reverse DNS): nslookup -port=8053 192.168.1.12 127.0.0.1. As we have configured BIND as an authoritative-only DNS server, any DNS request which is outside the local records of our zone should not be able to get fully resolved. To test this use dig -p 8053 @127.0.0.1 www.google.com which should return the status REFUSED and WARNING: recursion requested but not available message.

For security reasons, we restricted our BIND server to localhost only and did not allow it to connect to other DNS servers. Therefore you cannot use it as your only DNS solution for your private network. Instead, in the next recipe, we will learn how to combine Unbound with BIND to create an integrated and very secure all-in-one DNS server solution. But if you don't want to do this and use BIND as your single and full authoritative DNS server solution (which is not recommended on CentOS 7 anymore), you can do this by disabling or uninstalling Unbound, restoring the original named.conf.BAK configuration file, and enabling the following directives in the BIND configuration file: allow-query {localhost;192.168.1.0/24;}; (which enables the complete 192.168.1.0/24 network to make DNS requests), listen-on port 53 {any;}; (listen for requests on any network), listen-on-v6 port 8053 { none; }; (for disabling IPv6). If you want BIND to be forwarding everything, which it is not authoritative for, instead of using recursion to find out the answer, add the following directives as well (in this example we use the official Google DNS servers for any forwarding requests, but you can change this to fit your needs): forwarders { 8.8.8.8;};forward only;. Then restart the bind service.

Creating an integrated nameserver solution

So far in this chapter, we used Unbound as a caching-only DNS server solution because it is very secure and fast, and BIND as our authoritative-only DNS server because its zone management is highly configurable and customizable. BIND has been around for a long time and is the most used DNS software ever. However, a number of critical bugs have been found (and luckily fixed) in the past. Here in this recipe, we will combine Unbound with BIND to get the best of both worlds: Only the very secure Unbound service will be directly exposed to your private network and can take and serve DNS queries from your clients. The BIND service stays bound to localhost only as it was configured in a former recipe and is only allowed to resolve internal hostnames and does not have direct access to the Internet or your clients. If a client connects to your Unbound service and requests to resolve an internal hostname from your private network, Unbound will query the BIND server locally for the DNS resolution and cache the response. On the other hand, if a client requests to resolve an external domain name, Unbound itself will recursively query or forward other remote DNS servers and cache the response. The integration of both DNS server systems makes it the perfect all-round DNS server solution.

Getting ready

To complete this recipe, you will require a working installation of the CentOS 7 operating system and a console-based text editor of your choice. It is expected that a caching-only Unbound server (port 53) and an authoritative-only BIND server (port 8053) have been installed and are already running using recipes found in this chapter.

How to do it...

In this recipe, we will show you how to configure Unbound so it will be able to query our locally running authoritative-only BIND service whenever a client requests an internal hostname. Any other request should go out as a recursive DNS request to a remote root server to construct an answer:

1. Log in as root on our server running the Unbound and BIND service and open Unbound's main configuration file:

   ```
   vi /etc/unbound/unbound.conf
   ```

2. First put the following line somewhere in the `server:` clause:

   ```
   local-zone: "168.192.in-addr.arpa." nodefault
   ```

3. Next, we will have to allow Unbound to connect to localhost which is disabled by default, search for the line that reads: `# do-not-query-localhost: yes`, then activate and set it to no:

   ```
   do-not-query-localhost: no
   ```

4. Next, since our BIND server is not configured using DNSSEC, we need to tell Unbound to use it anyway (Unbound by default refuses to connect to DNS servers not using DNSSEC). Search for the line that starts with `# domain-insecure: "example.com"`, then activate it and change it so it reads as follows:

   ```
   domain-insecure: "centos7.home."

   domain-insecure: "168.192.in-addr.arpa."
   ```

5. Next, we need to tell Unbound to forward all the requests for our internal domain `centos7.home.` to the locally running BIND server (on port `8053`). Append the following at the file's end:

   ```
   stub-zone:
           name: "centos7.home."
           stub-addr: 127.0.0.1@8053
   ```

6. Also, we need to tell Unbound to do the same for any reverse lookup to our internal domain using BIND:

```
stub-zone:
        name: "1.168.192.in-addr.arpa."
        stub-addr: 127.0.0.1@8053
```

7. Save and close the file, and then restart the Unbound service:

```
unbound-checkconf && systemctl restart unbound
```

How it works

Congratulations! You now have a full authoritative and very secure DNS server solution using an integrated approach combining all the good parts from Unbound and BIND. In this recipe, we have shown you how to configure the Unbound service using stub-zones to connect to an internally running BIND service for both forward and reverse requests. A `stub-zone` is a special Unbound feature to configure authoritative data to be used that cannot be accessed using the public Internet servers. Its `name` field defines the zone name for which Unbound will forward any incoming DNS requests and the `stub-addr` field configures the location (IP address and a port) of the DNS server to access; in our example, this is the locally running BIND server on port `8053`. For Unbound to be able to connect to the localhost, we first had to allow this using the `do-not-query-localhost: no` directive, had to mark our forward and reverse domain as being `insecure`, and also had to define a new `local-zone`, which is necessary that Unbound knows that clients can send queries to a `stub-zone` authoritative server.

There's more...

In order to test our new Unbound/BIND DNS cluster, make one public and one internal hostname DNS request to the Unbound service from another computer in the same network (you can also run similar tests locally on the DNS server itself). If our Unbound/BIND DNS cluster has the IP `192.168.1.7`, you should be able to get correct answers for both `dig @192.168.1.7 www.packtpub.com` and `dig @192.168.1.7 client1.centos7. home` from any other computer in your network.

If you have to troubleshoot service problems or need to monitor the DNS queries of your new Unbound/BIND DNS server, you can configure logging parameters. For BIND, in the main configuration file `named.conf` you can set the verbosity of the logging output (or log level). This parameter is called `severity` and can be found within the `logging` directive. It is already set to `dynamic`; which gives the highest amount of logging messages possible. You can then read your current log using `tail -f /var/named/data/named.run`. For Unbound, you can set the level of verbosity in its main configuration file `unbound.conf` using the `verbosity` directive which is set to the lowest level of `1` but can be increased to `5`. To learn more about the different levels, use `man unbound.conf`. Use `journald` to read the Unbound logging information using the command `journalctl -f -u unbound. service` (press *Ctrl+c* key to exit the command).

We can not only log the system and service information but can also enable query logs. For Unbound just use a `verbosity` of 3 or above to record query information. For BIND, in order to activate the query log (query output will go to the log file `named.run`), use the command `rndc querylog on` (to turn it off, use `rndc querylog off`). Remember to turn off any excessive logging information, such as the query log, when configuring your DNS server on a productive system as it can decrease your service's performance. You can also install other third-party tools such as `dnstop` (from the `EPEL` repository) to monitor your DNS activity.

Populating the domain

In this recipe, we will show you how you can quickly add new local domain record entries to your authoritative BIND server which are currently unknown to your nameserver.

Getting ready

To complete this recipe, you will require a working installation of the CentOS 7 operating system and a console-based text editor of your choice. It is expected that Unbound and BIND have both been installed and are already running, and that you have read and applied the zone recipes in this chapter and have prepared the required forward and reverse zone files for resolving hostnames of your private network.

How to do it...

If you want to add new domain names to the IP address mappings to your DNS server, for example for new or unknown hosts in your local network, you have two alternatives. Since we have already created zone files for our local network, we can simply add new A (and/or CNAME) and corresponding PTR entries for every new subdomain within our base domain name into our forward and reverse zone file configuration using our text editor of choice. Alternatively, we can use the `nsupdate` command-line tool to add those records interactively without the need to restart the DNS server. In this section, we will show you how to prepare and work with the `nsupdate` tool. In our example, we will add a new subdomain `client4.centos7.home` for a computer with the IP address `192.168.1.14` to our DNS server's zone:

1. Log in as root on the server running your BIND service. Now first we need to activate `named` to be allowed to write into its zone files by SELinux:

    ```
    setsebool -P named_write_master_zones 1
    ```

2. Next, we need to fix some permission problems with the named configuration directory, otherwise `nsupdate` cannot update our zone files later:

    ```
    chown :named /var/named -R; chmod 775 /var/named -R
    ```

3. Since our BIND server is running on port `8053`, type the following command to start the interactive `nsupdate` session locally:

```
nsupdate -p 8053 -d -l
```

4. At the prompt (`>`), first connect to the local DNS server by typing the following (press *Return* to finish commands):

```
    local 127.0.0.1
```

5. To add a new forward domain to IP mapping to your DNS server, type the following:

```
update add client4.centos7.home. 115200 A 192.168.1.14
send
```

6. Now add the reverse relationship using the following command:

```
update add 14.1.168.192.in-addr.arpa. 115200 PTR client4.centos7.
home.
send
```

If both the update commands' outputs contained the message `NOERROR`, press *Ctrl+c* key to exit the interactive `nsupdate` session.

7. Finally, check if both the domain and IP resolution for the new zone entry work (this should also work remotely through the Unbound server):

```
dig -p 8053 @127.0.0.1  client4.centos7.home.
nslookup -port=8053 192.168.1.14 127.0.0.1
```

How it works...

In this fairly easy recipe, we showed you how easily you can add new domain name resolution records with the `nsupdate` tool dynamically at runtime without needing to restart your BIND DNS server.

So what did we learn from this experience?

In this recipe, we introduced you to the `nsupdate` command-line tool which is a utility for making changes to a running BIND DNS database without the need to edit the zone files or restart the server. If you have already configured the zone files in your DNS server, then this is the preferred way to make changes to the DNS server. It has several options, for example, you can connect to the remote DNS servers but for simplicity and for security reasons we will only use and allow the most simple form and only connect `nsupdate` to our BIND server locally (to connect to a BIND server remotely using `nsupdate`, you need to do more configuration, such as generate secure key-pairs, open the firewall, and so on).

After allowing `named` to write into its own zone files, which otherwise is prohibited by SELinux, and fixing some permission problems on the default named configuration directory, we started the `nsupdate` program with `-l` for local connection, and `-p 8053` to connect to our BIND DNS server on port `8053`. `-d` gives us debug output which can be useful for resolving any problems. We then got prompted by an interactive shell where we could run BIND specific `update` commands. First we set `local 127.0.0.1` which connects to our local server, than we used the commands `update add` to add a new forward A record to our running DNS server. The syntax is similar to defining records in the zone files. Here we used the line `update add <domain-name> <TTL> <type> <IP address>` to add a new A record with a TTL of three days (115200 seconds) for the domain `client4.centos7.home` to resolve to the IP address `192.168.1.14`. The next line was used to config some reverse resolution rules for our new domain and which adds the domain name as a `PTR` entry into our reverse zone. Here it is important to note that you need to define the domain part of the reverse `update add` rule the following way: `<host name for the rule>.<reverse C-class>.in-addr.arpa`. To finally execute our commands and make them permanent in our DNS server's database, without the need to restart the server, we used the `send` command for both the reverse and forward commands separately since they target different zones. Finally, we tested if the new entries into the DNS server's zone files were working by querying the BIND server.

Building a secondary (slave) DNS server

To guarantee high-availability in your network, it can be useful to operate more than one DNS server in your environment to catch up with any server failures. This is particularly true if you run a public DNS server where continuous access to the service is crucial and where it is not uncommon to have five and more DNS servers at once. Since configuring and managing multiple DNS servers can be time consuming, the BIND DNS server uses the feature of transferring zone files between the nodes so that every DNS server has the same domain resolving and configuration information. In order to do this, we need to define one primary and one or more secondary or slave DNS servers. Then we only have to adjust our zone file once on the primary server which will transfer the current version to all our secondary servers, keeping everything consistent and up-to-date. For a client it will then make no difference which DNS server they are connecting to.

Getting ready

To complete this recipe, you will require at least two CentOS 7 servers in the same network which can see and ping each other. An Internet connection will be required to download and install the BIND server software on all the computers we want to include in our DNS server *farm*. In this example, we have two servers, `192.168.1.7` which is already installed and configured as a BIND server, and `192.168.1.15` which will be our second BIND server within the subnet `192.168.1.0/24`. You should also have read and applied the zone file recipe from this chapter and created a forward and reverse zone file because this is what we want to transfer between DNS servers.

How to do it...

We begin this recipe by installing BIND on every CentOS 7 computer we want to include in our BIND DNS server cluster. To do this, follow the recipe *Setting up an authoritative-only DNS server* for all the remaining systems. Before we can start, we need to define which server will be our primary DNS server. For simplicity in our example, we will choose the server with the IP address `192.168.1.7`. Now let's make all our DNS server nodes aware of their role.

Changes to the primary DNS server

1. Let's log in as root on the primary server and open its main configuration:

    ```
    vi /etc/named.conf
    ```

2. Now we define which secondary DNS server(s) will be allowed to receive the zone files at all, write the following command somewhere between the options curly brackets in a new line (we only have one secondary DNS server with the IP address `192.168.1.15`, change accordingly):

    ```
    allow-transfer { 192.168.1.15; };
    notify yes;
    ```

3. Also, we must allow the other nameservers to connect to our primary nameserver. In order to do this, you need to change your `listen-on` directive to include the DNS server's primary network interface (in our example `192.168.1.7`, so change appropriately):

    ```
    listen-on port 8053 { 127.0.0.1;192.168.1.7; };
    ```

4. Save and close the file. Now open the new port `8053` in your server's firewall (or create a firewalld service for it, see *Chapter 6, Providing Security*):

    ```
    firewall-cmd --permanent --zone=public --add-port=8053/tcp --add-port=8053/udp;firewall-cmd --reload
    ```

5. Save and close the file. Next, update the zone files we created earlier to include the IP addresses of all the new nameservers we have available in the system. Change both the forward and reverse zone files, `/var/named/centos7.home.db` and `/var/named/db.1.168.192`, to include our new secondary DNS server. In the forward zone file, add the following lines (you can also use the `nsupdate` program to do this) into the appropriate sections:

    ```
    NS  ns2.centos7.home.

    ns2  A   192.168.1.15
    ```

6. In the reverse zone file, add instead into the appropriate sections:

    ```
    NS  ns2.centos7.home.

    15 PTR ns2.centos7.home.
    ```

7. Finally, restart BIND and recheck the configuration file:

```
named-checkconf && systemctl restart named
```

Changes to the secondary DNS server(s)

For simplicity and to demonstrate, just install `named` on any server you want to use as a BIND slave (we only show the important configuration here):

1. Log in to the new server as root, install BIND, and open its main configuration:

```
yum install bind; vi /etc/named.conf
```

2. Now locate the line `include /etc/named.rfc1912.zones;`. Immediately following this line, create a space for your work and add the following zones (replace the zone and file names appropriately):

```
zone "centos7.home" IN {
    type slave;
    masters port 8053 { 192.168.1.7; };
    file "/var/named/centos7.home.db";
};
zone "1.168.192.in-addr.arpa" IN {
    type slave;
    masters port 8053{ 192.168.1.7; };
    file "/var/named/db.1.168.192.db";
};
```

3. Save and close the file. Then fix some incorrect BIND folder permissions and enable `named` to write into its zone file directory before restarting BIND:

```
chown :named /var/named -R; chmod 775 /var/named -R
setsebool -P named_write_master_zones 1
named-checkconf && systemctl restart named
```

4. Now initiate a new zone transfer using:

```
rndc refresh centos7.home.
```

5. After waiting a while, to test if our secondary DNS server is working as expected, check if the master zone files have been transferred:

```
ls /var/named/*.db
```

6. Finally, we can now test if we can query our local domain on the secondary DNS server too:

```
dig @127.0.0.1 client2.centos7.home.
```

10
Working with Databases

In this chapter, we will cover:

- ▶ Installing a MariaDB database server
- ▶ Managing a MariaDB database
- ▶ Allowing remote access to a MariaDB server
- ▶ Installing a PostgreSQL server and managing a database
- ▶ Configuring remote access to a PostgresSQL
- ▶ Installing phpMyAdmin and phpPgAdmin

Introduction

This chapter is a collection of recipes that deliver the necessary steps to implement and maintain two of the most popular database management systems in the Linux world. The need for data is everywhere and is a *must have service* for almost any server, and this chapter provides the starting point required to deploy these database systems in any environment.

Installing a MariaDB database server

Supporting over 70 collations, more than 30 character sets, multiple storage engines, and deployment in virtualized environment, MySQL is a mission-critical database server that is used by production servers all over the world. It is capable of hosting a vast number of individual databases and it can provide support for various roles across your entire network. MySQL server has become synonymous with the **World Wide Web** (**WWW**), is used by desktop software, extends local services, and is one of the world's most popular relational database systems. The purpose of this recipe is to show you how to download, install, and lockdown MariaDB, which is the default implementation of MySQL in CentOS 7. MariaDB is open source and fully compatible with MySQL and adds several new features; for example, a non-blocking client API library, new storage engines with better performance, enhanced server status variables, and replication.

Getting ready

To complete this recipe, you will require a working installation of the CentOS 7 operating system with root privileges, a console-based text editor of your choice, and a connection to the Internet in order to download additional packages. It is expected that your server will be using a static IP address.

How to do it...

As the MariaDB **Database Management System** (**DBMS**) is not installed by default on CentOS 7, we will start this recipe by installing the required packages.

1. To begin, log in as root and type the following command to install the required packages:

    ```
    yum install mariadb-server mariadb
    ```

2. When complete, ensure the service starts at boot before starting the service:

    ```
    systemctl enable mariadb.service && systemctl start mariadb.service
    ```

3. Finally, begin the secure installation process with the following command:

    ```
    mysql_secure_installation
    ```

4. When you first run the previous command, you will be asked to provide a password but as this value has not been set, press the *Enter* key to represent the value (blank) none.

5. Now you will be asked a number of simple questions which will help you in the process of hardening your MariaDB DBMS system. It is a good advice to choose Yes (Y) to every question for maximum security unless you are already a MariaDB expert and really require a certain feature.

6. Finally, test if you can connect and login to the MariaDB service locally using the MariaDB command-line client called `mysql`. The test passes if the following command outputs all the MariaDB user names together with their associated hosts known to the MariaDB server (enter the administrator root password you set in the last step when prompted):

```
echo "select User,Host from user" | mysql -u root -p mysql
```

How it works...

MariaDB is a fast, efficient, multithreaded, and robust SQL database server. It supports multiple users and provides access to a number of storage engines, and by following a few short steps, you now know how to install, secure, and login to your MariaDB server.

So what did we learn from this experience?

We started the recipe by installing the necessary package for the MariaDB server (`mariadb-server`) and also the client shell interface (`mariadb`) for controlling and querying the server. Having done this, we then proceeded to ensure that the MariaDB daemon (`mariadb.service`) would start during the boot process before we actually started it. At this point we had a working installation, but in order to ensure that our installation was safe we then invoked the secure installation script in order to guide us through a few simple steps to harden our basic installation. As the basic installation process does not enable us to set a default password for the root user, we did it here as a first step in the script, so we could be certain that no one could access the MariaDB root user account without the required authorization. We then discovered that a typical MariaDB installation maintains an anonymous user. The purpose of this is to allow anyone to login to our database server without having to have a valid user account. It is typically used for testing purposes only, and unless you are in unique circumstances that require this facility, it is always advisable to remove this feature. Following this, and to ensure that the root user could not access our MariaDB server installation, we then opted to disallow remote root access before removing the test database and performing a reload of the privilege tables. Finally, we ran a small test to see if we could connect to the database with the root user and query some data from the `user` table (which is part of the standard `mysql` database).

Having completed the steps of the recipe, we have learned that the process of installing and securing the MariaDB server is very simple. Of course, there are always more things that can be done in order to make the installation useful but the purpose of this recipe was to show you that the most important part of installing your new database system was to make it secure. Remember, the act of running `mysql_secure_installation` is recommended for all MariaDB servers and it is advisable regardless of whether you are building a development server or one that is used in a production environment. As a server administrator, security should always remain your top priority.

Managing a MariaDB database

In this recipe, we will learn how to create a new database and database user for the MariaDB server. MariaDB can be used in conjunction with a wide variety of graphical tools (for example, the free MySQL Workbench), but in situations where you simply need to create a database, provide an associated user, and assign the correct permissions, it is often useful to perform this task from the command line. Known as the MariaDB shell, this simple interactive and text based-command line facility supports the full range of SQL commands and affords both local and remote access to your database server. The shell provides you with complete control over your database server, and for this reason it represents the perfect tool for you to start your MariaDB work.

Getting ready

To complete this recipe, you will require a working installation of the CentOS 7 operating system. It is expected that a MariaDB server is already installed and running on your server.

How to do it...

The MariaDB command-line tool supports executing commands in both the batch mode (reading from a file or standard input) and interactively (typing in statements and waiting for the results). We will use the latter in this recipe.

1. To begin, log in on your CentOS 7 server with any system user you like and type the following command in order to access the MariaDB server using the MariaDB shell with the main MariaDB administration user called `root` (use the password created in the previous recipe):

    ```
    mysql -u root -p
    ```

2. On successful login, you will be greeted with the MariaDB command-line interface. This feature is signified by the MariaDB shell prompt:

    ```
    MariaDB [(none)]>
    ```

3. In this first step, we will create a new database. To do this, simply customize the following command by substituting an appropriate value for the new `<database-name>` value using:

    ```
    CREATE DATABASE <database-name> CHARACTER SET utf8 COLLATE utf8_
    general_ci;
    ```

     If this is your first introduction to the MariaDB shell, remember to end each line with a semi-colon (;) and press the *Enter* key after typing each command.

4. Having created our database, we will now create a MariaDB user. Each user will consist of a username and a password that is completely independent of the operating system's user. For reasons of security, we will ensure that access to the database is restricted to localhost only. To proceed, simply customize the following command by changing the values `<username>`, `<password>`, and `<database-name>` to reflect your needs:

```
GRANT ALL ON <database-name>.* TO '<username>'@'localhost'
IDENTIFIED BY '<password>' WITH GRANT OPTION;
```

5. Next, make the MariaDB DBMS aware of your new user:

```
FLUSH PRIVILEGES;
```

6. Now simply type the following command to exit the MariaDB shell:

```
EXIT;
```

7. Finally, you can test the accessibility of your new `<username>` by accessing the MariaDB shell from the command-line in the following way:

```
mysql -u <username> -p
```

8. Now back at the MariaDB shell (`MariaDB [(none)] >`), type the following commands:

```
SHOW DATABASES;
```

```
EXIT;
```

How it works...

During the course of this recipe you were shown not only how to create a database, but also how to create a database user.

So what did we learn from this experience?

We started the recipe by accessing the MariaDB shell as the root user with the `mysql` command. By doing this, we were then able to create a database with a simple SQL function called `CREATE DATABASE`, providing a custom name for the `<database-name>` field. We also specified `utf8` as the character set of our new database together with a `utf8_general_ci` collation. A character set is how the characters are encoded in the database and a collation is a set of rules for comparing the characters in a character set. For historic reasons and to keep MariaDB backward-compatible with the older server versions, the default character set is `latin1` and `latin1_swedish_ci`, but for any modern databases you should always prefer to use `utf-8` instead as it is the most standard and compatible encoding for international character sets (non-English alphabets). However, this command can be modified to invoke the need to check if a database name is already in use by using: `CREATE DATABASE IF NOT EXISTS <database-name>`. In this way, you can then drop or remove a database by using the following command:

```
DROP DATABASE IF EXISTS <database-name>;
```

Having done this, it is simply a matter of adding a new database user with the appropriate permissions by running our GRANT ALL command. Here we provided <username> with full privileges via a defined <password> for localhost. As a specific <database-name> was elected, then this level of permission will be restricted to that particular database and using <database-name>.* allows us to specify these rules to all the tables (using the asterisks symbol) in this database. The general syntax in order to provide a chosen user with specific permission is:

```
GRANT [type of permission] ON <database name>.<table name> TO
'<username>'@'<hostname>';
```

For security reasons, here in this recipe we limit <hostname> to localhost but if you want to grant permissions to remote users you will need to change this value (see later). In our example, we set [type of permission] to ALL but you can always decide to minimize the privileges by providing a single or a comma-separated list of privilege-types offered in the following way:

```
GRANT SELECT, INSERT, DELETE ON <database name>.* TO
'<username>'@'localhost';
```

Using the previous technique, here is a summary of the permissions that can be employed:

 - ▶ ALL: Allows the <username> value with all available privilege-types
 - ▶ CREATE: Allows the <username> value to create new tables or databases
 - ▶ DROP: Allows the <username> value to delete tables or databases
 - ▶ DELETE: Allows the <username> value to delete rows from tables
 - ▶ INSERT: Allows the <username> value to insert rows into tables
 - ▶ SELECT: Allows the <username> value to read from tables
 - ▶ UPDATE: Allows the <username> value to update table rows

However, once the privileges were granted, the recipe then showed you that we must FLUSH the system in order to make our new settings available to the system itself. It is important to note that all commands within the MariaDB shell should end in a semicolon (;). Having completed our task, we simply exit the console using the EXIT; statement.

MariaDB is an excellent database system but like all services, it can be abused. So remain vigilant at all times, and by considering the previous advices, you can be confident that your MariaDB installation will remain safe and secure.

There's more...

Creating a restricted user is one way of providing database access but if you have a team of developers who require constant access to a development server, you may wish to consider providing a universal user who maintains superuser privilege. To do this, simply login to the MariaDB shell with your administrator user root, then create a new user in the following way:

```
GRANT ALL ON *.* TO '<username>'@'localhost' IDENTIFIED BY '<password>'
WITH GRANT OPTION;
```

By doing this, you will enable <username> to add, delete, and manage databases across your entire MariaDB server (the asterisks in *.* tell MariaDB to apply the privileges to all the databases and all their associated tables found on the database server), but given the range of administrative features, this new user account will restrict all activities to localhost only. So in simple terms, if you want to provide <username> with access to any database or to any table, always use an asterisk (*) in place of the database name or table name. Finally, every time you update or change a user permission, always be sure to use the FLUSH PRIVILEGES command before exiting the MariaDB shell with the EXIT; command.

Reviewing and revoking permissions or dropping a user

It is never a good idea to keep user accounts active unless they are used, so your first consideration within the MariaDB shell (login with your administrator user root) will be to review their current status by typing:

```
SELECT HOST,USER FROM mysql.user WHERE USER='<username>';
```

Having done this, if you intend to REVOKE permission(s) or remove a user listed here, you can do this with the DROP command. First of all, you should review what privileges the user of interest has by running:

```
SHOW GRANTS FOR '<username>'@'localhost';
```

You now have two options, starting with the ability to revoke the user's privileges as follows:

```
REVOKE ALL PRIVILEGES, GRANT OPTION FROM '<username>'@'localhost';
```

Then you may either reallocate the privilege using the formula provided in the main recipe or alternatively, you can decide to remove the user by typing:

```
DROP USER '<username>'@'localhost';
```

Finally, update all your privileges the usual way using FLUSH PRIVILEGES; before exiting the shell EXIT; command.

Allowing remote access to a MariaDB server

Unless you are running your MariaDB database server to drive some local web applications on the same server hardware, most working environments would be pretty useless if remote access to a database server were forbidden. In many IT surroundings you will find high-available, centralized dedicated database servers optimized in hardware (for example, huge amounts of RAM) and hosting multiple databases allowing hundreds of parallel connections from the outside to the server. Here in this recipe, we will show you how to make remote connections to the server possible.

Getting ready

To complete this recipe, you will require a working installation of the CentOS 7 operating system with root privileges. It is expected that a MariaDB server is already installed and running and you have read and applied the *Managing a MariaDB database* recipe for an understanding of permissions and how to test (local) database connections.

How to do it...

In our example, we want to access a MariaDB database server with the IP address
`192.168.1.12` from a client computer in the same network, with the IP address
`192.168.1.33`. Please change appropriately to fit your needs:

1. To begin, log in as root on your MariaDB database server and open the firewall for the incoming MariaDB connections:

   ```
   firewall-cmd --permanent --add-service=mysql && firewall-cmd
   --reload
   ```

2. Afterwards, we need to create a user account which can connect to our MariaDB server remotely (as we have prevented `root` from doing this in a further step for security reasons), login your database server using the MariaDB command line interface `mysql` as user `root` and type the following MariaDB statement (replacing the xxxx with a password of your choice, also feel free to adjust the username and remote IP of the client who wants to connect to the server—in our case the client has the IP `192.168.1.33`—accordingly):

   ```
   GRANT SELECT ON mysql.user TO 'johndoe'@'192.168.1.33' IDENTIFIED
   BY 'XXXX';

   FLUSH PRIVILEGES;EXIT;
   ```

3. Now we can test the connection from our client computer with the IP address of 192.168.1.33 in our network. This computer needs the MariaDB shell installed (on a CentOS 7 client, install the package `mariadb`) and needs to be able to ping the server running the MariaDB service (in our example, the IP 192.168.1.12). You can test connecting to the server by using the following command (on success, this will print out the content of the `mysql` user table):

```
echo "select user from mysql.user" | mysql -u johndoe -p mysql -h
192.168.1.12
```

How it works...

We started our journey by opening the standard MariaDB firewall port 3306 using the firewalld predefined MariaDB service, which is disabled by default on CentOS 7. After this, we configured which IP addresses were allowed to access our database server, which is done on a database level using the MariaDB shell. In our example, we used the GRANT SELECT command to allow the user johndoe at the client IP address 192.168.1.33 and with the password in quotes 'XXXX' to access the database with the name mysql and the table user to make SELECT queries only. Remember, here you can also apply wildcards in the <hostname> field using the % sign (which means any characters). For example, for defining any possible hostname combination in a Class C network, you can use the % sign like so 192.168.1.%. Granting access to the mysql.user database and table was just for testing purposes only and you should remove the user johndoe from this access permission whenever you have finished your tests, using: REVOKE ALL PRIVILEGES, GRANT OPTION FROM 'johndoe'@'192.168.1.33';. If you want you can also delete the user DROP USER 'johndoe'@'192.168.1.33'; because we don't need it anymore.

Installing a PostgreSQL server and managing a database

In this recipe, we will not only learn how to install the PostgreSQL DBMS on our server, but we will also discover how to add a new user and create our first database. PostgreSQL is considered to be the most advanced open source database system in the world. It is known for being a solid, reliable, and well-engineered system that is fully capable of supporting high-transaction and mission-critical applications. PostgreSQL is a descendant of the Ingres database. It is community-driven and maintained by a large collection of contributors from all over the world. It may not be as flexible or as pervasive as MariaDB, but because PostgreSQL is a very secure database system that excels in data integrity, it is the purpose of this recipe to show you how to begin exploring this forgotten friend.

Getting ready

To complete this recipe, you will require a working installation of the CentOS 7 operating system with root privileges, a console-based text editor of your choice, and a connection to the Internet in order to facilitate the download of additional packages. It is expected that your server will be using a static IP address.

How to do it...

PostgreSQL (also known as Postgres) is an object-relational database management system. It supports a large part of the SQL standard and it can be extended by the server administrator in many ways. However, in order to begin, we must start by installing the necessary packages:

1. Start by logging in your server as root and type:

    ```
    yum install postgresql postgresql-server
    ```

2. Having installed the database system, we must now enable the database server at boot by typing:

    ```
    systemctl enable postgresql
    ```

3. When you have finished, initialize the database system as follows:

    ```
    postgresql-setup initdb
    ```

4. Now complete this process by starting the database server:

    ```
    systemctl start postgresql
    ```

5. Now set a new initial password for our postgres administrator of your choice. As the default postgres user is currently using peer authentication, we need to execute any Postgres-related command with user postgres:

    ```
    su - postgres -c "psql --command '\password postgres'"
    ```

6. To get rid of the requirement, that the postgres user has to be logged in on a system user basis before he can execute Postgres-related commands such as psql, and to allow login with database user accounts in general, we need to change the authentication method for localhost from peer to md5 in the Postgres client authentication configuration file. You can do this manually or use the sed tool as shown next, after you have made a backup of the file first:

    ```
    cp /var/lib/pgsql/data/pg_hba.conf /var/lib/pgsql/data/pg_hba.conf.BAK
    ```

    ```
    sed -i 's/^\(local.*\)peer$/\1md5/g' /var/lib/pgsql/data/pg_hba.conf
    ```

7. Next, we have to restart the postgresql service in order to apply our changes:

    ```
    systemctl restart postgresql
    ```

8. Now you will be able to login to your Postgres server with user `postgres` without the need to login the `postgres` Linux system user first:

```
psql -U postgres
```

9. To exit the shell (`postgres=#`), type the following command (followed by the *Return* key):

```
\q
```

10. We will now issue a shell command to create a new database user, by substituting `<username>` with a relevant user name to fit your own needs (type in a new password for the user when prompted, repeat it, and afterwards enter the password for the administrator user `postgres` to apply these settings):

```
createuser -U postgres -P <username>
```

11. Now, also on the shell create your first database and assign it to our new user by replacing the `<database-name>` and `<username>` values with something more appropriate to your needs (enter the password for the `postgres` user):

```
createdb -U postgres <database-name> -O <username>
```

12. Finally, test if you can access the Postgres server with your new user by printing all the database names:

```
psql -U <username> -l
```

How it works...

PostgreSQL is an Object-Relational Database Management System and it is available to all CentOS servers. Postgres may not be as common as MariaDB, but its architecture and large array of features do make it an attractive solution for many companies concerned with data integrity.

So what did we learn from this experience?

We began this recipe by installing the necessary server and client `rpm` packages using `yum`. Having done this, we then proceeded to make the Postgres system available at boot before initializing the database system using the `postgresql-setup initdb` command. We completed this process by starting the database service. In the next stage, we were then required to set the password for the Postgres administrator user to harden the system. By default, the `postgresql` package creates a new Linux system user called `postgres` (which is also used as an administrative Postgres user account to access our Postgres DBMS), and by using `su - postgres - c` we were able to execute the `psql` commands as the `postgres` user, which is mandatory upon installation (this is called peer authentication).

Having set the admin password, to have more like a MariaDB shell-type of login procedure where every database user (including the administrator `postgres` user) can log in using the database `psql` client's user `-U` parameter, we changed this `peer` authentication to `md5` database password-based authentication for the localhost in the `pg_hba.conf` file (see the next recipe). After restarting the service, we then used Postgres's `createuser` and `createdb` command line tools to create a new Postgres user and connect it to a new database (we needed to provide the `postgres` user with the `-U` parameter because only he has the privileges for it). Finally, we showed you how to make a test connection to the database with your new user using the `-l` flag (which lists all the available databases). Also, you can use the `-d` parameter to connect to a specific database using the syntax: `psql -d <database-name> -U <username>`.

There's more...

Instead of using the `createuser` or `createdb` Postgres command-line tools, as we have been showing you in this recipe, to create your databases and users, you can also do the same using the Postgres shell. In fact, those command-line tools are actually just wrappers around the Postgres shell commands, and there is no effective difference between the two. `psql` is the primary command-line client tool for entering SQL queries or other commands on a Postgres server, similar to the MariaDB shell shown to you in another recipe in this chapter. Here, we will launch `psql` with a template called `template1`, the boilerplate (or default template) that is used to start building databases. After login (`psql -U postgres template1`), and typing in the administrator password you should be presented with the interactive Postgres prompt (`template1=#`). Now to create a new user in the `psql` shell, type:

```
CREATE USER <username> WITH PASSWORD '<password>';
```

To create a database, type:

```
CREATE DATABASE <database-name>;
```

The option to grant all privileges on the recently created database to the new user is:

```
GRANT ALL ON DATABASE <database-name> to <username>;
```

To exit the interactive shell, use: `\q` followed by pressing the *Return* key.

Having completed this recipe you could say that you not only know how to install PostgreSQL, but this process has served to highlight some simple architectural differences between this database system and MariaDB.

Configuring remote access to PostgreSQL

In this recipe, we will learn how to configure remote access to a Postgres server which is disabled by default. Postgres employs a method called host-based authentication and it is the purpose of this recipe to introduce you to its concepts in order to provide the access rights you need to run a safe and secure database server.

Getting ready

To complete this recipe, you will require a working installation of the CentOS 7 operating system with root privileges and a text editor of your choice. It is expected that PostgreSQL is already installed and running.

How to do it...

In the previous recipe, we have already modified the host-based authentication configuration pg_hba.conf file using sed to manage our Postgres's client authentication from peer to md5. Here we will make changes to it to manage remote access to our Postgres server.

1. To begin, log in as root and first open the firewall to allow any incoming PostgreSQL connections to the server:

    ```
    firewall-cmd --permanent --add-service=postgresql;firewall-cmd
    --reload
    ```

2. Now open the host-based authentication configuration file in your favorite text editor by typing:

    ```
    vi /var/lib/pgsql/data/pg_hba.conf
    ```

3. Scroll down to the end of the file and append the following line, to make these lines read as follows (substitute the XXX.XXX.XXX.XXX/XX value with a network address you want to grant access to. For example, if the IP address of your server was 192.168.1.12 then the network address would be 192.168.1.0/24):

    ```
    host      all          all          XXX.XXX.XXX.XXX/XX      md5
    ```

4. When you have finished, simply save and close the file in the usual way before opening the main Postgres configuration file by typing:

    ```
    vi /var/lib/pgsql/data/postgresql.conf
    ```

5. Add the following lines to the end of the file:

    ```
    listen_addresses = '*'
    port = 5432
    ```

6. When you have finished, save the file in the usual way before restarting the database server by typing the following command:

```
systemctl restart postgresql
```

7. On any other computer which is in the same network (defined by the XXX.XXX.XXX.XXX/XX value set previously), you can now test if the remote connection to your Postgres server is working using the `psql` shell (if your client computer is CentOS, you need to install it using `yum install postgresql`) by logging in on the server remotely and printing out some test data. In our example, the Postgres server is running with the IP address `192.168.1.12`.

```
psql -h 192.168.1.12 -U <username> -d <database-name>
```

How it works...

PostgreSQL is a safe and secure database system but where we access it (either remotely or locally) can often become a cause of confusion. It was the purpose of this recipe to lift the lid on host-based authentication and provide an easy-to-use solution that will enable you to get your system up-and-running.

So what did we learn from this experience?

We began the recipe by opening the Postgres service's standard ports in firewalld in order to make a connection from any remote computer possible in the first place. Then we opened Postgres's host-based authentication configuration file called `pg_hba.conf` with our favorite text editor. Remember, we already changed from `peer` to `md5` authentication for all local connections to provide user based authentication in a former recipe. The inserted host record line specifies a connection type, database name, a user name, a client IP address range, and the authentication method. Many of the previous commands may already be understood but it is important to realize that there are several different methods of authentication:

- **trust**: Allows the connection unconditionally and enables anyone to connect with the database server without the need for a password.

- **reject**: Allows the database server to reject a connection unconditionally, a feature that remains useful when filtering certain IP addresses or certain hosts from a group.

- **md5**: Implies that the client needs to supply an MD5-encrypted password for authentication.

- **peer and ident**: Access is granted if the client's logged in Linux user name from the operating system can be found as a database user in the system. ident is used for remote connections and peer for local connections.

Having completed this task, we then saved and closed the file before opening the main PostgreSQL configuration file located at `/var/lib/pgsql/data/postgresql.conf`. As you may or may not be aware, remote connections will not be possible unless the server is started with an appropriate value for `listen_addresses`, and where the default setting placed this on a local loopback address it was necessary to allow the database server to listen to all network interfaces (signified by the use of a star symbol or `*`) for incoming Postgres connections on the 5432 port. When finished, we simply saved the file and restarted the database server.

There is always much more to learn, but as a result of completing this recipe, you not only have a better understanding of host-based authentication but you have the ability to access your PostgreSQL database server both locally and remotely.

Installing phpMyAdmin and phpPgAdmin

Working with the MariaDB or Postgres command-line shell is sufficient for performing basic database administration tasks, such as user permission settings or creating simple databases as we have shown you in this chapter. The more complex your schemas and relationships between tables get and the more your data grows, the more you should consider using some graphical database user interfaces for better control and work performance. This is also true for novice database administrators as such tools provide you with syntax highlightning and validation and some tools even have graphical representations of your databases (for example, showing Entity Relationship Models). In this recipe, we will show you how to install two of the most popular graphical open-source database management software for MariaDB and PostgreSQL on the market, namely `phpMyadmin` and `phpPgAdmin`, which are web-based browser applications written in PHP.

Getting ready

To complete this recipe, you will require a working installation of the CentOS 7 operating system with root privileges, a console-based text editor of your choice, and a connection to the Internet in order to facilitate the download of additional packages. It is expected that your MariaDB or PostgreSQL server is already running using the recipes found in this chapter. Also, you will need a running Apache web server with PHP installed, which must be accessible from all the computers in your private network to deploy these applications (refer to *Chapter 12, Providing Web Services* for instructions). In addition, you need to have enabled the EPEL repositories for installing the correct software packages (refer to recipe *Using a third-party repository* in *Chapter 4, Managing Packages with YUM*). Finally, you will need one computer in your network with a graphical window manager and a modern web-browser to access these web applications.

How to do it...

In this recipe, we will first show you how to install and configure `phpMyAdmin` for remote access and afterwards how to do the same for `phpPgAdmin`.

Installing and configuring phpMyAdmin

To install and configure phpMyAdmin, perform the following steps:

1. Type in the following command to install the required package:

   ```
   yum install phpMyAdmin
   ```

2. Now create a copy of the main `phpMyadmin` configuration file:

   ```
   cp /etc/httpd/conf.d/phpMyAdmin.conf /etc/httpd/conf.d/phpMyAdmin.conf.BAK
   ```

3. Next, open the main `phpMyAdmin.conf` configuration file and add the line `Require ip XXX.XXX.XXX.XXX/XX` with your defined subnet's network address you want to grant access to the web application—for example, `Require ip 192.168.1.0/24` below the line `Require ip 127.0.0.1`. You have to do this twice in the file or you can use `sed` to do this automatically, as shown here. On the command-line define the environment variable `NET=` accordingly to fit it to your own subnet's network address.

   ```
   NET="192.168.1.0/24"
   ```

4. Then type the following line to apply your changes to the configuration file:

   ```
   sed -i "s,\(Require ip 127.0.0.1\),\1\nRequire ip $NET,g" /etc/httpd/conf.d/phpMyAdmin.conf
   ```

5. Afterwards, reload your Apache server and now you should be able to browse to the `phpMyAdmin` website from any other computer in your subnet using the server's IP running the web application, for example `192.168.1.12` (log in with your MariaDB administrator user called root or any other database user):

   ```
   http://192.168.1.12/phpMyAdmin
   ```

Installing and configuring phpPgAdmin

Following are the steps to install and configure phpPgAdmin:

1. Type in the following command to install the required package:

   ```
   yum install phpPgAdmin
   ```

2. Before editing the `phpPgAdmin` main configuration, make a backup of it first:

   ```
   cp /etc/httpd/conf.d/phpPgAdmin.conf /etc/httpd/conf.d/phpPgAdmin.conf.BAK
   ```

3. Allowing remote access to `phpPgAdmin` is very similar to `phpMyAdmin`. Here you can also add a `Require ip XXX.XXX.XXX.XXX/XX` line with your defined subnet's network address below the line `Require local` in the `phpPgAdmin.conf` file, or use the `sed` utility to do this automatically for you:

```
NET="192.168.1.0/24"
sed -i "s,\(Require local\),\1\nRequire ip $NET,g" /etc/httpd/
conf.d/phpPgAdmin.conf
```

4. Restart Apache and browse to the `phpPgAdmin` main page:

```
http://192.168.1.12/phpPgAdmin
```

How it works...

In this fairly simple recipe, we have shown you how to install two of the most popular graphical administration tools for MariaDB and Postgres, running as web applications in your browser (and written in PHP) on the same server where your database service is running, and enabled remote access to them.

So what did we learn from this experience?

Installing `phpMyAdmin` for administering MariaDB databases and `phpPgAdmin` for Postgres databases was as easy as installing the corresponding `rpm` packages using the `yum` package manager. As both the tools are not to be found in the official CentOS 7 repositories, you need to enable the third-party repository EPEL before you can access and install these packages. By default, when installing both the web applications, access is denied to any connection not being made from the server itself (local only). Since we want to have access to it from different computers in our network, having installed a web browser you need to allow remote connections first. For both the web applications, this can be achieved using the Apache `Require ip` directive which is part of the Apache `mod_authz_core` module. In both the configuration files for `phpMyAdmin` and `phpPgAdmin`, we defined a whole subnet, such as `192.168.1.0/24`, to allow connecting to the server, but you can also use a single IP address here which you want to allow access to. The `sed` commands inserted these important `Require` lines into the configuration file, but as said earlier you can also do this manually if you like by editing these files with your text editor of choice. After reloading the Apache configuration, you were then able to browse to the web pages using the two URLs shown in the recipe. On the start page of both the web sites, you can use any database user to log in without the need to enable remote privileges for them; any user with local permissions is sufficient.

In summary, we can say that we only showed you the basic configuration of both administration tools. There is always more to learn; for example, you should consider securing both PHP websites with SSL encryption or configuring your instances to connect to different database servers. Also, if you prefer desktop software for managing your databases, have a look at the open-source MySQL Workbench Community Edition, which can be downloaded from the official MySQL website for all major operating systems (Windows, OS X, Linux).

11

Providing Mail Services

In this chapter, we will cover:

- ▸ Configuring a domain-wide mail service with Postfix
- ▸ Working with Postfix
- ▸ Delivering the mail with Dovecot
- ▸ Using Fetchmail

Introduction

This chapter is a collection of recipes that deliver the necessary steps to implement and maintain one of the oldest and most versatile technologies on the Internet today. Everyone wants to send and receive e-mails and this chapter provides the necessary starting point required to deploy such a service in a timely and efficient manner.

Configuring a domain-wide mail service with Postfix

Postfix is a **Mail Transport Agent** (**MTA**) responsible for the transfer of e-mails between mail servers using the SMTP protocol. Postfix is now the default MTA on CentOS 7. Here, as with most other critical network services, its default configuration allows outgoing but does not accept incoming network connections from any host other than the local one. This makes sense if all you need is a local Linux user mailing system and for sending out mails to other external mail servers from localhost too. But if you want to run your own centralized mail server for your own private network and domain, this is quite restrictive. So the purpose of this recipe is to set up Postfix as a domain-wide mail service to allow e-mails sent from any host in your network and if the recipient is a valid e-mail address within your local domain, deliver them to the correct mailbox on the mail server.

Getting ready

To complete this recipe, you will require a working installation of the CentOS 7 operating system with root privileges, a console-based text editor of your choice, and a connection to the Internet to download additional software packages. You need to set up your local network properly and make sure that all the computers that want to send mails through your single-domain mailserver are in the same network and can ping this server. Also, setting your system time correctly is very important for any mail server. Apply the *Synchronizing the system clock with NTP and the chrony suite* recipe in *Chapter 2, Configuring the System* before beginning your configuration. Finally, you need to set a **Fully Qualified Domain Name** (**FQDN**) for your mail server. Refer to the *Setting your hostname and resolving the network* recipe in *Chapter 2, Configuring the System*. It is expected that your server will be using a static IP address and that it maintains one or more system user accounts. It is also assumed that you are working through this chapter recipe by recipe in the order in which they appear.

How to do it...

Postfix is already installed by default on all CentOS 7 flavors and it should be in a running state. In our example, we want to build a central mail server for our network 192.168.1.0/24 with the local domain name called `centos7.home`.

1. First login as root and test if Postfix is already working locally and can send local mails to your system users. Type the following command to send a mail to a Linux user specified by `<username>`:

   ```
   echo "This is a testmail" | sendmail <username>
   ```

2. On CentOS 7, Postfix is also already configured to send out mails to external e-mail addresses (but from localhost only) without any changes to the configuration file. For example, you could use right out-of-the-box:

   ```
   echo "This is a testmail" | sendmail contact@example.com
   ```

    If you don't have a trusted domain and certificate behind your Postfix server, in times of massive spam e-mails most external e-mail servers will reject or put such e-mails directly into the spam folders.

3. To see if the local mail message has been delivered successfully, show the latest mail log (Press *Ctrl+C* to exit the log):

   ```
   tail -f /var/log/maillog
   ```

4. Next, check if a FQDN for our server is available. This is mandatory, and if not set properly, refer to *Chapter 2, Configuring the System* to set one (in our example, this will output the name `mailserver.centos7.home`):

   ```
   hostname --fqdn
   ```

5. Now create a backup copy of the main Postfix configuration file before opening this file:

```
cp /etc/postfix/main.cf /etc/postfix/main.cf.BAK && vi /etc/
postfix/main.cf
```

6. First of all, we will want Postfix to listen on all network interfaces instead of only the local one. Activate or uncomment the following line (which means remove the # sign at the beginning of the line) that starts with `inet_interfaces` to read:

```
inet_interfaces = all
```

7. Now, some lines below, you will find the line that reads `inet_interfaces = localhost`. Deactivate it or comment it out by putting a # sign at the start of the line:

```
# inet_interfaces = localhost
```

8. Next we need to set the local domain-name of the mail server. For example, if our mailserver's FQDN is `mailserver.centos7.home` and this mailserver is responsible for delivering mail for the whole private `centos7.home` domain, the domain name will be (it's best to put it below the line that reads `#mydomain = domain.tld`):

```
mydomain = centos7.home
```

9. With the intention that this server may become a domain-wide mail server, you should now update the following line that starts with `mydestination` to read as follows (for example, in the `mydestination` section, comment out the first `mydestination` line and uncomment the second line):

```
mydestination = $myhostname, localhost.$mydomain, localhost,
$mydomain
```

10. Next, we need to specify the pathname of a mailbox file relative to a user's home directory. To do this, scroll down and locate the line that begins with `home_mailbox` and uncomment the following option (remove the # sign at the line's beginning):

```
home_mailbox = Maildir/
```

11. Save and close the file. Now we want to open the correct Postfix server ports in the firewall to allow the incoming SMTP connections to the server:

```
firewall-cmd --permanent --add-service=smtp && firewall-cmd
--reload
```

12. Next, restart the Postfix service as follows:

```
systemctl restart postfix
```

13. Afterwards, login to a different computer in the same network and install **Swiss Army Knife SMTP** (**swaks**) to test out our Postfix server connection remotely. On CentOS, type the following (it needs the EPEL repository to be installed in advance):

```
yum install swaks
```

14. Now, to test if you can connect to our new Postfix server using the standard SMTP mail port 25, with our Postfix server running on the IP address `192.168.1.100`, we are sending a mail remotely to a Linux system user `john` which has a system user account on our Postfix server:

```
swaks --server 192.168.1.100 --to john@centos7.home
```

15. Swaks creates output which should give us a hint if the mail transport has been successful. For example (the output has been truncated):

```
-> This is a test mailing
<-   250 2.0.0 Ok: queued as D18EE52B38
 -> QUIT
<-   221 2.0.0 Bye
```

16. You can also test that the last command has been successful by logging in as user `john` on the Postfix server, then checking and reading your local mailbox's inbox, which should contain a file with the test mail sent from the swaks tool (the filename will be different on your computer), as follows:

```
ls ~/Maildir/new
```

```
less ~/Maildir/new/14941584.Vfd02I1M246414.mailserver.centos7.home
```

How it works...

As we have seen, Postfix is installed and running on every CentOS 7 system by default and in its basic configuration the mail server is listening on the localhost address for incoming mails so you can already send out local mails between your server's local Linux system users without the need to contact an external MTA. It is already running because your system is already using it for a number of local services, such as the crond daemon or for sending out warnings about security breaches (for example, running a `sudo` command as a non-sudo user).

Before we can explain how this recipe works, we need to review some more basics about the Postfix MTA system in general. The Postfix MTA service can receive incoming e-mails from mail clients or other remote MTA servers using the SMTP protocol. If an incoming e-mail is destined for the MTA server's configured final destination domain (for example, a mail sent with the recipient address `john@centos7.home` is incoming to the `centos7.home` configured Postfix MTA server), it will deliver the mail to a local mailbox installed on the server (either in the filesystem or in a database system such as MariaDB). If the incoming mail is not destined for this server, it will be relayed (forwarded) to another MTA.

Remember that this is all a Postfix server is capable of doing and nothing more: receiving incoming SMTP connections from mail clients or other MTAs, delivering mail to local mailboxes on the server, and forwarding mail to other MTAs using SMTP. Contrary to common belief, Postfix cannot transfer the mails from its local mailboxes to the end users. Here we need another type of MTA called **delivery agent**, which uses different mail protocols, such as IMAP or POP3.

In this recipe, we configured our Postfix server so that the other computers and servers in the same network could also send mails to our Postfix server, which is blocked by default (by default only the server itself can send mails). If an incoming e-mail, sent from another computer in our network, has the same domain name in the recipient's e-mail address as our Postfix server has its FQDN in, then it gets delivered to the appropriate local mailbox defined by the recipient's part of the e-mail; all external e-mail addresses get relayed to an external MTA.

So what did we learn from this experience?

We began our journey by testing if we could send out local mails to system users. Here we logged in as our root user and sent a mail to a valid local system user using the sendmail program, which is included in the Postfix package. For every mail you send using sendmail, you should be able to see some new lines appearing in the `/var/log/maillog` file, which contains status information and other important logging text for the mail. If you sent a message from `root` to the user `john` and the FQDN of your server is `centos7.home`, new output lines appended to the log file should contain amongst other things a `from=<root@centos7.home>`, a `to=<john@centos7.home>` and if delivered successfully, a `status=sent` information. If no such logging information shows up, check the status of the Postfix service.

Afterwards, we displayed the FQDN for our server. It is very important to set this up correctly because this information will be used to authenticate the Postfix server when connecting to other MTAs or mail clients. MTAs check the FQDN which has been announced by their partner and some even refuse to connect if it is not provided or if it differs from the real DNS domain name of the server. After our initial test, we then started editing the main Postfix configuration file after we made a backup copy of it first. As said before, by default only the users sitting on the same server the Postfix service is running on can send mails between them as the server defaults to listening on the loopback device only. So first we enabled Postfix to listen to all the available network interfaces instead, using the `inet_interfaces = all` parameter. This ensured that all our clients in our network could connect to this server. Next, we set the domain name using the `mydomain` parameter we wanted to have for Postfix. In order for Postfix to work in our network, the domain name defined here in this variable must be the exact same value as the domain name for our server's network. Afterwards, we changed the `mydestination` parameter by choosing the line which adds the `$mydomain` parameter to the list of allowed domains. This will define all domains our Postfix mail server considers as the final destination. If a Postfix mail server is configured as the final destination for a domain, it will deliver the messages to the local mailboxes of the recipient users, which can be found in `/var/spool/mail/<username>` (we will change this location in the next step) instead of forwarding the mails to the other MTAs (as we added `$mydomain` to the list of final destinations in our example, we will deliver all mails sent to the `centos7.home` domain).

Here, you also need to remember that, by default, Postfix *trusts* all the other computers (SMTP clients) in the same IP subnetwork as the Postfix server is in to send mails to external e-mail addresses (relay mails to external MTAs) through our centralized server, which could be too relaxed for your network policy. Since e-mail spam is an ongoing problem on the Internet and we don't want to allow any user to abuse our mail server from sending spam (which an open relay mail server does; it this takes anything from any client and sends it to any mail server), we can further increase security by setting `mynetworks_style = host`, which only trusts and allows the localhost to send mails to external MTAs. Another way to reduce the spam risk might be to use the `mynetworks` parameter where you can specify which network or IP address is allowed to connect to our mail server and send e-mails through it; for example, `mynetworks = 127.0.0.0/8, 192.168.1.0/24`. To learn more about all the available Postfix settings, refer to the Postfix configuration parameter manual using the command `man 5 postconf`. Afterwards, we changed where the local mail should be stored. By default, all the incoming mails go to a centralized mailbox space located at `/var/spool/mail/<username>`. In order for local users to receive their mail in their own home directory, we used the `Maildir` parameter for the `home_mailbox` option, which changes this system to deliver all the mails to `/home/<username>/Maildir/` instead. Afterwards, we opened the standard SMTP protocol port in firewalld using the SMPT service, which Postfix uses for communication with the other MTAs or mail clients sending incoming mails through.

Postfix is already configured to start at boot, but to complete this part of the recipe we restarted the Postfix service for it to accept the new configuration settings. At this stage, the process of configuring Postfix was complete, but to test remote access we needed to log into another computer in the same network. Here we installed a small command line-based mail client called `swaks`, which can be used to test local or remote SMTP server connections. We ran our test by sending a mail to our remote Postfix mail server and supplied a recipient user and the IP address of our SMTP server. Having done this, you should have received a test message and as a result you should be happy to know that everything is working correctly. However, if you did happen to encounter any errors, you should refer to the mailserver log file located at `/var/log/maillog`.

There's more...

In this section of the recipe, we will change your e-mail sender address, encrypt SMTP connections, and configure your BIND DNS server to include our new mailserver's information.

Changing an e-mail's appearing domain name

If an MTA sends out an e-mail, Postfix automatically appends the hostname of the sender's e-mail address by default, if not provided explicitly otherwise, which is a great feature to track down which computer in your network sent the e-mail locally (otherwise it would be hard to find the origin of a mail if you got multiple computers sending out mails by a user called **root**). Often when sending messages to a remote MTA, you don't want to have your local hostname appear in the e-mail.

Here it is better to have only the domain name alone. In order to change this, go to the Postfix MTA you want to send mails from, open the Postfix configuration file `/etc/postfix/main.cf`, and enable this feature by uncommenting (removing the # sign at the beginning of the line) the following line to determine the origin (restart the Postfix service afterwards):

```
myorigin = $mydomain
```

Using TLS- (SSL) encryption for SMTP communication

Even if you are running your own Postfix server in a small or private environment, you should always be aware that normal SMTP traffic will be sent in clear text over the Internet, making it possible that anyone could sniff the communication. TLS will allow us to set up an encrypted SMTP connection between the server and the mail client, meaning that the complete communication will be made enciphered and impossible to be read by a third-party. In order to do this, if you have not already bought an official SSL certificate or generated some self-signed certificates for your domain, start by creating one here (read the *Generating self-signed certificates* recipe in *Chapter 6, Providing Security* to learn more). First login as root on your server and go to the standard certificate location: `/etc/pki/tls/certs`. Next, create a TLS/SSL keypair consisting of the certificate and its embedded public key as well as the private key (enter your Postfix's FQDN as the `Common name`, for example, `mailserver.centos7.home`) to do this type `make postfix-server.pem`. Afterwards, open the main Postfix configuration file `/etc/postfix/main.cf` with your favorite text editor and put in the following lines at the end of the file:

```
smtpd_tls_cert_file = /etc/pki/tls/certs/postfix-server.pem
smtpd_tls_key_file = $smtpd_tls_cert_file
smtpd_tls_security_level = may
smtp_tls_security_level = may
smtp_tls_loglevel = 1
smtpd_tls_loglevel = 1
```

Then save and close this file. Note that setting `smtpd_tls_security_level` to `may` will activate TLS encryption if available in the mail client program, otherwise it will use an unencrypted connection. You should only set this value to `encrypt` (which will enforce SSL/TLS encryption in any case) if you are absolutely sure that all your senders to your mail server are supporting this feature. If any sender (external MTA or mail client) does not support this feature, the connection will be refused. This means that e-mails from such sources will not be delivered into your local mailboxes. We also specified TLS encryption for outgoing SMTP connections from our Postfix server to other MTAs where possible using `smtp_tls_security_level = may`. By setting both the Postfix's client and server mode TLS log level to `1` we get more verbose output so we can check if the TLS connections are working. Some very old mail clients use an ancient port 465 for encrypting SMTP over SSL/TLS instead of the standard SMTP port 25.

In order to activate this feature, open `/etc/postfix/master.cf` and search, then uncomment (remove # at the start of each line) the following lines, so they read:

```
smtps          inet   n      -      n      -      -      smtpd
-o syslog_name=postfix/smtps
-o smtpd_tls_wrappermode=yes
```

Save and close the file, and then restart Postfix. Next, we need to open the SMTPS port in the firewall to allow incoming connections to our server. Since no SMTPS firewalld rule is available in CentOS 7, we will create our own service file first using the `sed` utility:

```
sed 's/25/465/g' /usr/lib/firewalld/services/smtp.xml | sed 's/Mail
(SMTP)/Mail (SMTP) over SSL/g' > /etc/firewalld/services/smtps.xml

firewall-cmd --reload

firewall-cmd --permanent --add-service=smtps; firewall-cmd --reload
```

You should now be able to test if an SMTPS connection can be made by using our `swaks` SMTP command line tool with the `-tls` parameter from a remote computer to our Postfix server running on IP 192.168.1.100, for example `swaks --server 192.168.1.100 --to john@centos7.home -tls`. This command line will test if the SMTP server supports TLS encryption (`STARTTLS`) and exit with an error message if it is not available for any reason. A working output would look as follows (truncated to only show you the most important lines):

```
 -> STARTTLS
<-  220 2.0.0 Ready to start TLS
=== TLS started with cipher TLSv1.2:ECDHE-RSA-AES128-GCM-SHA256:128
 ~> This is a test mailing
<~  250 2.0.0 Ok: queued as E36F652B38
```

You can then also recheck your TLS setup by going to the main mail log file on your Postfix server and watching for the following line corresponding to your swaks test mail from the last step (your output will be different):

```
Anonymous TLS connection established from unknown[192.168.1.22]:
TLSv1.2 with cipher ECDHE-RSA-AES256-GCM-SHA384 (256/256 bits)
```

Configure BIND to use your new mailserver

After our domain-wide Postfix server has been installed and configured, we should now announce this new mail service in our domain using a DNS server. Refer to *Chapter 8, Working with FTP* for details on how to set up and configure a BIND server, and especially read the section about the **Mail eXchanger** (**MX**) record if you haven't already. Then add a new MX entry to your BIND forward and corresponding reverse zone file. In your forward zone file, add the following lines for our Postfix server with the IP `192.168.1.100`:

```
IN      MX      10      mailhost.centos7.home.
mailhost                IN      A       192.168.1.100
```

In your reverse zone file, you could add the following lines instead:

```
100                    IN  PTR        mailhost.centos7.local.
```

Working with Postfix

In a previous recipe, we learned how to install and configure Postfix as our domain-wide e-mail server. When it comes to working with e-mails, there are lots of different tools and programs available for Linux and we already showed you how to send e-mails through the `sendmail` program as well as the `swaks` utility. Here in this recipe, we will show you how to work with one of the most commonly used mail utilities in Unix and Linux, called `mailx`, which has some useful features missing in the sendmail package for sending mails or reading your mailbox.

How to do it...

We will begin this recipe by installing the `mailx` package on our server running our domain-wide Postfix service, as it is not available on CentOS 7 by default.

1. Begin by logging in as root and typing the following command:

   ```
   yum install mailx
   ```

2. The easiest way is to use `mailx` with its standard input mode, as follows:

   ```
   echo "this is the mail body." | mail -s "subject" john@centos7.home
   ```

3. You can also send mails from a text file. This is useful when calling the `mailx` command from a shell script, using multiple recipients, or attaching some files to the e-mail:

   ```
   cat ~/.bashrc | mail -s "Content of roots bashrc file" john
   echo "another mail body" | mail -s "body" john,paul@example.com,chris
   echo "this is the email body" | mailx -s "another testmail but with attachment" -a "/path/to/file1" -a "/path/to/another/file" john@gmail.com
   ```

Connecting mailx to a remote MTA

One big advantage over the `sendmail` program is that we can use `mailx` to directly connect to and communicate with remote MTA mail servers. In order to test this feature, log in to another Linux-based computer, which should be in the same network as our Postfix server, install the `mailx` package, and send a mail through our Postfix server's IP address `192.168.1.100` (we have already opened the incoming SMTP firewall port in a previous recipe). In our example, we will send a local mail to the user `john`:

```
echo "This is the body" | mail -S smtp=192.168.1.100 -s "This is a remote test" -v john@centos7.home
```

Reading your local mails from the mailbox

Not only can the `mailx` program send e-mail messages to any SMTP server, it also provides a convenient mail reader interface for your local mailbox when started locally on the Postfix server. If you run the mail program with `-f` specifying a user mailbox, the program will start by showing you all the inbox e-mails. But remember that `mailx` can only read local mailboxes when the program is started on the same server your mailboxes are located at (if you want to use it to access your mailbox remotely you need to install an MTA access agent such as Dovecot—see later—with POP3 or IMAP). For example, login as Linux system user `john` on the Postfix server, and then, to open the mail reader with your user's local mailbox, type: `mailx -f ~/Maildir`.

You will now be presented with a list of all the mail messages in your current inbox. If you want to read a specific mail, you need to type in its number and press the *Return* key. After reading it, you can type *d* followed by *Return* to delete it or *r* followed by *Return* to reply to it. To go back to your current mail message overview screen, type *z* followed by *Return*. If you have more than one screen of mail messages, type *z-* (z minus) followed by *Return* to go back one page. Type *x* followed by *Return* to exit the program. To learn more, refer to the `mailx` manual (`man mailx`).

How it works...

In this recipe, we showed you how to install and use `mailx`, a program to send and read your Internet mail. It is based on an old Unix mail program called Berkely mail and provides the functionality of the POSIX `mailx` command. It should be installed on every serious CentOS 7 server because it has some advantages over the `sendmail` program and understands the protocols IMAP, POP3, and SMTP (If you need an even more user-friendly mail reader and sender, you can check out mutt. Type `yum install mutt` to install it. Then type `man mutt` to read its manual).

So what did we learn from this experience?

We started this recipe by installing the `mailx` package using the YUM package manager on our Postfix server. It includes the `mailx` command line program which can be run either with the command `mail` or `mailx`. Afterwards, we ran the program with the `-s` parameter, which specifies an e-mail subject and; also you need a recipient e-mail address as argument, either an external address or a local Linux system user name or mail. Without anything else, `mailx` suspects it's running on the same server as the mail server is on, so it implicitly sends the mail to the localhost MTA, which is Postfix in our example. Also, in its most simple form, `mailx` starts in interactive mode, which lets you type in the message body fields manually at the command line. This is good for quickly writing a mail for testing, but in most cases you will use `mailx` by piping in content from another source. Here we showed you how to do this by using the `echo` command to write a string to the Standard Input (STDIN) of `mailx`, but you can also `cat` a file content into it.

One often used example is to send some kind of file output or a log file content of a failing command to an administrator user or system reports at a certain scheduled time point using `cron`. Afterwards, we saw that we could also send mails to multiple recipients by comma-separating their e-mail addresses, and showed you how to send attachments along with your mail messages by using the `-a` option. In the next section, we then showed you how to send mails to a remote SMTP mail server using the `-S` option to set internal options (`variable=value`). This is a very useful feature if you haven't specified your standard mail server on your DNS server or for testing a remote mail server. Finally, in the last section we showed you how you could read your local mailbox on your Postfix server using `mailx`. It has a convenient browsing functionality to read, delete, and reply, and do advanced e-mail management for your local mailbox. You do this by typing in commands into the `mailx` interactive sessions followed by pressing the *Return* key. Remember, if you don't like this way of browsing your mails, you can also always read or filter your mails in your user's `~/Maildir` directory using command-line tools, such as `grep`, `less`, and so on. For example, to search all new mails for the case-intensive keyword `PackPub.com`, type `grep -i packtpub ~/Maildir/new`.

Delivering the mail with Dovecot

In a previous recipe, you were shown how to configure Postfix as a domain-wide mail transport agent. As we have learned in the first recipe of this chapter, Postfix only understands the SMTP protocol and does a remarkable job to transport messages from another MTA or mail user client to other remote mail servers or storing mails which are destinated to itself into its local mailboxes. After storing or relaying mails, Postfix jobs end. Postfix can only understand and speak the SMTP protocol and is not capable of sending messages to anything other than MTAs. Any possible recipient user for a mail message who wants to read his mails would now need to log in to the server running the Postfix service using ssh and look into his local mailbox directory, or alternatively use `mailx` locally to view his messages on a regular basis to see if there are any new mails. This is highly inconvenient and nobody would use such a system. Instead, the users choose to access and read their mail from their own workstations other than where our Postfix server is located. Therefore, another group of MTAs has been developed, sometimes are called **access agents** and which have the main functionality to synchronize or transfer those local mailbox messages from the server running the Postfix daemon over to external mailing programs where users can read them. These MTA systems use different protocols than SMTP, namely POP3 or IMAP. One such MTA program is Dovecot. Most professional server administrators would agree that Postfix and Dovecot are perfect partners and it is the purpose of this recipe to learn how to configure Postfix to work with Dovecot in order to provide a basic POP3/IMAP and a POP3/IMAP over SSL (POP3S/IMAPS) service for our mailboxes to provide an industry standard e-mail service for your users across the local network.

Getting ready

To complete this recipe, you will require a working installation of the CentOS 7 operating system with root privileges, a console-based text editor of your choice, and a connection to the Internet in order to download additional packages. It is also assumed that you are working through this chapter recipe by recipe in the order that they appear and for this reason it is expected that Postfix has been configured as a domain-wide MTA.

 This recipe serves as a guide to setting up a basic POP3S/IMAPS service for trusted users on a local network. It is not suitable for general Internet use without applying additional security measures.

How to do it...

Dovecot is not installed by default, and for this reason we must begin by installing the necessary packages by following the given steps:

1. To start, log in as root and type in the following command:

   ```
   yum install dovecot
   ```

2. Once installed, enable the Dovecot service at boot by typing:

   ```
   systemctl enable dovecot
   ```

3. Now open the main Dovecot configuration file in your favorite text editor, after creating a backup copy, by typing:

   ```
   cp /etc/dovecot/dovecot.conf /etc/dovecot/dovecot.conf.BAK
   ```
   ```
   vi /etc/dovecot/dovecot.conf
   ```

4. Begin by confirming the `protocols` we want to use by activating (removing the # sign at the beginning of the line) and modifying the following line, so it reads:

   ```
   protocols = pop3 imap imaps pop3s
   ```

5. Next, enable Dovecot to listen to all network interfaces instead of only the loopback address. Search for the line `#listen = *, ::`, then modify it so it reads:

   ```
   listen = *
   ```

6. Now save and close the file in the usual way before making a backup of the `10-mail.conf` file and afterwards opening it in your favorite text editor:

   ```
   cp /etc/dovecot/conf.d/10-mail.conf /etc/dovecot/conf.d/10-mail.conf.BAK
   ```
   ```
   vi /etc/dovecot/conf.d/10-mail.conf
   ```

7. Scroll down and uncomment (remove # character) the following line, so it reads:

```
mail_location = maildir:~/Maildir
```

8. Again, save and close the file in the usual way before creating a backup copy and then opening the following file in your favorite text editor:

```
cp /etc/dovecot/conf.d/20-pop3.conf /etc/dovecot/conf.d/20-pop3.conf.BAK
vi /etc/dovecot/conf.d/20-pop3.conf
```

9. Start by uncommenting the following line:

```
pop3_uidl_format = %08Xu%08Xv
```

10. Now scroll down and amend the following line:

```
pop3_client_workarounds = outlook-no-nuls oe-ns-eoh
```

11. Save and close the file in the usual way. Now we will allow plain text logins. To do this, make a backup before opening the following file:

```
cp /etc/dovecot/conf.d/10-auth.conf /etc/dovecot/conf.d/10-auth.conf.BAK
vi /etc/dovecot/conf.d/10-auth.conf
```

12. Change the line #disable_plaintext_auth = yes to state:

```
disable_plaintext_auth = no
```

13. Save and close the file. In our final configuration setting, we will tell Dovecot to use our self-signed server certificate. Just use your Postfix certificate from another recipe in this chapter or create a new one (otherwise skip this step):

```
cd /etc/pki/tls/certs; make postfix-server.pem
```

14. Open Dovecot's standard SSL config file after making a backup of the file:

```
cp /etc/dovecot/conf.d/10-ssl.conf /etc/dovecot/conf.d/10-ssl.conf.BAK
vi /etc/dovecot/conf.d/10-ssl.conf
```

15. Now change the following line (ssl = required) to read:

```
ssl = yes
```

16. Now change the following two lines to point to your server's own certificate path:

```
ssl_cert = < /etc/pki/tls/certs/postfix-server.pem
ssl_key = </etc/pki/tls/certs/postfix-server.pem
```

17. Save and close this file. Next, enable IMAP, IMAPS, POP3, and POP3S ports in our firewall to allow incoming connections on the corresponding ports. For POP3 and IMAP, we need to specify our own `firewalld` service files, since they are not available in CentOS 7 by default:

```
sed 's/995/110/g' /usr/lib/firewalld/services/pop3s.xml | sed 's/
over SSL//g' > /etc/firewalld/services/pop3.xml
sed 's/993/143/g' /usr/lib/firewalld/services/imaps.xml | sed 's/
over SSL//g' > /etc/firewalld/services/imap.xml
firewall-cmd --reload
for s in pop3 imap pop3s imaps; do firewall-cmd --permanent --add-
service=$s; done;firewall-cmd --reload
```

18. Now save and close the file before starting the Dovecot service:

```
systemctl start dovecot
```

19. Finally, to test our new POP3/SMTP network service, just login on another computer in the same network and run the following commands to use `mailx` to access the local mailboxes on the remote Postfix server, which is provided by Dovecot with the different access agent protocols. In our example, we want to access the local mailbox of the system user `john` on our Postfix server with the IP `192.168.1.100` (to login to john's account, you need his Linux user password) remotely:

```
mailx -f pop3://john@192.168.1.100
mailx -f imap://john@192.168.1.100
```

20. Next, to test the secure connections, use the following commands and type `yes` to confirm that the certificate is self-signed and not trusted:

```
mailx -v -S nss-config-dir=/etc/pki/nssdb -f pop3s://
john@192.168.1.100
mailx -v -S nss-config-dir=/etc/pki/nssdb -f imaps://
john@192.168.1.100
```

21. For all four commands, you should see the normal `mailx` inbox view of your mailbox with all your mail messages of user `john` as you would run the `mailx` command locally on the Postfix server to read local mails.

How it works...

Having successfully completed this recipe, you have just created a basic POP3/SMTP service, (with or without SSL encryption) for all the valid server users in your network, which will deliver local mails from the Postfix server to the client's e-mail program. Every local system user can directly authenticate and connect to the mail server and fetch their mail remotely. Of course, there is still much more that can be done to enhance the service, but you can now enable all local system account holders to configure their favorite e-mail desktop software to send and receive e-mail messages using your server.

POP3 downloads the mails from the server on a local machine and deletes them afterwards, whereas IMAP synchronizes your mails with your mail server without deleting them.

So what did we learn from this experience?

We started the recipe by installing Dovecot. Having done this, we then enabled Dovecot to run at boot before proceeding to make a few brief changes to a series of configuration files. Starting with the need to determine which protocol will be used in the Dovecot configuration file at `/etc/dovecot/dovecot.cf` here we will use: IMAP, POP3, IMAPS, and POP3S. As with most other essential networking services, after installation they only listen on the loopback device, so we enabled Dovecot to listen to all network interfaces installed in the server. In the `10-mail.conf` file we then confirmed the mailbox directory location for Dovecot (with the `mail_location` directive) as the location Postfix will put them into on receiving mails so Dovecot can find them here and pick them up. Following this, we then opened the POP3 protocol in `20-pop3.conf` by adding a fix relating to various e-mail clients (for example, for the Outlook client) using the `pop3_uidl_format` and `pop3_client_workarounds` directives. Finally, we enabled plain text authorization by making several changes to `/etc/dovecot/conf.d/10-auth.conf`. Remember that using plain text authorization with POP3 or IMAP without SSL encryption is considered insecure but because we were concentrating on a local area network (for a group of trusted server users) we should not necessarily see this as a risk. Afterwards, we enabled POP3 and IMAP over SSL (POP3S and IMAPS) by pointing the `ssl` directives in the `10-ssl.conf` file to some existing self-signed server certificates. Here we changed `ssl = required` to `ssl=yes` to not force the client connecting to the Dovecot service to use SSL encryption, as we do want to give the user the choice to enable encrypted authentication if he likes to but not make it mandatory for older clients. Afterwards, to make our Dovecot service available from the other computers in our network, we had to enable the four ports to allow POP3, IMAP, POP3S, and IMAPS, 993, 995, 110, 143, by using the predefined `firewalld` service files and creating the missing ones for IMAP and POP3 ourselves. Later, we started the Dovecot service and tested our new POP3/IMAP server using the `mailx` command remotely. By supplying an `-f` file parameter, we were able to specify our protocol and location. For using SSL connections, we needed to supply an additional `nss-config-dir` option pointing to our local Network Security Services database where certificates are stored in CentOS 7.

Remember, if you happen to encounter any errors, you should always refer to the log file located at `/var/log/maillog`. Using plain text authorization should not be used in a real corporate environment and POP3/IMAP over SSL should be preferred.

There's more...

In the main recipe, you were shown how to install Dovecot in order to enable trusted local system users with system accounts to send and receive e-mails. These users will be able to use their existing username as the basis of their e-mail address, but by making a few enhancements you can quickly enable aliases, which is a way to define alternative e-mail addresses for existing users.

To start building a list of user aliases, you should begin by opening the following file in your favorite text editor:

`vi /etc/aliases`

Now add your new identities to the end of the file, where `<username>` will be the name of the actual system account:

```
#users aliases for mail
newusernamea:     <username>
newusernameb:     <username>
```

For example, if you have a user called `john` who currently (only) accepts e-mails at `john@centos7.home`, but you want to create a new alias for `john` called `johnwayne@centos7.home`, you will write:

```
johnwayne:     john
```

Repeat this action for all the aliases, but when you have finished remember to save and close the file in the usual way before running the following command: `newaliases`.

Setting up e-mail software

There are a vast number of e-mail clients on the market and by now you will want to start setting up your local users to be able to send and receive e-mails. This isn't complicated by any means, but in order to have a good starting point you will want to consider the following principles. The format of the e-mail address will be `system_username@domain-name.home`.

The incoming POP3 settings will be similar to the following:

```
mailserver.centos7.home, Port 110
Username: system_username
Connection Security: None
Authentication: Password/None
```

For POP3S, just change the port to `995` and use `Connection Security: SSL/TLS`. For IMAP, just change the port to `143`, and for IMAPS use port `993` and `Connection Security: SSL/TLS`.

The outgoing SMTP settings will be similar to the following:

```
mailserver.centos7.home, Port 25
Username: system_username
Connection Security: None
Authentication: None
```

Using Fetchmail

So far in this chapter, we have shown you two different forms of MTA. First we introduced you to the Postfix MTA, which is a transport agent used for routing e-mails from a mail client to or between mail servers and delivering them to the local mailboxes on the mail server using the SMTP protocol. Then we showed you another type of MTA which sometimes called an access agent and which the Dovecot program can be used for. This delivers mails from the local Postfix mailboxes to any remote mail client programs using the POP3 or IMAP protocol. Now we will introduce you to a third type of MTA, which can be termed a retrieval agent, and explain what we will use the program Fetchmail for. Nowadays, almost everybody has more than one e-mail account, from one or more different mail providers, which can be hard to maintain if you need to login to all those different webmail sites or use different accounts in your mail program. This is where Fetchmail comes into play. It is a program, running on the same server as your domain-wide Postfix mail server and which can retrieve all your different e-mails from all your different mail providers and pass them into the local user mailboxes of your Postfix MTA. Once they are stored in their appropriate place, users can access all these mails in the usual way provided by the access agent Dovecot over POP3 or IMAP. Here in this recipe we will show you how to install and integrate Fetchmail into your server running the Postfix MTA.

Getting ready

To complete this recipe, you will require a working installation of the CentOS 7 operating system with root privileges, a console-based text editor of your choice, and a connection to the Internet in order to download additional packages. It is assumed that you are working through this chapter recipe by recipe in the order that they appear and for this reason it is expected that Postfix has been configured as a domain-wide MTA and Dovecot has been installed to provide a POP3/IMAP mail access service. In order to test Fetchmail in this recipe, we also need to have registered some external e-mail addresses: you need the name of the external e-mail server address and the port of your e-mail provider, as well as your user login credentials at hand. Often you can find this information from your mail provider's Frequently Asked Questions (FAQ) section on their webpage. Also, for some e-mail addresses you need to first enable POP3 or IMAP in your e-mail settings before you can use Fetchmail.

How to do it...

Fetchmail is not installed by default and for this reason we must begin by installing the necessary packages. Perform the following steps:

1. To begin, log in your mail server running your Postfix server and type:

   ```
   yum install fetchmail
   ```

2. Once installed, we will log into a system's user account for which we want to enable Fetchmail to download external mail from an external mail provider into his local mailbox, in our example it will be the system user john: su - john. Now let's configure Fetchmail with an external e-mail address. If your e-mail provider is called mailhost.com and it runs a POP3 server at pop.mailhost.com and IMAP on imap.mailhost.com with the username <user-name>, here (please substitute your own values) is an example command line to test connecting and fetching mails from this provider:

   ```
   fetchmail pop.mailhost.com -p pop3 -u <user-name> -k -v
   ```

3. If you want to use IMAP with the same provider instead:

   ```
   fetchmail imap.mailhost.com -p IMAP -u <user-name> -v
   ```

4. If the Fetchmail command was successful, all new messages will be downloaded from the server into your local mailbox in your user account.

How it works...

Here in this recipe, we showed you how to install and test Fetchmail, which provides automated mail retrieval capabilities for any user account having a local mailbox on our Postfix server. As a result, for a client connecting to the mail server using POP3 or IMAP, the mails fetched this way look like normal incoming e-mails. Fetchmail is often used to combine and bundle all your different mail accounts into one single account, but you can also use it if your mail provider does not have good virus or spam filter. Here you download the mails from your host's e-mail server, then process the mails using tools such as SpamAssassin or ClamAV before sending mails to your clients.

So what did we learn from this experience?

We began this recipe by installing the YUM package for Fetchmail. As we wanted to set up Fetchmail for a system user's mailbox called john, next we logged in as this user. Afterwards, we tested the Fetchmail program by running a simple command line to fetch mail from a single mail provider. As said before, for a successful login to your external mail provider, you need to know the exact login information (server address, port, username, and password, as well as the type of protocol) of the server before you can use Fetchmail.

Remember that, while some e-mail providers let the user decide if he wants to connect securely using SSL or not, some hosters such as gmail.com only allow secure connections. This means that the example command shown here in this recipe is likely to fail on every major e-mail provider if they don't support POP3/IMAP access without SSL connections. Proceed to the next section in order to learn how to use Fetchmail with SSL POP3/IMAP encryption.

You should always prefer SSL encryption if your mail provider offers both. Also, some providers such as gmail.com only let the user use their services via webmail and disable POP3/IMAP service features by default; you need to enable them in your account's settings on your provider's website (see later).

We specified with the -p parameter which mail protocol to use with the fetchmail command. With the -u parameter, we specified the user identification to be used when logging in to the mailserver, which is completely dependent on our e-mail provider. For POP3, we applied the -k flag to ensure that the e-mails only get fetched from the server but never deleted (which is the default when using the POP3 protocol). Finally, we used -v to make the output more verbose and give us more information for our simple test. If your e-mail provider supports SSL, you also need to add a -ssl flag to the Fetchmail command as well as the root certificate of the mail server (see the next section for more information). If you run the previous command, Fetchmail will immediately start asking the mail server for any mail in the inbox on the server and download anything to your user's local mailbox.

There's more...

In this section, we will show you how to configure Fetchmail to download all your e-mails from some real-life mail providers using POP3S, IMAPS, and the POP3 and IMAP protocols to your local mailbox on the Postfix server using a configuration file. Finally, we will show you how to automate the Fetchmail process.

Configuring Fetchmail with gmail.com and outlook.com e-mail accounts

Here we will configure the different external mail accounts which Fetchmail will download from: the popular gmail.com and outlook.com e-mail providers and a hypothetical one at my-email-server.com.

As we learned in the main recipe that Fetchmail processes configuration options on the command line by default, this should not be your preferred way of using Fetchmail to download your mail from different mail accounts automatically. Normally Fetchmail should be running as a service in daemon mode in the background at boot time or with a cron job and polls a list of mail servers defined in a special configuration file at specific time intervals. With this you can conveniently configure multiple mail servers and a long list of other options.

At the time of writing this book, for gmail.com to work with Fetchmail you need to login to the gmail.com website with your user account and first enable IMAP by going to your accounts settings in **Forwarding and POP/IMAP**. Also, enable **Allow less secure apps** under **Sign-in & security** in **My account**. For outlook.com, login to your mail account on the webpage, then click on **options**, again click on **options**, then click on **Connect devices and apps with POP**, and then click on **enable POP**.

Both outlook.com and gmail.com use secure POP3S and IMAPS protocols, so you need to download and install the root certificates they are signing their SSL certificates with on your Fetchmail server first in order to be able to use their services. Here we can install the Mozilla CA certification bundle, which has been compiled by the Mozilla foundation and includes the most commonly used root server certificates used by all major websites and services, such as those used by our mail providers. For gmail.com we need the Equifax Secure Certificate Authority root certificate and for outlook.com we need the root server certificate from Globalsign. Fetchmail needs these root certificates to verify the validity of any other SSL certificate downloaded from the e-mail server. Login as root on your Postfix server and install the following package:

```
yum install ca-certificates
```

Afterwards, login as a Linux system user, for example, john, who we will create a new Fetchmail configuration file for, and who already has a local Postfix mailbox directory on our server located in his home directory under ~/Maildir. Now before configuring any account in the Fetchmail configuration file, you should always first test if the connection and authentication to the specific account are working with the Fetchmail command line, as shown in the previous recipe. For testing our different mail providers' accounts, we need three different command line calls. For testing if your provider is using SSL encryption, you need the -ssl flag; a typical output for a mail provider who is not allowing non-SSL connections could be:

```
Fetchmail: SSL connection failed.
Fetchmail: socket error while fetching from <userid>@<mailserver>
Fetchmail: Query status=2 (SOCKET)
```

If your google and outlook username is johndoe at both mail providers for testing google with the IMAPS protocol try (enter your e-mail user's password when prompted):

```
fetchmail imap.gmail.com -p IMAP --ssl -u johndoe@gmail.com -k -v
```

If the login was successful, the output should be similar to (truncated):

```
Fetchmail: IMAP< A0002 OK johndoe@gmail.com authenticated (Success)
9 messages (2 seen) for johndoe at imap.gmail.com.
Fetchmail: IMAP> A0005 FETCH 1:9 RFC822.SIZE
```

For testing `outlook.com` with POP3S, use:

```
fetchmail pop-mail.outlook.com -p POP3 --ssl -u johndoe@outlook.com -k
-v
```

On success, the output should be similar to (it has been truncated):

```
Fetchmail: POP3> USER johndoe@outlook.com
Fetchmail: POP3< +OK password required
Fetchmail: POP3< +OK mailbox has 1 messages
```

For our third hypothetical e-mail account at `my-email-server.com`, we will use POP3 or IMAP without SSL so test it using our account:

```
fetchmail pop3.my-email-server.com -p POP3 -u johndoe -k -v
fetchmail imap.my-email-server.com -p IMAP -u johndoe  -v
```

You should also check if all the fetched mails from your external providers have been downloaded correctly. View your system user's local mailbox using the `mailx` command (`mailx -f ~/Maildir`). After we successfully verify that Fetchmail is able to connect to the servers and fetch some mails, we now can proceed to create a local Fetchmail configuration file in our system user's home directory in order to automate this process and configure multiple mail addresses. Start by opening a new empty file using `vi ~/.fetchmailrc`. Remember that all the commands which can be put on the command line can also be used with slightly different names in the configuration file (and much more). Now put in the following content (replace `john` with your actual Linux system user, `johndoe` with your e-mail user account name, and `secretpass` with your actual mail password for this account):

```
set postmaster "john"
set logfile fetchmail.log
poll imap.gmail.com with proto IMAP
user 'johndoe@gmail.com' there with password 'secretpass' is john here
ssl
fetchall
poll pop-mail.outlook.com with proto POP3
user 'johndoe@outlook.com' there with password 'secretpass' is john
here
ssl
fetchall
poll pop3.my-email-server.com with proto POP3
user 'johndoe@my-email-server.com' there with password 'secretpass' is
john here
fetchall
```

Save and close this file. In this file, we used the following important commands:

- `postmaster`: Defines the local Linux user which will receive all the warning or error mails if Fetchmail runs into problems.

- `logfile`: Defines a filename for a log file, which can be very helpful for us to supervise and debug Fetchmail output when it's running continuously over a long period of time in the background.

- `poll` section: Specifies downloading mails from a specific mail provider. For every mail account, you will define one such poll section. As you can see here, the syntax is very similar to the one used on the command line when we tested the single connections. With `proto` we define the `mail` protocol, `user` is the login user for the mail account, `password` is the login password of your account, and with the `is <username> here` parameter you specify which local system user account this mail account is tied to. For SSL connections you need the `ssl` flag, and we specified the `fetchall` parameter to make sure we also download all the e-mail messages flagged as `read` by the e-mail provider as otherwise Fetchmail would not download e-mails that have already been read.

Next change the permissions of the `.fetchmailrc` file because it contains passwords and should therefore not be read by anyone other than our own user:

```
chmod 600 ~/.fetchmailrc
```

Finally, we execute Fetchmail with the settings given in our configuration file. For testing, we will use a very verbose parameter here: `fetchmail -vvvv`. All the new mails from all your different e-mail providers should now be fetched, so afterwards you should go through the output and see if every server was ready and could be polled just as the single tests we did on the command line tests earlier. All the new mails should have been downloaded to the local mailbox, so in order to read your local mails you can use the `mailx` command as usual, like: `mail -f ~/Maildir`.

Automating Fetchmail

As just said, we can now manually start the polling process every time we want by just typing in `fetchmail` on the command line. This will poll and fetch all new mails from the mail servers specified in our new configuration file and then after processing each entry once it will exit the program. Now what's still missing is a mechanism to continuously query our mail servers at a specific interval updating our mailbox whenever new mails can be fetched. Here you can use two approaches. Either run the `fetchmail` command as a cron job or as an alternative you can start Fetchmail in daemon mode (use the parameter `set daemon` in your `.fetchmailrc` config file to activate it.) and put it in the background. This way Fetchmail will run constantly and wake up at a given time point and start the polling until everything finishes processing and then go back to sleep until the next interval has been reached.

As both methods are basically the same, here we will show you how to run Fetchmail as a cron job, which is much easier to set up because we don't have to create some custom systemd service files (currently in CentOS 7 there is no `fetchmail systemd` service available out-of-the box). For every system user (for example, `john`) who has a `fetchmail` configuration file, to start the e-mail server polling process every 10 minutes type in the following command once to register the cron job:

```
crontab -l | { cat; echo "*/10 * * * * /usr/bin/fetchmail &> /dev/null
"; } | crontab -
```

Do not set the Fetchmail polling cycle shorter than every 5 minutes; otherwise, some mail providers may block or ban you, as it just overloads their systems.

12

Providing Web Services

In this chapter, we will cover the following:

- ▶ Installing Apache and serving web pages
- ▶ Enabling system users and building publishing directories
- ▶ Implementing name-based hosting
- ▶ Implementing CGI with Perl and Ruby
- ▶ Installing, configuring, and testing PHP
- ▶ Securing Apache
- ▶ Setting up HTTPS with Secure Sockets Layer (SSL)

Introduction

This chapter is a collection of recipes that provides the necessary steps to serve web pages. From installing a web server to delivering a dynamic page through SSL, this chapter provides the starting point required to implement an industry standard hosting solution anywhere and at any time.

Installing Apache and serving web pages

In this recipe, we will learn how to install and configure the Apache web server to enable the serving of static web pages. Apache is one of the world's most popular open source web servers. It runs as the backend for over half of all the Internet's web sites and can be used to serve both static and dynamic web pages. Commonly referred to as `httpd`, it supports an extensive range of features. It is the purpose of this recipe to show you how easily it can be installed using the YUM package manager so that you can maintain your server with the latest security updates. Apache 2.4 is available on CentOS 7.

Getting ready

To complete this recipe, you will require a working installation of the CentOS 7 operating system with root privileges, a console-based text editor of your choice, and a connection to the Internet in order to download additional packages. It is expected that your server will be using a static IP address and a hostname.

How to do it...

Apache is not installed by default and for this reason we will begin by installing the necessary packages using the YUM package manager.

1. To begin, log in as root and type the following command:

   ```
   yum install httpd
   ```

2. Create a home page by typing:

   ```
   vi /var/www/html/index.html
   ```

3. Now add the required HTML. You can use the following code as a starting point but it is expected that you will want to modify it to suit your own needs:

   ```
   <!DOCTYPE html>
   <html lang="en">
   <head><title>Welcome to my new web server</title></head>
   <body><h1>Welcome to my new web server</h1>
   <p>Lorem ipsum dolor sit amet, adipiscing elit.</p></body>
   </html>
   ```

4. You can now remove the Apache 2 test page with the following command:

   ```
   rm -f /etc/httpd/conf.d/welcome.conf
   ```

5. Having completed these steps, we will now consider the need to configure the httpd service for basic usage. To do this, open the httpd configuration file in your favorite text editor by typing (after you have made a backup of the file):

   ```
   cp /etc/httpd/conf/httpd.conf /etc/httpd/conf/httpd.conf.BAK
   ```
   ```
   vi /etc/httpd/conf/httpd.conf
   ```

6. Now scroll down to find the line ServerAdmin root@localhost. The traditional approach to setting this value is based on the use of the webmaster identity, so simply modify the e-mail address to reflect something more relevant to your own needs. For example, if your server's domain name was www.centos7.home then your entry will look similar to this:

   ```
   ServerAdmin webmaster@centos7.home
   ```

7. Now scroll down a few more lines to find the `ServerName` directive as follows: `#ServerName www.example.com:80`. Uncomment this line (which means remove the leading # sign at its beginning) and replace the value `www.example.com` with something more appropriate to your own needs. For example, if your server's domain name was `www.centos7.home` then your entry will look as follows:

ServerName www.centos7.home:80

8. Next, we will expand the `DirectoryIndex` directive a bit more. Find the line `DirectoryIndex index.html`, which is part of the `<IfModule dir_module>` block, then change it to:

DirectoryIndex index.html index.htm

9. Save and close the file, and then type the following command to test the config file:

apachectl configtest

10. Next, let's configure our web server's firewall by allowing incoming `http` connections (this defaults to port 80) to the server:

firewall-cmd --permanent --add-service http && firewall-cmd --reload

11. Now proceed to set the `httpd` service to start at boot and start the service:

systemctl enable httpd && systemctl start httpd

12. You can now test `httpd` from any computer in the same network as your web server (both systems should be able to see and ping each other), pointing your browser at the following URL by replacing `XXX.XXX.XXX.XXX` with the IP address of your server in order to see our own custom Apache test page we created:

http://XXX.XXX.XXX.XXX.

13. Alternatively, if you don't have a web browser, you can check if Apache is up and running using `curl` by fetching our test page on any computer in your network:

curl http://XXX.XXX.XXX

How it works...

Apache is a software package that enables you to publish and serve web pages, and is more commonly known as `httpd`, Apache2 or simply Apache. It was the purpose of this recipe to show you how easily CentOS enables you to get started with your very first website.

So what did we learn from this experience?

We began the recipe by installing Apache via the YUM package manager and the package named `httpd`. Having done this, we learned that on CentOS 7 the default location to serve static HTML is `/var/www/html` so our first task was to create a suitable home page, which we put in `/var/www/html/index.html`. Here we used a basic HTML template to get you started and it is expected that you would like to customize the look and feel of this page yourself. Following this, we then removed the default Apache 2 welcome page found in `/etc/httpd/conf.d/welcome.conf`. Following this, the next stage was to open the `httpd.conf` configuration file in our favorite text editor after making a backup of it so we could revert our changes if any problems occurred. First we defined the server's e-mail address and the server name, which often appear in the error messages on the server-generated web pages; for this reason it should reflect your domain name. Next, we adjusted the `DirectoryIndex` directive, which defines which files will be sent first to the browser if a directory is requested. Often people request not a specific web page but a directory instead. For example, if you browse to `www.example.com`, you request a directory, while `www.example.com/welcome.html` is a specific web page. By default Apache sends the `index.html` in the requested directory but we expanded this since a lot of websites use the `.htm` extension instead. Finally, we saved and closed the `httpd` configuration file in the usual way before proceeding to check if the Apache configuration file contained any errors by using the `apachectl configtest` command. This should print out a `Syntax OK` message so we could enable the `httpd` service to start at boot time. We had to open the standard HTTP port 80 in our firewalld to allow incoming HTTP requests to the server, and finally we then started the `httpd` service. Remember, you can also always reload Apache's configuration file if it has been changed without fully restarting the service, by using: `systemctl reload httpd`. Having completed these steps, it was simply a matter of opening your browser from another computer in the same network and electing a method of viewing our new Apache start page. You can use your server's IP address (for example, `http://192.168.1.100`), while those with hostname support can type the hostname (for example, `http://www.centos7.home`) instead. Apache's access and error log files can be found in `/var/log/httpd`. To get a live view of who is currently accessing your web server, open `/var/log/httpd/access_log`; to see all the errors, type `/var/log/httpd/error_log`.

Apache is a big subject and we cannot cover every nuance, but over the coming recipes we will continue to expose additional functionalities that will enable you to build a web server of choice.

Enabling system users and building publishing directories

In this recipe, we will learn how Apache provides you with the option to allow your system users to host web pages within their home directories. This approach has been used by ISPs since the outset of web hosting and in many respects it continues to flourish due to its ability to avoid the more complex method of virtual hosting. In the previous recipe you were shown how to install the Apache web server, and with the desire to provide hosting facilities for system users, it is the purpose of this recipe to show you how this can be achieved in CentOS 7.

Getting ready

To complete this recipe, you will require a working installation of the CentOS 7 operating system with root privileges and a console-based text editor of your choice. It is expected that your server will be using a static IP address that supports a hostname or domain name and that the Apache web server is already installed and currently running. Also, at least one system user account should be available on the server.

How to do it...

To provide the functionality offered by this recipe, no additional packages are required but we will need to make some modifications to the Apache configuration file.

1. To begin, log in as root and open the Apache userdir configuration file in your favorite text editor by typing the following command, after you have created a backup copy of it first:

    ```
    cp /etc/httpd/conf.d/userdir.conf /etc/httpd/conf.d/userdir.conf.BAK
    vi /etc/httpd/conf.d/userdir.conf
    ```

2. In the file, locate the directive that reads as `UserDir disabled`. Change it to the following:

    ```
    UserDir public_html
    ```

3. Now scroll down to the `<Directory "/home/*/public_html">` section and replace the existing block with the one here:

    ```
    <Directory /home/*/public_html>
        AllowOverride All
        Options Indexes FollowSymLinks
        Require all granted
    </Directory>
    ```

4. Save and exit the file. Now log in as any system user to work with your publishing web directory (`su - <username>`), and then create a web publishing web folder in your home directory and a new home page for your user:

    ```
    mkdir ~/public_html && vi ~/public_html/index.html
    ```

5. Now add the required HTML. You can use the following code as a starting point but it is expected that you will modify it to suit your own needs:

    ```
    <!DOCTYPE html>
    <html lang="en">
    <head><title>Welcome to my web folder's home page</title></head>
    <body><h1>Welcome to my personal home page</h1></body>
    </html>
    ```

6. Now modify the permissions of the Linux system user's `<username>` home folders by typing:

    ```
    chmod 711 /home/<username>
    ```

7. Set the read/write permissions for `public_html` 755 so Apache can execute it later:

    ```
    chmod 755 ~/public_html -R
    ```

8. Now log in as root again using `su - root` to configure SELinux appropriately for the use of http home directories:

    ```
    setsebool -P httpd_enable_homedirs true
    ```

9. As root, change the SELinux security context for your user's web public directory (this needs `policycoreutils-python` package to be installed) with the username `<user>`:

    ```
    semanage fcontext -a -t httpd_user_content_t /home/<user>/public_html
    ```

    ```
    restorecon -Rv /home/<user>/public_html
    ```

10. To complete this recipe, simply reload the `httpd` service configuration:

    ```
    apachectl configtest && systemctl reload httpd
    ```

11. You can now test your setup by browsing to (substitute <username> appropriately):
    `http://<SERVER IP ADDRESS>/~<username>` in any browser.

How it works...

In this recipe, we learned how easy it is to host your own peers by enabling user directories on the Apache web server.

So what did we learn from this experience?

We began the recipe by making a few minor configuration changes to Apache's `userdir. conf` in order to set up the user directory support. We activated the user directories by adjusting the `UserDir` directive from disabled to pointing to the name of the HTML web directory within each user's home directory, which will contain all our user's web content, and call this `public_html` (you can change this directory name to anything you like but `public_ html` is the de facto standard for naming it). Then we proceeded to modify the `<Directory /home/*/public_html>` tag. This directive applies all its enclosed options to the parts of the filesystem defined in the beginning tag `/home/*/public_html`. In our example, the following options are enabled for this directory: `Indexes` are used whenever a directory does not have `index.html`. This will show the file and folder content of the directory as HTML. As we will see in the recipe *Securing Apache*, this should be avoided for your web root whereas, for serving user directories, this can be a good choice if you just want to make your home folder accessible to your peers so they can quickly share some files (if you have any security concerns, remove this option). The `FollowSymLinks` option allows symbolic links (man `ln`) from this `public_html` directory to any other directory or file in the filesystem. Again, avoid this in your web root folder but for home directories it can be useful if you need to make files or folders accessible within the `public_html` folder without the need to copy them into it (user directories often have disk quotas). Next we configured access control to the `public_html` folder. We did so by setting `Require all granted`, which tells Apache that in this `public_html` folder anyone from everywhere can access the contents through the HTTP protocol. If you want to restrict access to your `public_html` folder then you can replace `all granted` with different options. To allow access based on a hostname use, for example `Require host example.com`. With the `ip` parameter we can restrict the `public_html` folder to an internally available network only, for example `Require ip 192.168.1.0/24`. This is particularly useful if your web server has multiple network interfaces and one IP address is used for connecting to the public Internet and another one for your internal private network. You can add multiple `Require` lines within a `Directory` block. Remember to always set at least `Require local` which allows local access.

Having saved our work, we then began to make various changes to the home directories. First we created the actual `public_html` folder within our user's home directory, which will be the actual personal web publishing folder later. Next, we changed its permissions to `755` which means that our user can do everything in the folder but all the other users and groups can only read and execute its content (and change into this folder). This type of permission is needed because all the files in the `public_html` folder will be accessed by a user named `apache` with the group `apache` if someone requests its content via the Apache web server later. If no read or execute permissions are set for the `other users` flag (man `chmod`), we will get an `Access denied` message in our browser. This will also be the case if we do not change the permissions for the parent `/home/<username>` directory in advance because parent directory permissions can affect its child subfolder permissions. A normal user home directory in CentOS Linux has the permissions `700` which means that the home directory's owner can do anything but everyone else is completely locked out of the home folder and its content.

As written before, the Apache user needs access to the subfolder `public_html` so we have to change the permissions to `711` for the home folder so that everyone else can at least change into the directory (and then access the subfolder `public_html` as well since this is set to be read/write accessible). Next, we set the security context of our new web folder for SELinux. On systems running SELinux, it's mandatory to set all the Apache web publishing folders to the `httpd_user_content_t` SELinux label (along with their contents) in order to make them available to Apache. Also, we made sure to set the correct SELinux Boolean to enable Apache home directories (which is enabled by default): `httpd_enable_homedirs` is `true`. Read *Chapter 14, Working with SELinux* to learn more about SELinux.

You should be aware that the previous process of managing the home directories should be repeated for each user. You will not have to restart Apache every time you enable a new system user but, having completed these steps for the first time, it will be simply a matter of reloading the configuration of the `httpd` service to reflect the initial changes made to the configuration file. From this point on, your local system users can now publish web pages using a unique URL based on their username.

Implementing name-based hosting

Normally, if you install Apache as shown in the previous recipe, you can host exactly one website that is accessible as the server's IP address or the domain name Apache is running on, for example, `http://192.168.1.100` or `http://www.centos7.home`. Such a system is very wasteful for your server resources as you would need individual servers with Apache installed for every single domain you want to host. **Name-based** or **virtual hosting** is used to host multiple domains on the same Apache web server. If a number of different domain names have already been assigned to your Apache web server's IP address using a DNS server or through a local `/etc/hosts` file, virtual hosts can be configured for every available domain name to direct the user to a specific directory on the Apache server containing the site's information. Any modern webspace provider uses this kind of virtual hosting to divide one web server's space into multiple sites. There is no limit to this system and to the number of sites to create from it as long as your web server can handle its traffic. In this recipe, we will learn how to configure name-based virtual hosting on the Apache web server.

Getting ready

To complete this recipe, you will require a working installation of the CentOS 7 operating system with root privileges and a console-based text editor of your choice. It is expected that your server will be using a static IP address and Apache is installed and currently running, and that you have enabled system users publishing directories in an earlier recipe. Virtual host names cannot work without previously setting up one or more domains or subdomains outside Apache.

For testing, you could set up your /etc/hosts (see the *Setting your hostname and resolving the network* recipe in *Chapter 2, Configuring the System*) or configure some A or CNAMES in your BIND DNS server (refer to *Chapter 9, Working with Domains*) to use different domain names or subdomains, such as www.centos7.home, all pointing to your Apache web server's IP address.

 A common misconception is that Apache can create domain names for your Apache web server on its own. This is not true. The different domain names you want to wire to different directories using virtual hosts need to be set up in a DNS server or /etc/hosts file to point to your Apache server's IP address before you can use them with virtual hosts.

How to do it...

For the purpose of this recipe we will be building some local virtual hosts with the following Apache example subdomain names: www.centos7.home, web1.centos7.home, web2.centos7.home and <username>.centos7.home for the corresponding web publishing folders /var/www/html, /var/www/web1, /var/www/web2, and /home/<username>/public_html for the domain's network name centos7.home. These names are interchangeable and it is expected that you will want to customize this recipe based on something more appropriate to your own needs and circumstances.

1. To begin, log in as root on your Apache server and create a new configuration file that will hold all our virtual host definitions:

   vi /etc/httpd/conf.d/vhost.conf

2. Now put in the following content, customizing the centos7.home value and the username <username> to fit your own needs:

```
<VirtualHost *:80>
    ServerName centos7.home
    ServerAlias www.centos7.home
    DocumentRoot /var/www/html/
</VirtualHost>
<VirtualHost *:80>
    ServerName  web1.centos7.home
    DocumentRoot /var/www/web1/public_html/
</VirtualHost>
<VirtualHost *:80>
    ServerName  web2.centos7.home
    DocumentRoot /var/www/web2/public_html/
</VirtualHost>
<VirtualHost *:80>
    ServerName  <username>.centos7.home
```

```
        DocumentRoot /home/<username>/public_html/
    </VirtualHost>
```

3. Now save and close the file in the usual way before proceeding to create the directories for both virtual hosts that are currently missing:

   mkdir -p /var/www/web1/public_html /var/www/web2/public_html

4. Having done this, we can now create default index pages for the missing subdomains web1 and web2 by using our favorite text editor, as follows:

   echo "\<html\>\<head\>\</head\>\<body\>\<p\>Welcome to Web1\</p\>\</body\>\</html\>" > /var/www/web1/public_html/index.html

   echo "\<html\>\<head\>\</head\>\<body\>\<p\>Welcome to Web2\</p\>\</body\>\</html\>" > /var/www/web2/public_html/index.html

5. Now reload the Apache web server:

   apachectl configtest && systemctl reload httpd

6. Now, for simple testing purposes, we will just configure all our new Apache web server's subdomains in the hosts file of the client computer that wants to access these virtual hosts, but remember that you can also configure these subdomains in a BIND DNS server. Login to this client computer (it needs to be in the same network as our Apache server) as root and add the following lines to the /etc/hosts file, assuming our Apache server has the IP address 192.168.1.100:

   192.168.1.100 www.centos7.home

   192.168.1.100 centos7.home

   192.168.1.100 web1.centos7.home

   192.168.1.100 web2.centos7.home

   192.168.1.100 john.centos7.home

7. Now on this computer, open a browser and test things out by typing the following addresses into the address line (replace <username> with the username you defined for the virtual host): http://www.centos7.home, http://web1.centos7.home, http://web2.centos7.home and http://<username>.centos7.home.

How it works...

The purpose of this recipe was to show you how easy it is to implement name-based virtual hosting. This technique will boost your productivity and using this approach will give you unlimited opportunities to domain-based web hosting.

So what did we learn from this experience?

We began by creating a new Apache configuration file to hold all our virtual host configuration. Remember, all files ending with the `.conf` extension in the `/etc/httpd/conf.d/` directory will be loaded automatically when Apache is started. Following this, we then proceeded to put in the relevant directive blocks, starting with our default server root `centos7.home` and the alias `www.centos7.home`. The most important option in any virtual host block is the `ServerName` directive, which maps an existing domain name for our web server's IP address to a specific directory on the filesystem. Of course, there are many more settings you can include, but the previous solution provides the basic building blocks that will enable you to use it as the perfect starting point. The next step was to then create individual entries for our `centos7.home` subdomains `web1`, `web2`, and `<username>`. Remember, each virtual host supports the typical Apache directives and can be customized to suit your needs. Refer to the official Apache manual (install the YUM package `httpd-manual`, then go to the location `/usr/share/httpd/manual/vhosts/`) to learn more. After we created our virtual host blocks for every subdomain we wanted, we then proceeded to create the directories to hold the actual content and created a basic `index.html` in each directory. In this example, our `web1` and `web2` content directories were added to `/var/www`. This is not to imply that you cannot create these new folders in another place. In fact most production servers generally place these new directories in the home folder, as shown with our `/home/<username>/public_html` example. However, if you do intend to take this approach, remember to modify the permissions and ownership, as well as SELinux labels (outside `/var/www` you need to label Apache directories as `httpd_sys_content_t`) of these new directories so that they can be used as they were intended. Finally, we reloaded the Apache web service so that our new settings would take immediate effect. We could then directly use the subdomain names in our browser to browse to our virtual hosts when correctly set up in `/etc/hosts` on the client or on a BIND DNS server.

Implementing CGI with Perl and Ruby

In the previous recipes in this chapter, our Apache service only served static content, which means that everything requested by a web-browser already existed in a constant state on the server, for example as plain HTML text files that don't change. Apache simply sends the content of a specific file from the web server to the browser as a response where it then gets interpreted and rendered. If there were no way to change the contents sent to the client, the Internet would be really boring and not the huge success it is today. Not even the simplest example of dynamic content, such as showing a web page with the web server's current local time would be possible.

Therefore, early in the 1990's, some smart people started inventing mechanisms to make communication possible between a web server and some executable programs installed on the server to generate web pages dynamically. This means that the content of the HTML sent to the user can change in response to different contexts and conditions. Such programs are often written in scripting languages such as Perl or Ruby but can be written in any other computer language as well, such as Python, Java, or PHP (see later). Because Apache is written in pure C and C++, it cannot execute or interpret any other programming language such as Perl directly. Therefore, a bridge between the server and the program is needed to define how some external programs can interact with the server. One of these methods is called the **Common Gateway Interface** (**CGI**) which is a very old way to serve dynamic content. Most Apache web servers use some form of CGI applications and in this recipe we will show you how to install and configure CGI for use with Perl and Ruby to generate our first dynamic content.

 There also exist some special Apache web server modules such as `mod_perl`, `mod_python`, `mod_ruby`, and so on which should be generally preferred as they directly embed the interpreter of the language into the web server process and therefore are a lot faster in comparison to any interface technology such as CGI.

Getting ready

To complete this recipe, you will require a working installation of the CentOS 7 operating system with root privileges, a console-based text editor of your choice, and a connection to the Internet in order to facilitate the download of additional packages.

It is expected that your server will be using a static IP address, Apache is installed and currently running, and that your server supports one or more domains or subdomains.

How to do it...

As both scripting languages Perl as well as Ruby are not installed by default on CentOS 7 Minimal, we will start this recipe by installing all required packages using YUM.

1. To begin, log in as root and type the following command:

    ```
    yum install perl perl-CGI ruby
    ```

2. Next, restart the Apache web server:

    ```
    systemctl restart httpd
    ```

3. Next, we need to configure SELinux appropriately for the use of CGI scripts:

    ```
    setsebool -P httpd_enable_cgi 1
    ```

4. Then we need to change the correct security context for our `cgi-bin` directory for SELinux to work:

```
semanage fcontext -a -t httpd_sys_script_exec_t /var/www/cgi-bin
restorecon -Rv /var/www/cgi-bin
```

Creating your first Perl CGI script

1. Now create the following Perl CGI script file by opening the new file `vi /var/www/cgi-bin/perl-test.cgi` and putting in the following content:

```
#!/usr/bin/perl
use strict;
use warnings;
use CGI qw(:standard);
print header;
my $now = localtime;
print start_html(-title=>'Server time via Perl CGI'),
h1('Time'),
p("The time is $now"),
end_html;
```

2. Next, change the file's permission to 755, so our `apache` user can execute it:

```
chmod 755 /var/www/cgi-bin/perl-test.cgi
```

3. Next, to test and actually see what HTML is being generated from the preceding script, you can execute the `perl` script directly on the command line; just type:

```
/var/www/cgi-bin/perl-test.cgi
```

4. Now open a browser on a computer in your network and run your first Perl CGI script, which will print the local time by using the URL:

```
http://<server name or IP address>/cgi-bin/perl-test.cgi
```

5. If the script is not working, have a look at the log file `/var/log/httpd/error_log`.

Creating your first Ruby CGI script

1. Create the new Ruby CGI script file `vi /var/www/cgi-bin/ruby-test.cgi` and put in the following content:

```
#!/usr/bin/ruby
require "cgi"
cgi = CGI.new("html4")
cgi.out{
    cgi.html{
```

```
cgi.head{ cgi.title{"Server time via Ruby CGI"} } +
cgi.body{
        cgi.h1 { "Time" } +
        cgi.p { Time.now}
    }
  }
}
```

2. Now change the file's permission to 755 so our apache user can execute it:

    chmod 755 /var/www/cgi-bin/ruby-test.cgi

3. To actually see what HTML is being generated from the preceding script, you can execute the Ruby script directly on the command line; just type /var/www/cgi-bin/ruby-test.cgi. When the line offline mode: enter name=value pairs on standard input is shown, press *Ctrl+D* to see the actual HTML output.

4. Now open a browser on a computer in your network and run your first Ruby CGI script which will print the local time by using the following URL:

    http://<server name or IP address>/cgi-bin/ruby-test.cgi

5. If it is not working, have a look at the log file /var/log/httpd/error.log.

How it works...

Here in this recipe we showed you how easy it is to create some dynamic web sites using CGI. When a CGI resource is accessed, the Apache server executes that program on the server and sends its output back to the browser. The main advantage of this system is that CGI is not restricted to any programming language but works as long as a program is executable on the Linux command line and generates some form of text output. The big disadvantage of CGI technology is that it is a very old and outdated technology: every user request to a CGI resource starts a new process of the program. For example, every request to a Perl CGI script will start and load a new interpreter instance into memory, which will produce a lot of overhead, therefore making CGI only usable for smaller websites or lower parallel user request numbers. As said before, there are other technologies to deal with this issue, for example FastCGI or Apache modules such as mod_perl.

So what did we learn from this experience?

We began this recipe by logging in as root and installing the perl interpreter and the CGI.pm module for it as it is not included in the Perl standard library (we will use it in our script), as well as by installing the ruby interpreter for the Ruby programming language. Afterwards, to make sure our Apache web server takes notice of our new programming languages installed on the system, we restarted the Apache process.

Next, we made sure that SELinux is enabled to work with CGI scripts and then we provided the standard Apache `cgi-bin` directory `/var/www/cgi-bin` with the proper SELinux context type to allow system-wide execution. To learn more about SELinux, read *Chapter 14, Working with SELinux*. In this directory we then put our Perl and Ruby CGI scripts and made them executable afterwards for the Apache user. In the main Apache configuration file, the `/var/www/cgi-bin` directory has been defined as the standard CGI directory by default, which means that every executable file you put into this directory, with proper access and execution permissions and the `.cgi` extension, is automatically defined as a CGI script and can be accessed and executed from your web browser, no matter which programming or scripting language it has been written in. To test our scripts, we then opened a web browser and went to the URL `http://<server name or IP address>/cgi-bin/` with the name of the `.cgi` script to follow.

There's more...

If you would like to allow execution of CGI scripts in other web directories as well, you need to add the following two lines (`Options` and `AddHandler`) to any virtual host or existing `Directive` directive, or create a new one in the following way (remember that you then also have to set the SELinux `httpd_sys_script_exec_t` label on the new CGI location as well):

```
<Directory "/var/www/html/cgi-new">
    Options +ExecCGI
    AddHandler cgi-script .cgi
</Directory>
```

Installing, configuring, and testing PHP

Hypertext Preprocessor (**PHP**) remains one of the most popular server-side scripting languages designed for web development. It already supports some nice features, such as connecting to relational databases like MariaDB out-of-the-box which can be used to implement modern web applications very fast. While a current trend can be seen for larger enterprises to move away from PHP in favor of some newer technologies such as Node.js (server-side JavaScript), it is still the superior scripting language on the consumer market. Every hosting company in the world provides some kind of LAMP stack (Linux, Apache, MySQL, PHP) to run the PHP code. Also, a lot of very popular web applications are written in PHP, such as WordPress, Joomla, and Drupal, so it's fair enough to say that PHP represents a must-have feature for almost any Apache web server. Here in this recipe, we will show you how to get started with installing and running PHP in your Apache web server with the module `mod_php`.

Getting ready

To complete this recipe, you will require a working installation of the CentOS 7 operating system with root privileges and a console-based text editor of your choice and a Internet connection. It is expected that your server will be using a static IP address and Apache is installed and currently running, and that your server supports one or more domains or subdomains.

How to do it...

We will begin this recipe by installing the PHP Hypertext Processor together with the Apache mod_php module, both not installed by default on CentOS 7 minimal.

1. To begin, log in as root and type the following command:

    `yum install mod_php`

2. Now let's open the standard PHP configuration file after we have made a backup of the original file first:

    `cp /etc/php.ini /etc/php.ini.bak && vi /etc/php.ini`

3. Find the line `; date.timezone` = and replace it with your own timezone. A list of all the available PHP time zones can be found at `http://php.net/manual/en/ timezones.php`. For example (be sure to remove the leading `;` as this is disabling the interpretation of a command; this is called commenting out) to set the timezone to the city Berlin in Europe use:

    `date.timezone = "Europe/Berlin"`

4. To make sure the new module and settings have been properly loaded, restart the Apache web server:

    `systemctl restart httpd`

5. To be consistent with the CGI examples from the former recipe, here we will create our first dynamic PHP script which will print out the current local server time in the script `vi /var/www/html/php-test.php`, and run the popular PHP function `phpinfo()` that we can use to print out important PHP information:

    ```
    <html><head><title>Server time via Mod PHP</title></head>
    <h1>Time</h1>
    <p>The time is <?php print Date("D M d, Y G:i a");?></p><?php
    phpinfo(); ?></body></html>
    ```

6. To actually see what HTML is being generated from the preceding script, you can execute the PHP script directly on the command line; just type: `php /var/www/ html/php-test.php`.

7. Now open a browser on a computer in your network and run your first PHP script which will print the local time by using the following URL: `http://<server name or IP address>/php-test.php`.

How to do it...

In this recipe, we showed you how easy it is to install and incorporate PHP into any Apache web server by using the `mod_php` module. This module enables an internal PHP interpreter, which directly runs in the Apache process and is much more efficient than using CGI, and should always be your preferred method whenever is available.

So what did we learn from this experience?

We began this recipe by installing the `mod_php` module using YUM, which will install PHP as a dependency as well as both are not available on any standard CentOS 7 minimal installations. Installing `mod_php` added the `/etc/php.ini` configuration file which we then opened after making a backup of the original file first. This file is the main PHP configuration file and should be edited with care because a lot of settings can be security relevant to your web server. If you are just starting out with PHP, leave everything as it is in the file and don't change anything despite the `date.timezone` variable. We set this to reflect our current time zone and it is necessary for PHP because it is used by a lot of different time and date functions (we will use some date functions in our first PHP script as well, see below). Next, we restarted the Apache web server which automatically reloads the PHP configurations as well. Afterwards, we created our first PHP script and put it in the main web root folder `/var/www/html/php-test.php`; this prints out the current server time as well as the result of the `phpinfo()` PHP function. This gives you a well categorized tabular overview of your current PHP installation, helping you diagnose server-related problems or see which modules are available in PHP.

In comparison to CGI, you may ask yourself why we don't have to put the PHP scripts into any special folder such as `cgi-bin`. By installing `mod_php`, an Apache configuration file called `/etc/httpd/conf.d/php.conf` gets deployed into the Apache configuration folder, which exactly answers this question, it specifies that PHP scripts will get executed as valid PHP code whenever they get the extension `.php` from anywhere in every web directory.

Securing Apache

Even though the Apache HTTP server is one of the most mature and safe server applications included in CentOS 7, there is always room for improvement and a large number of options and techniques are available to harden your web server's security even more. While we cannot show the user every single security feature as it is outside of the scope this book, in this recipe, we will try to teach what is considered to be good practice when it comes to securing your Apache web server for a production system.

Getting ready

To complete this recipe, you will require a working installation of the CentOS 7 operating system with root privileges and a console-based text editor of your choice. It is expected that your server will be using a static IP address and Apache is installed and currently running, and that your server supports one or more domains or subdomains.

How to do it...

Most of the security options and techniques have to be set up in the main Apache configuration file, so we will begin this recipe by opening it in our favorite text editor.

Configuring httpd.conf to provide better security

1. To begin, log in as root and open the main Apache config file:

   ```
   vi /etc/httpd/conf/httpd.conf
   ```

2. Now go to your main document root. To do so, search the directive called:

   ```
   <Directory "/var/www/html">
   ```

3. Within the beginning `<Directory "/var/www/html">` and closing `</Directory>` tags find the line `Options Indexes FollowSymLinks`, then disable (comment out) this line by putting a # in front of it, so it reads:

   ```
   #   Options Indexes FollowSymLinks
   ```

4. Now scroll down to the end of the configuration file and insert the following line one line before the line `# Supplemental configuration`. We do not want our server to leak any detailed information through the header, so we type:

   ```
   ServerTokens Prod
   ```

5. Afterwards, reload the Apache configuration to apply your changes:

   ```
   apachectl configtest && systemctl reload httpd
   ```

Removing unneeded httpd modules

Even the most stable, mature, and well-tested programs can include bugs and cause vulnerabilities, as the latest news about the Heartbleed bug in OpenSSL or Shellshock in Bash have shown, and the Apache web server is no exception. Therefore, it is often beneficial to remove all unneeded software to limit the functionality, and thus the likelihood of security problems in your system. For the Apache web server, we can remove all unneeded modules to increase security (this can also increase performance and memory consumption). Let's start this process by reviewing all the currently installed Apache modules.

1. To show all currently installed and loaded Apache modules, type as user root:

   ```
   httpd -M
   ```

2. All the modules outputted by the preceding command are loaded into the Apache web server by special configuration files in the /etc/httpd/conf.modules.d folder where they are grouped together by their primary target into the following files:

   ```
   00-base.conf, 00-dav.conf, 00-lua.conf, 00-mpm.conf, 00-proxy.
   conf, 00-ssl.conf, 00-systemd.conf, 01-cgi.conf, 10-php.conf
   ```

3. So instead of going through all the modules individually, this file structure in the conf.modules.d folder can make our life much easier because we can disable/enable whole groups of modules. For example, if you know that you will not need any Apache DAV modules because you will not provide any WebDAV server, you can disable all DAV-related modules by renaming the extension of the 00-dav.conf configuration file since only files with the ending .conf are read and loaded automatically by Apache. In order to do so, type:

   ```
   mv /etc/httpd/conf.modules.d/00-dav.conf /etc/httpd/conf.
   modules.d/00-dav.conf.BAK
   ```

4. Afterwards, reload the Apache configuration to apply your changes to the modules directory:

   ```
   apachectl configtest && systemctl reload httpd
   ```

5. If you need more fine-grained control, you can also enable/disable single modules in all the configuration files in this directory as well. For example, open 00-base.conf in your favorite text editor and disable a single line by adding a # to the beginning of the line of choice you want to disable. For example:

   ```
   # LoadModule userdir_module modules/mod_userdir.so
   ```

6. If you decide to use some disabled modules files later, just rename the .BAK file to the original file name or remove the # in a specific module config file before reloading httpd once again.

Protecting your Apache files

Another really simple way to increase the security of your Apache web server is to protect your server-side scripts and configurations. In our scenario, we have one user (root) who alone is responsible and maintains the complete Apache web server, websites (for example, uploading new HTML pages to the server), server-side scripts, and configurations. Therefore, we will give him/her full file permissions (read/write/execute). The `apache` user still needs proper read and execute permissions to serve and access all Apache related files, thus minimizing the risk that your Apache web server is exposing some potential security risks to other system users or can get compromised through HTTP hacks. Do this in two steps:

1. First we will change or reset the ownership of the complete Apache configuration directory and the standard web root directory to owner `root` and group `apache`:

   ```
   chown -R root:apache /var/www/html /etc/httpd/conf*
   ```

2. Afterwards, we will change the file permissions so no one other than our dedicated `apache` user (and also `root`) can read those files:

   ```
   chmod 750 -R /var/www/html /etc/httpd/conf*
   ```

How it works...

We began this recipe by opening the main Apache configuration file `httpd.conf` to change settings for our main Apache root web content directory `/var/www/html`. Here we disabled the complete `Options` directive which included the `Indexes` as well as the `FollowSymLinks` parameter. As we have learned, if you request a directory instead of a file from the Apache server, `index.html` or the `index.htm` file within this directory will be sent automatically. Now the `Indexes` option configures the Apache web server in such a way that if no such file can be found in the requested directory, Apache will auto-generate a listing of the directory's content, as if you had typed `ls` (for list directory) in that directory on the command line, and show it to the user as a HTML page. We don't want this feature in general because it can expose secret or private data to unauthorized users and a lot of system administrators will tell you that indexing is considered to be a security threat in general. The `FollowSymLinks` directive should also not be used in production systems because if you make a mistake with it, it can easily expose parts of the file system, such as the complete root directory. Finally, we add another measurement to increase the server's base security and this is done by disabling the server version banner information. When the Apache web server generates either a web page or an error page, valuable information, for example the Apache server version and the activated modules, is sent automatically to the browser and a possible attacker can gain valuable information about your system. We stopped this from happening by simply setting `ServerTokens` to `Prod`. Afterwards, we showed you how to disable Apache modules to reduce the general risk of bugs and exploitations of your system. Finally, we showed how to adjust your Apache file permissions which can also be a good general protection.

There are lots of other things to consider when it comes to hardening your Apache web server but most of these techniques, such as Limiting HTTP request methods, `TraceEnable`, setting cookies with `HttpOnly` and secure flags, disabling the HTTP 1.0 protocol or SSL v2, or modifying the HTTP header with useful security-related HTTP or custom headers such as `X-XSS-Protection`, are much more advanced concepts and can restrict a general purpose Apache web server too much.

Setting up HTTPS with Secure Sockets Layer (SSL)

In this recipe, we will learn how to add a secure connection to the Apache web server by creating a self-signed SSL certificate using OpenSSL. This is often a requirement for web servers if the sites running on them transfer sensitive data such as credit card or login information from the web browser to the server. In a previous recipe you were shown how to install the Apache web server, and with the growing demand for secure connections, it is the purpose of this recipe to show you how to enhance your current server configuration by teaching you how to extend the features of the Apache web server.

Getting ready

To complete this recipe, you will require a working installation of the CentOS 7 operating system with root privileges, a console-based text editor of your choice, and a connection to the Internet in order to facilitate the download of additional packages. It is expected that Apache web server has been installed and that it is currently running. Here we will create a new SSL certificate for Apache. If you want to learn more about it, refer to *Chapter 6, Providing Security* for advice on generating self-signed certificates. As a correct domain name is crucial for SSL to work, we will continue naming our Apache web server's configured domain name `centos7.home` to make this recipe work (change it to fit your own needs).

How to do it...

Apache does not support SSL encryption by default and for this reason we will begin by installing the necessary package `mod_ssl` using the YUM package manager.

1. To begin, log in as root and type the following command:

```
yum install mod_ssl
```

2. During installation of the mod_ssl package, a self-signed certificate as well as the key pair for the Apache web server are generated automatically; these lack a proper common name for your web server's domain name. Before we can re-generate our own required SSL files using the `Makefile` in the next steps, we need to delete those files:

```
rm /etc/pki/tls/private/localhost.key /etc/pki/tls/certs/
localhost.crt
```

3. We are now required to create our intended self-signed certificate and server key for our Apache web server. To do this, type the following command:

```
cd /etc/pki/tls/certs
```

4. To create the self-signed Apache SSL keypair, consisting of the certificate and its embedded public key as well as the private key, type:

```
make testcert
```

5. In the process of creating the certificate, first you will be asked to enter a new passphrase and then to verify it. Afterwards, you need to type it in again for the third time. As usual, enter a secure password. You will then be asked a number of questions. Complete all the required details by paying special attention to the common name value. This value should reflect the domain name of your web server or the IP address the SSL certificate is for. For example, you may type:

```
www.centos7.home
```

6. When the process of creating your certificate is complete, we will proceed by opening the main Apache SSL configuration in the following way (after making a backup):

```
cp /etc/httpd/conf.d/ssl.conf /etc/httpd/conf.d/ssl.conf.BAK
```
```
vi /etc/httpd/conf.d/ssl.conf
```

7. Scroll down to the section that begins with `<VirtualHost _default_:443>` and locate the line `# DocumentRoot "/var/www/html"` within this block. Then activate it by removing the # character, so it reads:

```
DocumentRoot "/var/www/html"
```

8. Right below, find the line that reads `#ServerName www.example.com:443`. Activate this line and modify the value shown to match the common name value used during the creation of your certificate, as follows:

```
ServerName www.centos7.home:443
```

9. Save and close the file, next we need to enable the HTTPS port in our firewalld to allow incoming HTTP SSL connections over port `443`:

```
firewall-cmd --permanent --add-service=https && firewall-cmd
--reload
```

10. Now restart the Apache `httpd` service to apply your changes. Note that if prompted you have to enter the SSL passphrase you added when you created the SSL test certificate:

`systemctl restart httpd`

11. Well done! You can now visit your server with a secure connection by replacing all the available HTTP URLs we have defined for the server using HTTPS instead. For example, go to `https://www.centos7.home` instead of `http://www.centos7.home`.

 When you browse to this website, you will get a warning message that the signing certificate authority is not known. This exception is to be expected when using self-signed certificates and can be confirmed.

How it works...

We began the recipe by installing `mod_ssl` using the YUM package manager, which is the default Apache module to enable SSL. The next step was then to go to the standard location where all the system's certificates can be found in CentOS 7, that is, `/etc/pki/tls/certs`. Here we can find a `Makefile`, which is a helper script for conveniently generating self-signed SSL test certificates and which hides away complicated command line parameters for the OpenSSL program from you. Remember that the `Makefile` currently lacks a `clean` option and therefore every time we run it, we need to delete any old versions of the generated files from a former run manually, otherwise it will not start doing anything. After deleting the old Apache SSL files, we used `make` with the `testcert` parameter, which creates self-signed certificates for the Apache web server and puts them in the standard locations, already configured in the `ssl.conf` file (the `SSLCertificateFile` and `SSLCertificateKeyFile` directives), so we didn't have to change anything here. During the process, you were asked to provide a password before completing a series of questions. Complete the questions but pay special attention to the Common name. As was mentioned in the main recipe, this value should reflect either the domain name of your server or your IP address. In the next phase, you were required to open Apache's SSL configuration file in your favorite text editor which can be found at `/etc/httpd/conf.d/ssl.conf`. In it we enabled the `DocumentRoot` directive to put it under SSL control and activated the `ServerName` directive with an expected domain value that must be the same as the one we defined as our common name value. We than saved and closed the configuration file and enabled the HTTPS ports in our firewall, thus allowing incoming connections over the standard HTTPS `443` port. Having completed these steps, you can now enjoy the benefits of a secure connection using a self-signed server certificate. Just type `https://` instead of `http://` for any URL address available on your Apache web browser. However, if you are intending to use an SSL Certificate on a production server for members of the public, then your best option is to purchase an SSL certificate from a trusted Certificate Authority.

There's more...

We learned that since our SSL certificate is protected by a passphrase, so whenever we need to restart our Apache web server, we need to enter the password. This is impractical for server restarts as Apache will refuse to start without a password. To get rid of the password prompt, we will provide the passphrase in a special file and make sure it is only accessible by root.

1. Create a backup of the file that will contain your password:

    ```
    cp /usr/libexec/httpd-ssl-pass-dialog /usr/libexec/httpd-ssl-pass-
    dialog.BAK
    ```

2. Now overwrite this password file with the following content, replacing XXXX in the following command line with your current SSL passphrase:

    ```
    echo -e '#!/bin/bash\necho "XXXX"' > /usr/libexec/httpd-ssl-pass-
    dialog
    ```

3. Finally, change the permissions so that only root can read and execute them:

    ```
    chmod 500 /usr/libexec/httpd-ssl-pass-dialog
    ```

13
Operating System-Level Virtualization

In this chapter, we will cover:

- ▶ Installing and configuring Docker
- ▶ Downloading an image and running a container
- ▶ Creating your own images from Dockerfiles and uploading to Docker Hub
- ▶ Setting up and working with a private Docker registry

Introduction

This chapter is a collection of recipes that provides the essential steps to install, configure, and work with Docker, which is an open platform to build, ship, share, and run distributed applications through operating-system-level virtualization, a technology that has been around for many years in the Linux world and can provide speed and efficiency advantages over traditional virtualization technologies.

Installing and configuring Docker

Traditional virtualization technologies provide *hardware virtualization*, which means they create a complete hardware environment so each **virtual machine** (**VM**) needs a complete operating system to run it. Therefore they have some major drawbacks because they are heavyweight and produce a lot of overhead while running. This is where the open-source Docker containerization engine offers an attractive alternative. It can help you build applications in Linux containers, thus providing application virtualization.

This means that you can bundle any Linux program of choice with all its dependencies and its own environment and then share it or run multiple instances of it, each as a completely isolated and separated process on any modern Linux kernel, thus providing native runtime performance, easy portability, and high scalability. Here, in this recipe, we will show you how to install and configure Docker on your CentOS 7 server.

Getting ready

To complete this recipe, you will require a working installation of the CentOS 7 operating system with root privileges, a console-based text editor of your choice, and a connection to the Internet in order to download additional `rpm` packages and a test Docker image.

How to do it...

While Docker is available as a package in the official CentOS 7 repository, we will use the official Docker repository to install it on our system instead.

1. To begin, log in as root and update your YUM packages before downloading and executing the official Docker Linux installation script using the following command:

   ```
   yum update && curl -sSL https://get.docker.com/ | sh
   ```

2. Next, enable Docker at boot time before starting the Docker daemon (the first time you start, it will take a while):

   ```
   systemctl enable docker && systemctl start docker
   ```

3. Finally, after starting Docker you can verify that it's working by typing:

   ```
   docker run hello-world
   ```

How it works...

When installing any software on CentOS 7, most of the time it is a very good advice to use the packages available in your official CentOS repository instead of downloading and installing from third-party locations. Here by installing Docker using the official Docker repository instead we made an exception. We did this because Docker is a very young project and is evolving fast, and it keeps changing a lot. While you can use Docker for running every Linux application, including critical web servers or programs dealing with confidential data, bugs found or introduced into the Docker program can have severe security consequences. By using the official Docker repository, we make sure we always get the latest updates and patches available as fast as possible right from the developers of this fast-moving project. So anytime you type `yum update` in the future, your package manager will automatically query and check the Docker repos to see if there is a new version of Docker available for you.

So what did we learn from this experience?

We started this recipe by logging into our server as root and updated the YUM package's database. Then we used a command to download and execute the official Docker installation script from `https://get.docker.com/` in one step. What this script does is add the official Docker repository to the YUM package manager as a new package source and then automatically install Docker in the background. Afterwards, we enabled the Docker service at boot-time and started it by using `systemd`. Finally, to test our installation, we issued the command `docker run hello-world`, which downloads a special image from the official Docker registry to test our installation. If everything went fine, you should see the following success message (output truncated):

Hello from Docker

This message shows that your installation appears to be working correctly.

Downloading an image and running a container

A common misconception is that Docker is a system for running containers. Docker is only a build-tool to wrap up any piece of Linux based software with all its dependencies in a complete filesystem that contains everything it needs to run: code, runtime, system tools, and system libraries. The technology to run Linux containers is called operating-system-level virtualization and provides multiple isolated environments built in every modern Linux kernel by default. This guarantees that it will always run the same, regardless of the environment it is deployed in; thus making your application portable. Therefore, when it comes to distributing your Docker applications into Linux containers, two major conceptional terms must be introduced: **Docker images** and **containers**. If you ever wanted to set up and run your own WordPress installation, in this recipe we will show you how to do so the fastest way possible by downloading a pre-made WordPress image from the official Docker hub; we will then run a container from.

Getting ready

To complete this recipe, you will require a working installation of the CentOS 7 operating system with root privileges, a console-based text editor of your choice, and a connection to the Internet in order to facilitate the download of additional Docker images. It is expected that Docker has already been installed and is running.

How to do it...

The official WordPress image from Docker Hub does not contain its own MySQL server. Instead it relies on it externally, so we will start this recipe by installing and running a MySQL docker container from Docker Hub.

1. To begin, log in as root and type the following command by replacing `<PASSWORD>` in the following command with a strong MySQL database password of your own choice (at the time of writing, the latest WordPress needs MySQL v.5.7; this can change in the future, so check out the official WordPress Docker Hub page):

   ```
   docker run --restart=always --name wordpressdb -e MYSQL_ROOT_
   PASSWORD=<PASSWORD> -e MYSQL_DATABASE=wordpress -d mysql:5.7
   ```

2. Next, install and run the official WordPress image and run an instance of it as a Docker container, connecting it to the MySQL container (providing the same `<PASSWORD>` string from the previous step):

   ```
   docker run --restart=always -e WORDPRESS_DB_PASSWORD=<password> -d
   --name wordpress --link wordpressdb:mysql -p 8080:80 wordpress
   ```

3. Now the MySQL and WordPress container should already be running. To check the currently running containers, type:

   ```
   docker ps
   ```

4. To get all the Docker WordPress container settings, use:

   ```
   docker inspect wordpress
   ```

5. To check the container's log file for our WordPress container, run the following command:

   ```
   docker logs -f wordpress
   ```

6. Open a browser on a computer in the same network as the server running the Docker daemon and type in the following command to access your Wordpress installation (replace IP address with the one from your Docker server):

   ```
   http://<IP ADDRESS OF DOCKER SERVER>:8080/
   ```

How it works...

A Docker image is a collection of all the files that make up a software application and its functional dependencies, as well as information about any changes as you modify or improve on its content (in the form of a change log). It is a non-runnable, read-only version of your application and can be compared to an ISO file. If you want to run such an image, a Linux container will be created out of it automatically by cloning the image. This is what then actually executes. It's a real scalable system because you can run multiple containers from the same image. As we have seen, Docker is really not only the tools you need to work with images and containers but a complete platform as it also provides tools to access already pre-made images of all kinds of Linux server software. This is really the beauty of the whole Docker system because most of the time you don't have to reinvent the wheel twice trying to create your own docker image from scratch. Just go to the Docker Hub (`https://hub.docker.com`), search for a software you want to run as a container, and when you find it then just use the `docker run` command, providing the Docker Hub name of the image, and you are done. Docker really can be a life-saver when thinking about all the endless hours trying to get the latest trendy programs to work with all the dependencies you need to compile and trying to get it to install.

So what did we learn from this experience?

We started our journey by using the `docker run` command which downloaded two images from the remote Docker Hub repos and put them into a local image store (called `mysql:5.7` and `wordpress`) and then run them (create containers out of them). To get a list of all the images downloaded on our machine, type `docker images`. As we have seen, both `run` command lines provided the `-e` command line parameter, which we need to set some essential environment variables that will then be visible within the container. These include the MySQL database we want to run and the MySQL root password to set and access them. Here we see a very important feature of Docker: containers that can communicate which each other! Often you can just stack your application together from different Docker container pieces and make the whole system very easy to use. Another important parameter was `-p` which is used to create a port mapping from our host port `8080` to the internal HTTP port 80 and opens the firewall to allow incoming traffic on this port as well. `--restart=always` is useful to make the image container restartable, so the containers automatically get restarted on reboot of the host machine. Afterwards, we introduced you to Docker's `ps` command line parameter which prints out all running Docker containers. Here the command should print out two running containers called `wordpressdb` and `wordpress`, together with their `CONTAINER_ID`. This ID is a unique MD5 hash we will use all the time in most of the Docker command line inputs whenever we need to reference a specific container (in this recipe we referenced by container name which is also possible). Afterwards, we showed you how to print out a container's configuration by using the `inspect` parameter. Then, to get the Wordpress container's log file in an open stream, we used the `log -f` parameter. Finally, since the `-p 8080:80` mapping allows incoming access to our server at port 8080, we could then access our Wordpress installation from any computer in the same network using a browser. This will open the Wordpress installation screen.

Note that if you have any connection problems while downloading any containers from Docker at any time, such as `dial tcp: lookup index.docker.io: no such host`, restart the Docker service before trying again.

There's more...

In this section, we will show you how to start and stop a container and how to attach to your container.

Stopping and starting a container

In the main recipe, we used Docker's `run` command which is actually a wrapper for two other Docker commands: `create` and `start`. As the names of these commands suggest, the `create` command creates (clones) a container from an existing image and if it does not exist in the local image cache then it downloads it from a given Docker registry (such as the predefined Docker hub), while the `start` command actually starts it. To get a list of all the containers (running or stopped) on your computer, type: `docker ps -a`. Now identify a stopped or a started container, and find out its specific `CONTAINER_ID`. Then we can start a stopped container or stop a running one by providing the correct `CONTAINER_ID` such as `docker start CONTAINER_ID`. Examples are: `docker start 03b53947d812` or `docker stop a2fe12e61545` (the `CONTAINER_ID` hashes will vary on your computer).

Sometimes you need to remove a container; for example, if you want to completely change its command line parameters when creating from an image. For removing a container, use the `rm` command (but remember that it has to be stopped before): `docker stop b7f720fbfd23; docker rm b7f720fbfd23`

Attaching and interacting with your container

Linux containers are completely isolated processes running in a separated environment on your server and there is no way to log in to it like logging into a normal server using `ssh`. If you need to access your containers BASH shell then you can run the `docker exec` command, which is particularly useful for debugging problems or modifying your container (for example, installing new packages or updating programs or files in it). Note that this only works on running containers and you need to know your container's ID before (type `docker ps` to find out) you run the following command: `docker exec -it CONTAINER_ID /bin/bash`, for example `docker exec -it d22ddf594f0d /bin/bash`. Once successfully attached to the container, you will see a slightly changed command-line prompt with the `CONTAINER_ID` as hostname; for example, `root@d22ddf594f0d:/var/www/html#`. If you need to exit your container, type `exit`.

Creating your own images from Dockerfiles and uploading to Docker Hub

Besides images and containers, Docker has a third very important term called a **Dockerfile**. A Dockerfile is like a recipe on how to create an environment for a specific application, which means that it contains the blueprint and exact description on how to build a specific image file. For example, if we would like to containerize a webserver-based application, we would define all the dependencies for it, such as the base Linux system that provides the system dependencies such as Ubuntu, Debian, CentOS, and so on (this does not mean we *virtualize* the complete operating system but just use the system dependencies), as well as all applications, dynamic libraries, and services such as PHP, Apache, and MySQL in the Dockerfile and also all special configuration options or environment variables. There are two ways to build your own custom images. One, you could download an existing base image as we did in the previous Wordpress recipe and then attach to the container using BASH, install your additional software, make the changes to your configuration files, and then commit the container as a new image to the registry. Alternatively, here in this recipe, we will teach you how to build your own Docker image from a new Dockerfile for an Express.js web application server and upload it to your own Docker Hub account.

Getting ready

To complete this recipe, you will require a working installation of the CentOS 7 operating system with root privileges, a console-based text editor of your choice, and a connection to the Internet in order to communicate with the Docker Hub. It is expected that Docker is already installed and is running. Also, for uploading your new image to the Docker Hub, you need to create a new Docker Hub user account there. Just go to `https://hub.docker.com/` and register there for free. In our example, we will use a fictitious new Docker Hub user ID called `johndoe`.

How to do it...

1. To begin, log in as root and create a new directory structure using your Docker Hub user ID (substitute the `johndoe` directory name appropriately with your own ID), and open an empty Dockerfile where you put in your image's building blueprint:

   ```
   mkdir -p ~/johndoe/centos7-expressjs

   cd $_ ; vi Dockerfile
   ```

2. Put in the following content into that file:

   ```
   FROM centos:centos7

   RUN yum install -y epel-release;yum install -y npm;

   RUN npm install express --save
   ```

```
COPY . ./src
EXPOSE 8080
CMD ["node", "/src/index.js"]
```

3. Save and close the file. Now create your first Express.js web application, which we will deploy on the new container. Open the following file in the current directory:

```
vi index.js
```

4. Now put in the following JavaScript content:

```
var express = require('express'), app = express();
app.get('/', function (req, res) {res.send('Hello CentOS 7
cookbook!\n');});
app.listen(8080);
```

5. Now to build an image from this Dockerfile, stay in the current directory and use the following command (don't forget the dot at the end of this line and replace johndoe with your own Docker Hub ID):

```
docker build -t johndoe/centos7-expressjs .
```

6. After successfully building the image, let's run it as a container:

```
docker run -p 8081:8080 -d johndoe/centos7-expressjs
```

7. Finally, test if we can make an HTTP request to our new Express.js web application server running in our new container:

```
curl -i localhost:8081
```

8. If the Docker image is successfully running on the Express.js server, the following HTTP response should occur (truncated to the last line):

```
Hello CentOS 7 cookbook!
```

Uploading your image to the Docker Hub

1. After creating a new Docker Hub account ID called johndoe, we will start to login to the site using the following command—stay in the directory where you put your Dockerfile from the last step—for example ~/johndoe/centos7-expressjs (provide the username, the password, and the registration e-mail when asked):

```
docker login
```

2. Now, to push your new image created in this recipe to the Docker Hub (again replace johndoe with your own user ID), use:

```
docker push johndoe/centos7-expressjs
```

3. After uploading, you will be able to find your image on the Docker Hub web page search. Alternatively, you can use the command line:

```
docker search expressjs
```

How it works...

Here in this short recipe, we showed you how to create your first Dockerfile which will create a CentOS 7 container to serve Express.js applications, which is a modern alternative to LAMP stacks where you program JavaScript on the client-and server-side.

So what did we learn from this experience?

As you can see, a Dockerfile is an elegant way to describe all the instructions on how to create an image. The commands are straight-forward to understand and you use special keywords to instruct Docker what to do in order to produce an image out of it. The FROM command tells Docker which base image we should use. Fortunately, someone has already created a base image from the CentOS 7 system dependencies (this will be downloaded from Docker Hub). Next, we used the RUN command, which just executes commands as on a BASH command-line. We use this command to install dependencies on our system in order to run Express.js applications (it's based on the Node.js rpm package which we access by installing the EPEL repository first). The COPY command copies files from our host machine to a specific location on the container. We need this to copy our index.js file which will create all our Express. js web server code in a later step on to the container. EXPOSE, as the name implies, exposes an internal container port to the outside host system. Since by default Express.js is listening on 8080, we need to do this here. While all these commands shown up to this point will only be executed once when creating the image, the next command CMD will be run every time we start the container. The command node /src/index.js will be executed and instructs the system to start the Express.js web server with the index.js file (which we already provided in this directory by copying it from the host machine). We don't want to go into any details about the JavaScript part of the program—it just handles HTTP GET requests and returns the Hello World string. In the second part of this recipe, we showed you how to push our new created image to the Docker Hub. In order to do so, login with your Docker user account. Then we can push our image to the repository.

As this is a very simple Dockerfile, there is much more to learn about this subject. To see a list of all the commands available in the Dockerfile, use man Dockerfile. Also, you should visit the Docker Hub and browse the Dockerfiles (under the section *Source Repository hosted on GitHub*) of some interesting projects to learn how to create some highly sophisticated image files with just a handful of commands on your own.

Setting up and working with a private Docker registry

While we have learned in a former recipe in this chapter how easy it is to upload our own images to the official Docker Hub, everything we put there will be exposed to the public. If you work on a private or closed-source project within a corporate environment or just want to test things out before publishing to everyone, chances are high that you would prefer your own, protected or cooperate-wide private Docker registry. Here in this recipe we will show you how you can set up and work with your own Docker registry that will be available in your own private network and which will be protected by TLS encryption and which will use user authentication so you can control exactly who can use it (push and pull images to and from it).

Getting ready

To complete this recipe, you will require a working installation of the CentOS 7 operating system with root privileges, a console-based text editor of your choice, and a connection to the Internet in order to facilitate the download of additional packages. In our example, we will install the Docker Registry on a server with the IP address `192.168.1.100`. Change the recipe's commands appropriately to fit your needs. You need to have set a FQDN for this server, otherwise the registry will not work. For simplicity, we will use the `/etc/hosts` approach instead of setting up and configuring a DNS server (see *Chapter 9, Working with Domains* if you would like to do this instead). Also, you need an Apache web server on your Docker server running which must be accessible from your whole private network.

How to do it...

Complete all the following steps in this recipe with user root on every computer in your network you want to connect to the Docker registry!

1. On each computer you want to access your Docker registry, as well as on our Docker registry server itself, with the IP address `192.168.1.100`, define the domain name of the Docker registry, which in our example will be `dockerserver.home` (replace the `dockerserver.home` part appropriately if you use a different domain name):

    ```
    echo "export DCKREG=dockerserver.home" >> ~/.bash_profile
    source ~/.bash_profile
    ```

2. Now we will define the FQDN of our Docker server registry on each computer in our network we want to use the registry on (as well as on the Docker registry server itself). Log in as root on every machine and type the following command. Skip this step if you have already defined your Docker registry's server's domain name via a BIND DNS server (change the IP address of your Docker service `192.168.1.100` appropriately):

```
echo "192.168.1.100 $DCKREG" >>  /etc/hosts
```

Steps to be done on our Docker registry server (192.168.1.100)

1. First create a TLS certificate for our Docker registry certificate (use the FQDN you defined in DCKREG when asked for a `Common name` (for name; for example your name or your server's hostname) `[]:dockerserver.home`):

```
cd; mkdir -p ~/certs; openssl req -newkey rsa:4096 -nodes -sha256
-keyout certs/domain.key -x509 -days 365 -out certs/domain.crt
```

2. Next, we need to copy the new certificate to the Docker trusted certificate's location as well as to the system's default trusted certificate location and rebuild the certificate index:

```
mkdir -p /etc/docker/certs.d/$DCKREG\:5000

cp  ~/certs/domain.crt /etc/docker/certs.d/$DCKREG\:5000/ca.crt

cp ~/certs/domain.crt /etc/pki/ca-trust/source/anchors/docker-
registry.crt

update-ca-trust
```

3. Also, copy the certificate to our Apache web server so we can easily access it from the Docker clients later:

```
cp ~/certs/domain.crt /var/www/html/docker-registry.crt
```

4. Next, we will finally download, create, and run our Docker registry as a container:

```
mkdir ~/auth; touch ~/auth/htpasswd docker run -d -p 5000:5000
--restart=always --name registry -v /

root/certs:/certs -v /root/auth:/auth -v /reg:/var/lib/registry -e
REGISTRY_HTTP_TLS_CERTIFICATE=/certs/domain.crt -e

 REGISTRY_HTTP_TLS_KEY=/certs/domain.key -e "REGISTRY_AUTH_
HTPASSWD_REALM=Registry Realm" -e REGISTRY_AUTH_HTPASSWD_PATH=/
auth/htpasswd -e REGISTRY_AUTH=htpasswd registry:2
```

5. Now check if the registry is running (in the output you should find it listening on `[::]:5000, tls`):

```
docker logs registry
```

6. For setting up user authentication for our registry, use the following command (here we use `johndoe` as the username and `mysecretpassword` as the password for authentication. Change these two values to fit your needs. Repeat this command for every user account you want to have later for your users to login):

```
cd; docker run -it --entrypoint htpasswd -v $PWD/auth:/auth -w /
auth registry:2 -Bbc /auth/htpasswd johndoe mysecretpassword
```

7. Next restart the registry to apply your user account changes:

```
docker restart registry
```

8. Now create a new firewalld service and activate it in our firewall to make incoming connections to our new Docker registry port `5000` possible:

```
sed 's/80/5000/g' /usr/lib/firewalld/services/http.xml | sed
's/WWW (HTTP)/Docker registry/g' | sed 's/<description>.*<\/
description>//g' > /etc/firewalld/services/docker-reg.xml
```

```
firewall-cmd --reload
```

```
firewall-cmd --permanent --add-service=docker-reg; firewall-cmd
--reload
```

Steps to be done on every client needing access to our registry

1. Finally we can test connecting to our own new TLS-enhanced private Docker registry with user authentication by logging in on any computer in the same network as our Docker registry with root.

2. The first step is to install Docker on every client that wants to connect to the Docker registry:

```
yum update && curl -sSL https://get.docker.com/ | sh
```

3. Next, on every client wanting to connect to our new Docker registry, set up the server's certificate on the client first before we are able to connect to it (this step has been tested on CentOS 7 clients only):

```
mkdir -p /etc/docker/certs.d/$DCKREG\:5000
```

```
curl http://$DCKREG/docker-registry.crt -o /tmp/cert.crt
```

```
cp /tmp/cert.crt /etc/docker/certs.d/$DCKREG\:5000/ca.crt
```

```
cp /tmp/cert.crt /etc/pki/ca-trust/source/anchors/docker-registry.
crt
```

```
update-ca-trust
```

4. For testing, we start by pulling a new small test image from the official Docker Hub. Log in to the official Docker Hub by using your Docker Hub account (see a previous recipe in this chapter):

```
docker login
```

5. Now pull a small image called `busybox`:

```
docker pull busybox
```

6. Afterwards, switch the Docker registry server to use our own that we set up in this recipe (enter the username and password, for example, `johndoe / mysecretpassword`. Leave the e-mail field blank):

```
docker login $DCKREG:5000
```

7. Next, to push a Docker image from our client to our new private Docker registry, we need to tag it to be in our registry's domain:

```
docker tag busybox $DCKREG:5000/busybox
```

8. Finally, push the image to our own registry:

```
docker push $DCKREG:5000/busybox
```

9. Congratulations! You have just pushed your first image to your private Docker repository. You can now pull this image `$DCKREG:5000/busybox` on any other client set up to communicate to our repository. To get a list of all the available images, use (change the account information accordingly):

```
curl https://johndoe:mysecretpassword@$DCKREG:5000/v2/_catalog
```

How it works...

In this recipe we showed you how to set up your own Docker registry running in a Docker container on the server. It is very important to understand that you will need to configure a FQDN for your registry server because it is mandatory for the whole system to work.

So what did we learn from this experience?

We began by configuring the Docker registry's FQDN on every computer using the `/etc/hosts` approach. Then we created a new certificate on the Docker registry server which will be used to communicate securely using TLS encryption between clients and registry. Next we installed the new generated certificate on the `httpd` server, so it is accessible to all the clients later; also in a specific Docker directory to make it accessible for Docker as well; and in the default trusted certificate location of the server where we also rebuilt the certificate cache for this server. Afterwards, we used the `docker run` command to download, install, and run our new Docker registry in a docker container itself on this server. We provided a list of parameters to configure TLS encryption and user authentication.

In the next step, we attached to the registry to create new `htpasswd` accounts. You can repeat this step whenever you need new accounts for your registry. Don't forget to restart the registry container afterwards. Next, on every client we want to make communications to our new Docker registry, we need to install the server's certificate also in the same places as on the server itself; thus we downloaded it from the HTTP source implemented previously and copied it to the various locations. To test things out on the client, next we connected to the official Docker Hub to download a random image we wanted to push to our own registry in the next step. We downloaded the `busybox` image to our own image cache and afterwards switched to connecting to our new private Docker registry. Before we could upload the image to the new location, we had to give it a proper tag that fitted the new server name and then we were able to push the image to our new Docker registry. The server is now available at port 5000 in the complete network. Remember that, if you don't want to use your own registry any more on the clients, you can always switch back to the official `docker` repository using `docker login`.

There is so much more to learn about Docker. In the recipes of this chapter we only scratched the surface of the Docker platform. If you want to learn more about it, consider going to `https://www.Packtpub.com` and check out one of the many titles available at this website about it.

14

Working with SELinux

In this chapter, we will cover the following topics:

- ▶ Installing and configuring important SELinux tools
- ▶ Working with SELinux security contexts
- ▶ Working with policies
- ▶ Troubleshooting SELinux

Introduction

This chapter is a collection of recipes that strive to demystify **Security-Enhanced Linux** (**SELinux**), a mature technology for hardening your Linux system using additional security features added to the basic security system. It has been around for many years in the CentOS world but nevertheless is a somewhat little-known and confusing topic for a lot of system administrators.

Installing and configuring important SELinux tools

The most significant security feature of any Linux system is providing access control—often called **Discretionary Access Control** (**DAC**)—which allows the owner of an object (such as a file) to set security attributes for it (for example, deciding who can read or write to a file using the `chown` and `chmod` commands). While this old and very simple security system was sufficient in ancient UNIX times, it does not meet all the modern requirements of security, where servers and services are constantly connected to the Internet.

Often, security breaches can be initiated by attackers exploiting buggy or misconfigured applications and the permissions to them. This is why the SELinux has been developed. Its main purpose is to enhance the security of the DAC system in Linux. It does so by adding an additional security layer on top of DAC, which is called **Mandatory Access Control** (**MAC**), and which can provide fine-grain access control to every single component of your system. SELinux has already been enabled on CentOS 7 and is absolutely recommended for any server connected directly to the Internet. Here in this recipe, we will install additional tools and configure them to better manage your SELinux system, and help in the troubleshooting and monitoring process.

Getting ready

To complete this recipe, you will require a working installation of the CentOS 7 operating system with root privileges and a connection to the Internet in order to download additional packages. For the best learning experience, it is also preferred that you work through this chapter recipe by recipe, in the order that they appear, because they build upon each other.

How to do it...

Throughout this book, we already applied programs such as `semanage` from the `rpm` `policecoreutils-python` package to manage our SELinux environment. If you missed installing it, we will begin this recipe by doing so (skip step 1 if you have already done this before):

1. Log in as root and install the following basic toolkit to work with SELinux:

    ```
    yum install policycoreutils-python
    ```

2. Now, we need some additional tools that will also be needed later in the course of this chapter:

    ```
    yum install setools setools-console setroubleshoot*
    ```

3. Next, install and configure the SELinux manual pages as they are not available by default on CentOS 7, but are important for getting detailed information about specific policies, security contexts, and SELinux Booleans later. First, we need to install another package:

    ```
    yum install policycoreutils-devel
    ```

4. Afterwards, let's generate all the man pages for all SELinux security context policies currently available on the system, and then update the manual pages database afterwards:

    ```
    sepolicy manpage -a -p /usr/share/man/man8; mandb
    ```

How it works...

By following this recipe, we installed all the tools needed for our daily work with SELinux. Also, we generated all available SELinux manual pages, which will be our primary source of information when working with SELinux, and also for troubleshooting SELinux services later.

SELinux has two primary and fundamental terms that we need to understand before diving into the remaining recipes in this chapter: **labels** (or more technically, security contexts) and **policies**. From SELinux's perspective, a Linux system is divided into a number of different objects. Objects, for example, are all files, processes, users, sockets, and pipes in a system. In a SELinux context, every such object gets a special label. SELinux policies are the rules to control access to these objects using the labels defined on them: On every access attempt to such an object (for example, a file read), all SELinux policies available to the system will be searched if there is a rule for the specific label to make access control decisions (allow or deny the access).

So, what did we learn from this experience?

A lot of system administrators seem to avoid SELinux *like the plague*, and a trend in a lot of instruction manuals and tutorials leans towards disabling it altogether right after the installation of CentOS 7 because people seem to fear it and don't want to mess with it, or are even frustrated if some networking service is not working correctly out-of-the-box. Often, they blame SELinux for any connection problems, so it often looks easier to disable it altogether rather than find out the true reasons by delving into the inner workings of SELinux. If you are disabling it, you are missing out one of the most critical security features of CentOS 7 that can prevent a lot of harm to your system in the event of an attack! In the last few years, the SELinux project has evolved very much and is easier to use than ever. A lot of convenient tools for working with it have emerged, and we get more of a complete set of policies to work with all the major applications and services available. By installing these tools, we are now ready to use SELinux and work with it in the most convenient way possible.

There's more...

There are three different modes when it comes to SELinux. While **Enhanced** is the only true mode that really protects us and enhances our server's security, there are two other modes: **Disabled** and **Permissive**. Disabled means SELinux is turned off, which will never be an option for us in this book and is not discussed any further as it does not make sense to get rid of this fantastic CentOS feature. When disabled, our system is not enhanced by SELinux and the good old DAC system is the only source of protection we have at hand. Permissive mode means SELinux is turned on, the policy rules are loaded, and all objects are labeled with a specific security context, but the system is not enforcing these policies. This is like a dry-run parameter that a lot of Linux based command-line tools have: it simulates the system under SELinux enhanced security protection, and the system logs every SELinux policy violation as it would when running for real. This is a great way to debug the system, or to analyze the consequences that a normal, enforced run would have had on the system.

Often, it is used if you are unsure about the impact of using SELinux. As this mode does not really provide us with any additional security, we will eventually need to switch to **Enforcing** mode if we want enhanced security! Again, this is the only mode that protects us; SELinux is fully running with all the policies loaded and is enforcing these rules on the system. You should always aim for Enforcing mode on any system! To view the current mode, use the command `sestatus`. We can see the current SELinux mode in the `Current mode` line in the output. On CentOS 7, SELinux is in Enforcing mode by default, which again tells us that the system is fully protected by it. To change this mode to permissive mode, use the command `setenforce permissive`. Now, validate your setting using `sestatus` again. To revert your changes back to Enforcing mode, use `setenforce enforcing`. Setting the SELinux mode using `setenforce` is only setting it temporarily, and it will not survive a reboot (take a look at the `Mode from config` file in the `sestatus` output). To change this permanently, open the `/etc/selinux/config` file and change the `SELINUX=` configuration parameter.

Working with SELinux security contexts

As we have learned from the previous recipe in this chapter, SELinux is all about labels and policies. In this recipe, we will show you how to work with these labels, also known as security contexts.

Getting ready

To complete this recipe, you will require a working installation of the CentOS 7 operating system with root privileges. It is assumed that you are working through this chapter recipe by recipe, so by now you should have installed the SELinux tools from the previous recipe and generated all the SELinux man pages for the policies. As you may notice, some of the commands that we will show you in this recipe have already been applied in other recipes in this book. We will explain them here in detail. For using the `netstat` program, install the package, `net-tools`, with the YUM package manager.

How to do it...

As we have learned in a previous recipe, almost every component in a SELinux system is an object (files, directories, processes, users, and so on). We will begin this recipe by showing you how to print out the SELinux labels for all kinds of objects using the `-Z` command-line flag, which a lot of basic Linux commands on a SELinux system support.

1. To begin with, log in as root and type the following commands to explore SELinux security context information from various kinds of objects:

   ```
   id -Z

   ls -Z
   ```

```
ps -auxZ

netstat -tulpenZ
```

2. Next, to list all available security context names for the files and directories on your system, use the following command (which we filtered for `httpd` labels only):

```
semanage fcontext -l | grep httpd
```

3. Next, let's create a new empty file that we can work with:

```
touch /tmp/selinux-context-test.txt
```

4. Show the current security context of the new file (should contain the type `user_tmp_t`):

```
ls -Z /tmp/selinux-context-test.txt
```

5. Finally, change the `user_tmp_t` type to a random `samba_share_t` label name:

```
semanage fcontext -a -t samba_share_t /tmp/selinux-context-test.txt

restorecon -v /tmp/selinux-context-test.txt
```

6. Perform a test to validate your changes:

```
ls -Z /tmp/selinux-context-test.txt
```

How it works...

Here in this recipe, we have shown you how to display labels (security contexts) of various SELinux object types, how to show all available label names, and how to modify or set them on the example of the file object. Working on a SELinux enhanced system on a daily basis, most administrators would confirm that the most important objects we have to manage security contexts for are files, directories, and processes. Also, you need to remember that every SELinux object can have only one security context.

So, what did we learn from this experience?

As we have have seen, we can use the `-Z` parameter on a lot of different standard Linux command-line tools to print out their SELinux security context. Here, we have shown you examples to display labels for users, files and directories, processes, and network connections, which we could query with the `id`, `ls`, `ps`, and `netstat` commands. In the output of these commands, we see that every security context label of every such object consists of three values: user (flagged by `_u`), role (`_r`), and type (`_t`). The type field is used as the main mechanism to do all our access control decisions in the standard SELinux type (which is called targeted), so we often call the whole SELinux access control process **type enforcement** (**TE**).

The other values user and role in an object's label are only necessary for very advanced SELinux configurations not discussed here. In order to show all the available context types for use on our system, use the command-line `seinfo -t`. These SELinux types are a very important concept that we need to understand. For file and directory objects, they are used to *bundle* together groups of objects related to each other, and that should be protected or treated the same so that we can define specific policy rules on them. For example, we can assign each file in the standard mail spool directory, `/var/spool/mail`, of the type `mail_spool_t`, and then create an access rule policy in which we will use this type to allow specific access. In the context of processes, type values are called domains. Here, types are used as a way to isolate and *sandbox* processes: any process that has a specified domain name can only communicate and interact with other processes in the same domain (with some exceptions, such as transitions not discussed here). This *isolating* of processes via domains greatly reduces security risks. When processes get compromised, they can only damage themselves and nothing else.

> SELinux is sometimes called a sandboxing system. Starting from the assumption that software will always have bugs, SELinux provides ways to isolate components of the software such that a breach in one component doesn't compromise another.

If you type in `ps -auxZ`, you will also see that there are processes that run in a domain called `unconfined_t`. Processes running with this label are not protected by SELinux policies, which means that, if an unconfined process is compromised, SELinux does not prevent an attacker from gaining access to other system resources and data. Here, security falls back to standard DAC rules, which will be your only and exclusive protection instead.

After we discussed how to display security contexts, next in the recipe we showed you how you can set and change them. In some older documentation as well as in some SELinux policy `man` pages, you will encounter examples with a tool called `chcon`, which is used to modify the security context of your objects. The usage of this tool is not the recommended approach any more, and you should always replace such command line examples with the newer `semanage fcontext -a -t` command-line in combination with the `restorecon` program. For `semanage`, you provide the label type name with `-t`, and then provide the filename you want to set it for. Then, with `restorecon`, you provide the filename to which you want to apply the change made by `semanage` earlier. This is needed because security context can be set on two levels. It can be set to the policy and on a filesystem level. The `chcon` command sets the new context directly on the filesystem, while the policy context does not get altered. This can be a problem, for example, if you want to reset or change the security context of your filesystem later (this is called relabeling)—which means that all the security context will be applied from the policy to the filesystem, overwriting all your changes made with `chcon`. So it is better to use `semanage`, which will write to the policy, and then use `restorecon`, which will synchronize the policy labels to the filesystem, keeping everything up-to-date. If you want to set labels for directories instead of single files, you can use regular expressions; to see some examples and further command-line options; type `man semanage-fcontext` and browse to the `EXAMPLES` section.

Working with policies

At the core of every SELinux system are the policies. These are the exact rules that define the access rights and relationships between all our objects. As we have learned earlier, all our system's objects have labels, and one of them is a type identifier that can then be used to enforce rules laid down by policies. In every SELinux enabled system, by default, all access to any object is prohibited unless a policy rule has been defined otherwise. Here, in this recipe, we will show you how we can query and customize SELinux policies. As you may notice, some of the commands have already been applied in other recipes in this book, such as for the httpd or ftpd daemons. Here, you will find out how policies work.

Getting ready

To complete this recipe, you will require a working installation of the CentOS 7 operating system with root privileges. It is assumed that you are working through this chapter recipe by recipe, so by now you should have installed the SELinux tools from the previous recipe and generated all SELinux man pages for the policies. For our tests here, we will use the Apache web server, so please make sure it is installed and running on your system (Refer to recipe *Installing Apache and serving web pages* in *Chapter 12, Providing Web Services*).

How to do it...

1. To begin, log in as root and type the following command to show all SELinux Boolean policy settings, filtered by the httpd daemon only:

    ```
    semanage boolean -l | grep httpd
    ```

2. To get more information about a specific policy and its contained Booleans, read the corresponding man page; for example, for httpd type the following:

    ```
    man httpd_selinux
    ```

3. Here, within the manual pages for the httpd policy, we will, among others, find detailed information about every httpd policy Boolean available. For example, there is a section about httpd_use_nfso. To toggle single policy features, use the setsebool command together with the policy Boolean name with the on or off parameter, as shown here:

    ```
    setsebool httpd_use_nfs on
    setsebool httpd_use_nfs off
    ```

How it works...

Here in this recipe, we have shown you how to work with SELinux Booleans. Remember that SELinux follows the model of least privilege, which means that SELinux policies enable only the least amount of features to any object; like a system service, they need to perform their task and nothing more. These features of a policy can be controlled (activated or deactivated) using corresponding SELinux Booleans at runtime without the need to understand the inner workings of policy writing. It is a concept to make policies customizable and extremely flexible. In other recipes in this book, we have already worked with enabling SELinux Booleans to add special policy features, such as enabling Apache or FTP home directories, which are all disabled by default.

What did we learn from this experience?

SELinux Booleans are like switches to enable or disable certain functionalities in your SELinux policy. We started this recipe using the `semanage` command to show all Booleans available on the system, and we filtered by `http` to get only those related to this service. As you can see, there are a huge number of Booleans available in your system, and most of them are disabled or off (the model of least privilege); to get more information about a specific policy and its Boolean values, use the SELinux man pages that we installed in a previous recipe. Sometimes, it can be difficult to find a specific man page of interest. Use the following command to search for man page names that are available: `man -k _selinux | grep http`. In our example, `httpd_selinux` is the correct man page to get detailed information about the `httpd` policy. Finally, if we decide to switch a specific SELinux Boolean feature, we will use the `setsebool` command. You should remember that setting Booleans in this way only works until reboot. To make those settings permanent, use the `-p` flag, for example, `setsebool -P httpd_use_nfs on`.

There's more...

With all our knowledge from the previous recipes so far, we are now able to show an example where we put everything together. Here, we will see SELinux security contexts and policies in action for the `httpd` service. If the Apache web server is running, we can get the SELinux domain name of the `httpd` process using the following line:

ps auxZ | grep httpd

This will show us that the `httpd` domain (type) is called `httpd_t`. To get the SELinux label of our web root directory, type in the following command:

ls -alZ /var/www/html

This will tell us that the security context type of our Apache web server's web root directory is called `httpd_sys_content_t`. Now, with this information, we can get the exact rules for the Apache domain from our policy:

sesearch --allow | grep httpd_t

This will print out every `httpd` policy rule available. If we filter the output for the `httpd_sys_content_t` context type, the following line comes up for files again:

allow httpd_t httpd_sys_content_t : file { ioctl read getattr lock open }

This shows us which source target context is allowed to access, which destination target context, and with which access rights. In our example for the Apache web server, this specifies that the `httpd` process that runs as domain `httpd_t` can access, open, and modify all the files on the filesystem that match the `httpd_sys_content_t` context type (all files in the `/var/www/html` directory match this criterion). Now, to validate this rule, create a temporary file and move it to the Apache web root directory: `echo "CentOS7 Cookbook" > /tmp/test.txt;mv /tmp/test.txt /var/www/html`. Any file inherits the security context of the directory in which it is created. If we had created the file directly in the web root directory, or had copied the file instead of moving it (copying means creating a copy), it would automatically be in the correct `httpd_sys_content_t` context and fully accessible by Apache. But, as we moved the file from the `/tmp` directory, it will stay as the `user_tmp_t` type in the web root directory. If you now try to fetch the URL, for example,, `curl http://localhost/test.txt`, you should get a 403 forbidden message. This is because the `user_tmp_t` type is not part of the `httpd_t` policy rule for file objects, because, as said before, everything that is not defined in a policy rule will be blocked by default. To make the file accessible, we will now change its security context label to the correct type:

semanage fcontext -a -t httpd_sys_content_t /var/www/html/test.txt

restorecon -v /var/www/html/test.txt

Now, again fetch `curl http://localhost/test.txt`, which should be accessible, and print out the correct text: CentOS7 cookbook.

Remember that, if you copy a file, the security context type is inherited from the targeted parent directory. If you want to preserve the original context when copying, use `cp -preserve=context` instead.

Troubleshooting SELinux

In this recipe, you will learn how to troubleshoot SELinux policies, which is most often needed when access to some SELinux objects has been denied and you need to find out the reasons for it. In this recipe, we will show you how to work with the `sealert` tool, which will create human-readable and understandable error messages to work with.

Getting ready

To complete this recipe, you will require a working installation of the CentOS 7 operating system with root privileges. It is assumed that you are working through this chapter recipe by recipe, so by now you should have installed the SELinux tools and applied the *Working with policies* recipe in this chapter, as we will produce some SELinux denial events in order to show you how to use the log file tools.

How to do it...

1. To begin, login as root and provoke a SELinux denial event:

   ```
   touch /var/www/html/test2.html

   semanage fcontext -a -t user_tmp_t /var/www/html/test2.html

   restorecon -v /var/www/html/test2.html

   curl http://localhost/test2.html
   ```

2. Now, let's generate an up-to-date human readable log file:

   ```
   sealert -a /var/log/audit/audit.log
   ```

3. In the program's output, you will get a detailed description of any SELinux problem and, at the end of each so called alert, you will even find a suggested solution to fix the problem; in our example, the alert of interest should read (the output is truncated) as shown next:

   ```
   SELinux is preventing /usr/sbin/httpd from open access on the file
   /var/www/html/test2.html.
   ```

   ```
   /var/www/html/test2.html default label should be httpd_sys_
   content_t
   ```

How it works...

Here in this recipe, we showed you how easily one can troubleshoot SELinux problems using the `sealert` program. We started by provoking a SELinux deny access problem by creating a new file in the web root directory and assigning it a wrong context type of value `user_tmp_t`, which has no access rule defined in the `httpd` policy. Then, we used the `curl` command to try and fetch the website and actually produce the **Access Vector Cache** (**AVC**) denial message in the SELinux logs. Denial messages are logged when SELinux denies access. The primary source where all SELinux logging information is stored is the audit log file, which can be found at `/var/log/audit/audit.log`, and easier-to-read denial messages will also be written to `/var/log/messages`. Here, instead of manually grepping for error messages and combining both log files, we use the `sealert` tool, which is a convenience program that will parse the audit and messages log file and present valuable AVC content in a human-readable format. At the end of each alert message, you will also find a suggested solution to the problem. Please note that those are auto-generated messages and should always be questioned before applying.

15
Monitoring
IT Infrastructure

In this chapter, we will cover the following topics:

- ▸ Installing and configuring Nagios Core
- ▸ Setting up NRPE on remote client hosts
- ▸ Monitoring important remote system metrics

Introduction

This chapter is a collection of recipes that provide the necessary steps to set up the de-facto industry standard, open source network monitoring framework: Nagios Core.

Installing and configuring Nagios Core

In this recipe, we will learn how to install Nagios Core version 4, an open-source network monitoring system that checks whether hosts and services are working and notifies users when problems occur or services become unavailable. Nagios provides solutions to monitor your complete IT infrastructure and is designed with an architecture that is highly extendable and customizable and goes far beyond simple bash scripts to monitor your services. (Refer to the *Monitoring important server infrastructure* recipe in *Chapter 3, Managing the System*.)

Getting ready

To complete this recipe, you will require a working installation of the CentOS 7 operating system with root privileges, a console-based text editor of your choice, and a connection to the Internet in order to facilitate the download of additional packages. Nagios Core 4 is not available in the official sources but from the EPEL repository; make sure to have installed it before (refer to the *Using a third-party repository* recipe in *Chapter 4, Managing Packages with YUM*). For the Nagios web frontend, you need a running Apache2 web server as well as PHP (refer to the recipes from *Chapter 12, Providing Web Services*) installed on your Nagios server. In our example, the Nagios server has the IP address 192.168.1.7, and it will be able to monitor all IT infrastructure in the complete 192.168.1.0/24 subnet.

How to do it...

Nagios Core 4 is not available by default, so let's begin by installing all the required packages:

1. To do so, log in as root and type the following command:

    ```
    yum install nagios nagios-plugins-all nagios-plugins-nrpe nrpe
    ```

2. First, create a new user account called `nagiosadmin`, which is needed for authentication to the web frontend (enter a secure password when prompted), then reload the Apache configuration:

    ```
    htpasswd /etc/nagios/passwd nagiosadmin  && systemctl reload httpd
    ```

3. Now, add an e-mail address for the `nagiosadmin` web user to the Nagios configuration, open the following file, and search and replace the string, `nagios@ localhost`, with an appropriate e-mail address you want to use here (it can be a domain-wide or external e-mail address):

    ```
    vi /etc/nagios/objects/contacts.cfg
    ```

4. Now, we need to adjust the main configuration file to activate `/etc/nagios/ servers` as our server's definition configuration directory, where we will put all our server config files later, but first, make a backup:

    ```
    cp /etc/nagios/nagios.cfg  /etc/nagios/nagios.cfg.BAK
    sed -i -r 's/^#cfg_dir=(.+)servers$/cfg_dir=\1servers/g'
    /etc/nagios/nagios.cfg
    ```

5. We will have to create the server's config directory that we just defined in the last step:

    ```
    mkdir /etc/nagios/servers
    chown nagios: /etc/nagios/servers;chmod 750 /etc/nagios/servers
    ```

6. Afterwards, to check the correctness of the `nagios.cfg` syntax, run the following:

    ```
    nagios -v /etc/nagios/nagios.cfg
    ```

7. Finally, enable the Nagios daemon on boot and start the service:

```
systemctl enable nagios && systemctl start nagios
```

How it works...

Here in this recipe, we have shown you how to install the Nagios Core v4 server (Core is the open-source version of the Nagios project) on CentOS 7. Besides the main Nagios package, we also required the NRPE package and all the Nagios plugins on our Nagios server. After installing, we created a user account, which is able to log in to the web frontend, and we set the e-mail address for this user in the main Nagios configuration file. Next, we activated the `/etc/nagios/servers` directory using `sed`, where all our server definition files will be put in a later recipe in this chapter. Then, we created the directory and changed permissions to the Nagios user. To test the Nagios server installation, open a web browser on a computer in the same subnet 192.168.1.0/24 as your Nagios server, open the following URL (in our example, the Nagios server has the IP 192.168.1.7, so change accordingly), and then log in with your newly created `nagiosadmin` user account to `http://192.168.1.7/nagios`.

Setting up NRPE on remote client hosts

The **Nagios Remote Plugin Executor** (**NRPE**) is a system daemon that uses a special client-server protocol and should be installed on all client hosts that you want to monitor via your Nagios server remotely. It allows the central Nagios server to trigger any Nagios checks on these client hosts securely and with low overhead. Here, we will show you how to set up and configure any CentOS 7 client to use NRPE; if you've got more than one computer in your network that you want to monitor, you need to apply this recipe for every instance.

Getting ready

To complete this recipe, you will require a computer other than your Nagios server with an installation of the CentOS 7 operating system and root privileges, which you want to monitor, and which needs a console-based text editor of your choice installed on it, along with a connection to the Internet in order to facilitate the download of additional packages. This computer needs to have access to our Nagios server over the network. In our example, the Nagios server has the IP address `192.168.1.7`, and our client system will have the IP address `192.168.1.8`.

How to do it...

1. Log in as root on your CentOS 7 client system and install all Nagios plugins as well as NRPE on it:

```
yum install epel-release;yum install nrpe nagios-plugins-all
nagios-plugins-nrpe
```

2. Afterwards, open the main NRPE config file (after making a backup first):

    ```
    cp /etc/nagios/nrpe.cfg /etc/nagios/nrpe.cfg.BAK && vi /etc/
    nagios/nrpe.cfg
    ```

3. Find the line that starts with `allowed_hosts`, and add the IP address of your Nagios server separated by a comma so that we can communicate with it (in our example `,192.168.1.7`, so change it accordingly); it should read as follows:

    ```
    allowed_hosts=127.0.0.1,192.168.1.7
    ```

4. Save and close the file, then enable NRPE at boot and start it:

    ```
    systemctl enable nrpe && systemctl start nrpe
    ```

5. Then enable the NRPE port in firewalld. To do this, create a new firewalld service file for NRPE:

    ```
    sed 's/80/5666/g' /usr/lib/firewalld/services/http.xml | sed
    's/WWW (HTTP)/Nagios NRPE/g' | sed 's/<description>.*<\/
    description>//g' > /etc/firewalld/services/nrpe.xml
    firewall-cmd --reload
    firewall-cmd --permanent --add-service=nrpe; firewall-cmd --reload
    ```

6. Finally, test the NRPE connection. To do this, log in as root on your Nagios server (for example, at `192.168.1.7`) and execute the following command to check NRPE on our client (`192.168.1.8`):

    ```
    /usr/lib64/nagios/plugins/check_nrpe -H 192.168.1.8 -c check_load
    ```

7. If the output prints out an `OK - load average` message with some numbers, you have successfully configured NRPE on the client!

How it works...

Here in this recipe, we have shown you how to install NRPE on your CentOS 7 clients that you want to monitor with your Nagios servers. If you want to monitor other Linux systems running other distributions such as Debian or BSD, you should be able to find appropriate packages using their own package managers or compile NRPE from source. Besides the NRPE package, we also installed all the Nagios plugins on this machine since NRPE is only the daemon for running monitoring commands on client computers, but it does not include them. After installation, NRPE is listening only on localhost (`127.0.0.1`) connections by default, so we then had to change this to also listen to connections from our Nagios server, which runs with the IP `192.168.1.7`, using the `allowed_hosts` directive in the main NRPE configuration file. The NRPE port `5666` is needed for incoming connections from the Nagios server, so we also had to open it in the firewall. Since no firewalld rule is available for it by default, we created our own new service file and added it to the current firewalld configuration. Afterwards, we could test our NRPE installation from our Nagios server by running a `check_nrpe` command using the client's IP address and a random check command (`check_load` returns the system's load).

Monitoring important remote system metrics

The Nagios plugin `check_multi` is a convenient tool to execute multiple checks within a single check command that generates an overall returned state and output from it. Here in this recipe, we will show you how to set it up and use it to quickly monitor a list of important system metrics on your clients.

Getting ready

It is assumed that you've gone through this chapter recipe by recipe, therefore by now, you should have a Nagios server running and another client computer that you want to monitor, which can already be accessed via its NRPE service externally by our Nagios server. This client computer that you want to monitor needs an installation of the CentOS 7 operating system with root privileges and a console-based text editor of your choice installed on it, as well as a connection to the Internet in order to facilitate the download of additional packages. The client computer will have the IP address `192.168.1.8`.

How to do it...

The `check_multi` Nagios plugin is available from Github, so we will begin this recipe to install the `git` program by downloading it:

1. Log in as root on your client computer and install Git if not done already:

   ```
   yum install git
   ```

2. Now, download and install the `check_multi` plugin by compiling it from the source:

   ```
   cd /tmp;git clone git://github.com/flackem/check_multi;cd /tmp/
   check_multi
   ```

   ```
   ./configure --with-nagios-name=nagios --with-nagios-user=nagios
   --with-nagios-group=nagios --with-plugin-path=/usr/lib64/nagios/
   plugins --libexecdir=/usr/lib64/nagios/plugins/
   ```

   ```
   make all;make install;make install-config
   ```

3. Next, we install another very useful plugin called `check_mem`, which is not available in the CentOS 7 Nagios plugin `rpms`:

   ```
   cd /tmp;git clone https://github.com/justintime/nagios-plugins.git
   ```

   ```
   cp /tmp/nagios-plugins/check_mem/check_mem.pl  /usr/lib64/nagios/
   plugins/
   ```

4. Next, let's create a `check_multi` command file that will contain all your desired client checks that you want to combine in a single run; open the following file:

   ```
   vi /usr/local/nagios/etc/check_multi/check_multi.cmd
   ```

5. Put in the following content:

```
command[ sys_load::check_load ] = check_load -w 5,4,3 -c 10,8,6
command[ sys_mem::check_mem ] = check_mem.pl -w 10 -c 5 -f -C
command[ sys_users::check_users ] = check_users -w 5 -c 10
command[ sys_disks::check_disk ] = check_disk -w 5% -c 2% -X nfs
command[ sys_procs::check_procs ] = check_procs
```

6. Next, test out the command file that we just created in the last step using the following commandline:

```
/usr/lib64/nagios/plugins/check_multi -f   /usr/local/nagios/etc/
check_multi/check_multi.cmd
```

7. If everything is correct, it should print out the results of your five plugin checks and an overall result, for example, OK - 5 plugins checked. Next, we will install this new command in the NRPE service on our client so that the Nagios server is able to execute it remotely by calling its name. Open the NRPE configuration file:

```
vi /etc/nagios/nrpe.cfg
```

8. Add the following line to the end of the file right below the last # command line to expose a new command called check_multicmd to our Nagios server:

```
command[check_multicmd]=/usr/lib64/nagios/plugins/check_multi -f
/usr/local/nagios/etc/check_multi/check_multi.cmd
```

9. Finally, let's reload NRPE:

```
systemctl restart nrpe
```

10. Now, let's check whether we can execute our new check_multicmd command that we defined in the last step from our Nagios server. Log in as root and type the following command (change the IP address of your client, 192.168.1.8, appropriately):

```
/usr/lib64/nagios/plugins/check_nrpe  -H 192.168.1.8 -c "check_
multicmd"
```

11. If the output is the same as running it locally on the client itself (take a look at the former step), we can successfully execute remote NRPE commands on our client through our server, so let's define the command on our Nagios server system for real so that we can start using it within the Nagios system. Open the following file:

```
vi /etc/nagios/objects/commands.cfg
```

12. Put in the following content at the end of the file to define a new command called check_nrpe_multi, which we can use in any service definition:

```
define command {
    command_name check_nrpe_multi
```

```
    command_line $USER1$/check_nrpe -H $HOSTADDRESS$ -c "check_
multicmd"

}
```

13. Next, we will define a new server definition for the client that we want to monitor on our Nagios server (give the config file an appropriate name, for example, its domain name or IP address):

    `vi /etc/nagios/servers/192.168.1.8.cfg`

14. Put in the following content, which will define a new host with its service, using our new Nagios command that we just created:

```
define host {
        use                     linux-server
        host_name                host1
        address                 192.168.1.22
        contact_groups           unix-admins
}
define service {
        use generic-service
        host_name host1
        check_command check_nrpe_multi
        normal_check_interval 15
        service_description check_nrpe_multi service
}
```

15. Finally, we need to configure all persons who should get notification e-mails for our new service in case of errors. Open the following file:

    `vi /etc/nagios/objects/contacts.cfg`

16. Put in the following content at the end of the file:

```
define contactgroup{
        contactgroup_name       unix-admins
        alias                   Unix Administrators
 }
define contact {
        contact_name                    pelz
        use                             generic-contact
        alias                           Oliver Pelz
        contactgroups                   unix-admins
```

```
                    email                    oliverpelz@mymailhost.com
    }
```

17. Now, restart the Nagios service:

```
systemctl restart nagios
```

How it works...

We started this recipe by installing the `check_multi` and `check_mem` plugins from their author's Github repositories; they are plain command-line tools. Nagios performs checks by running such external commands, and it uses the return code along with output from the command as information on whether the check was successful or not. Nagios has a very flexible architecture that can be easily extended using plugins, add-ons, and extensions. A central place to search for all kinds of extensions is at `https://exchange.nagios.org/`. Next, we added a new command file for `check_multi`, where we put five different system `check_` commands in. These checks act as a starting point for customizing your monitoring needs and will check system load, memory consumption, system users, free space, and processes. All available `check_` commands can be found at `/usr/lib64/nagios/plugins/check_*`. As you can see in our command file, the parameters of those `check_` commands can be very different, and explaining them all is out of the scope of this recipe. Most of them are used to set threshold values to reach a certain state, for example, the `CRITICAL` state. To get more information about a specific command, use the `--help` parameter with the command. For example, to find out what all the parameters in the `check_load -w 5,4,3 -c 10,8,6` command are doing, use run `/usr/lib64/nagios/plugins/check_load --help`. You can easily add any number of new check commands to our command file from existing plugins, or you can download and install any new commands, if you like. There are also a number of command file examples shipped with the `check_multi` plugin, which are very useful for learning, so please have a look at the directory: `/usr/local/nagios/etc/check_multi/*.cmd`.

Afterwards, we checked the correctness of our new command file that we just created by dry-running it as an `-f` parameter from the `check_multi` command locally on the client. In its output, you will find all the single outputs as if you would have run these five commands individually. If one single check fails, the complete `check_multi` will do. Next, we defined a new NRPE command in the NRPE config file called `check_multicmd` that can then be executed from the Nagios server, which we tested in the next step from our Nagios server. For a test to be successful, we expect the same results as we got when calling the command from the client itself. Afterwards, we defined this command in our `commands.cfg` on the Nagios server so that we can reuse it as much as we like in any service definition by referencing the command's name, `check_nrpe_multi`. Next, we created a new server file named as the IP address (you can name it anything you like as long it has the `.cfg` extension in the directory) of the client we want to monitor: `192.168.1.8.cfg`. It contains exactly one host definition and one or multiple service definitions, which are linked by the value of `host_name` of the host with the `host_name` value in your service definitions.

In the host definition, we defined a `contact_groups` contact that links to the `contacts.cfg` file's contact group and contact entry. These will be used to send notification e-mails if the checked service has any errors. The most important value in the service definition is the `check_command check_nrpe_multi` line, which executes the command that we created before as our one and only check. Also, the `normal_check_interval` is important as it defines how often the service will be checked under normal conditions. Here, it gets checked every 15 minutes. You can add as many service definitions to a host as you like.

Now, go to your Nagios web frontend to inspect your new host and service. Here, go to the **Hosts** tab, where you will see the new host, **host1**, that you defined in this recipe, and it should give you information about its status. If you click on the **Services** tab, you will see the **check_nrpe_multi** service. It should show the **Status** as **Pending, OK,** or **CRITICAL**, depending on the success of the single checks. If you click on its **check_nrpe_multi** link, you will see details about the checks.

Here in this chapter, we could only show you the very basics of Nagios, and there is always more to learn, so please read the official Nagios Core documentation at `https://www.nagios.org`, or check out the book *Learning Nagios 4, Packt Publishing*, by Wojciech Kocjan.

Index

D

data backups
maintaining 64, 65
database
managing 203-206
Database Management System (DBMS) 196
delivery agent 217
DHCP
about 143
running 143-146
Disabled mode 277
Discretionary Access Control (DAC) 275
disk quotas
group quotas, enabling 103
limiting system, setting up 102
project (directory) quotas, enabling 103-105
user quotas, enabling 103
using 102
working 105-107
DNS server
about 32, 145
authoritative-only DNS server,
configuring 176-185
caching-only Unbound DNS server,
configuring 173, 174
forwarding only DNS server,
configuring 174-176
primary DNS server changes, making 191
secondary DNS server changes,
making 192, 193
secondary (slave) DNS server, building 190
Docker
configuring 261-263
installing 261-263
URL 263
Dockerfiles
images, creating from 267, 268
Docker Hub
images, uploading to 267-269
URL 265, 267
Docker registry server
setting up 271, 272
domain
about 171
populating 188-190
Domain Name System server. *See* **DNS server**

domain-wide mail service
BIND, configuring for new mailserver 220
configuring, with Postfix 213-218
e-mail's appearing domain name,
modifying 218
TLS- (SSL) encryption, used for SMTP
communication 219, 220
Dovecot
e-mail software, setting up 228, 229
used, for delivering mail 223-228
Dynamic Host Control Protocol. *See* **DHCP**

E

ELRepo
about 87
reference link 87
Enforcing mode 278
Enhanced mode 277
existing firewalld service (ssh)
changing 126
Ext4 98
extensions
URL 294

F

fail2ban
configuring 119-121
installing 119-121
Fetchmail
about 229
automating 234, 235
configuring, with Gmail account 231-234
configuring, with Outlook account 231-234
using 229-231
file amount (inodes) 105
files
navigating, with less controls 24
sharing, WebDAV using for 146-149
synchronizing 62, 63
file size (blocks) 105
filesystem
accessing 18
capacity, extending 109-113
formatting 98-101
maintaining 107-109
mounting 98-101

system clock
synchronizing, with chrony suite 29-32
synchronizing, with NTP 29-32

T

tasks
scheduling, with cron 59-61
third-party repository
using 85-87
Top-level Domain name (TLD) 181
type enforcement (TE) 279

U

Unbound DNS Security Extensions (DNSSEC) 175
unneeded httpd modules
removing 255
USB installation media
creating, on OS X 4-6
creating, on Windows 4-6
users
managing 57-59
troubleshooting 168, 169

V

very secure FTP daemon (vsftpd) 159
Vim
about 24
working with 25
virtual block device
creating 96, 97
virtual FTP users
about 163
working with 163-166
virtual machine (VM) 261
volume group (vg) 112
vsftpd server
securing, with SSH - SFTP 133
securing, with SSL-FTPS 132

W

Web-based Distributed Authoring and Versioning (WebDAV)
using, for file sharing 146-149
web pages
serving 237-240
Windows
checksum, confirming on 2-4
USB installation media, creating on 4-6
Windows Internet Naming Service (WINS) 157
World Wide Web (WWW) 76, 196

Y

Yellowdog Updater Modified (YUM)
about 21
optimizing 80-82
priorities, knowing 82-84
repository, creating 87-90
used, for installing packages 77, 78
used, for removing packages 79, 80
used, for searching packages 75, 76
used, for updating system 73-75

Thank you for buying
CentOS 7 Linux Server Cookbook
Second Edition

About Packt Publishing

Packt, pronounced 'packed', published its first book, *Mastering phpMyAdmin for Effective MySQL Management*, in April 2004, and subsequently continued to specialize in publishing highly focused books on specific technologies and solutions.

Our books and publications share the experiences of your fellow IT professionals in adapting and customizing today's systems, applications, and frameworks. Our solution-based books give you the knowledge and power to customize the software and technologies you're using to get the job done. Packt books are more specific and less general than the IT books you have seen in the past. Our unique business model allows us to bring you more focused information, giving you more of what you need to know, and less of what you don't.

Packt is a modern yet unique publishing company that focuses on producing quality, cutting-edge books for communities of developers, administrators, and newbies alike. For more information, please visit our website at www.packtpub.com.

About Packt Open Source

In 2010, Packt launched two new brands, Packt Open Source and Packt Enterprise, in order to continue its focus on specialization. This book is part of the Packt open source brand, home to books published on software built around open source licenses, and offering information to anybody from advanced developers to budding web designers. The Open Source brand also runs Packt's open source Royalty Scheme, by which Packt gives a royalty to each open source project about whose software a book is sold.

Writing for Packt

We welcome all inquiries from people who are interested in authoring. Book proposals should be sent to author@packtpub.com. If your book idea is still at an early stage and you would like to discuss it first before writing a formal book proposal, then please contact us; one of our commissioning editors will get in touch with you.

We're not just looking for published authors; if you have strong technical skills but no writing experience, our experienced editors can help you develop a writing career, or simply get some additional reward for your expertise.

CentOS System Administration Essentials

ISBN: 978-1-78398-592-0   Paperback: 174 pages

Become an efficient CentOS administrator by acquiring real-world knowledge of system setup and configuration

1. Centralize user accounts in openLDAP and understand how Directory can be at the back-end of many services.

2. Learning Puppet to centralize server configuration will free up your time as configuration is handled just once on the configuration server.

3. A step-by-step guide that covers the very popular Linux Distribution CentOS 6.5 with easy-to-follow instructions.

Troubleshooting CentOS

ISBN: 978-1-78528-982-8   Paperback: 190 pages

A practical guide to troubleshooting the CentOS 7 community-based enterprise server

1. Gain exposure to insider tips and techniques to quickly detect the reason for poor network/storage performance.

2. Troubleshooting methodologies, defining, and isolating problems.

3. Identify key issues that impact performance, storage, scalability, capacity.

Please check **www.PacktPub.com** for information on our titles

CentOS High Availability

ISBN: 978-1-78528-248-5   Paperback: 174 pages

Leverage the power of high availability clusters on CentOS Linux, the enterprise-class, open source operating system

1. Install, configure, and manage a multi-node cluster running on CentOS Linux.

2. Manage your cluster resources and learn how to start, stop, and migrate resources from one host to another.

3. Designed as a step-by-step guide, this book will help you become a master of cluster nodes, cluster resources, and cluster services on CentOS 6 and CentOS 7.

SELinux Cookbook

ISBN: 978-1-78398-966-9   Paperback: 240 pages

Over 70 hands-on recipes to develop fully functional policies to confine your applications and users using SELinux

1. Design custom SELinux policies and understand the reference policy interface constructions to build readable SELinux policy rules.

2. Experience the wide range of security controls SELinux offers by customizing web application confinement.

3. Step-by-step recipes exploring the SELinux environment.

Please check **www.PacktPub.com** for information on our titles

Made in the USA
Columbia, SC
08 December 2020